Through Fire and Water

The Life and Faith of a
Naval Surgeon in War and Peace

Dr Mark Houghton

malcolm down
PUBLISHING

We went through fire and water,
but you brought us to a place of abundance.

Psalm 66:12

Dedication

To Esther, my wonderful wife, friend and co-labourer in all matters. You handle the Houghtons with grace and good humour.

Copyright © Mark Houghton 2025

First published 2025 by Malcolm Down Publishing Ltd.
www.malcolmdown.co.uk

28 27 26 25 24   7 6 5 4 3 2 1

The right of Mark Houghton to be identified as the author of this work has been asserted by him in accordance with the Copyright, Designs and Patents Act 1988.

All rights reserved. No part of this publication may be reproduced, stored in a retrieval system, or transmitted in any other form or by any means, electronic, mechanical, photocopying, recording or otherwise, without the prior permission of the publisher.

British Library Cataloguing in Publication Data
A catalogue record for this book is available from the British Library.

Paperback: ISBN 978-1-917455-07-7
Hardback: ISBN 978-1-917455-19-0

Unless otherwise indicated, Scripture quotations taken from New International Version (Anglicised edition) Copyright ©1979, 1984, 2011 by Biblica.
Used by permission of Hodder & Stoughton Publishers, an Hachette UK company.
All rights reserved.
'NIV' is a registered trademark of Biblica.
UK trademark number 1448790.

Cover design by Esther Kotecha
Art direction by Sarah Grace

Printed in the UK

Endorsement

Mark Houghton has written a fabulous biography of his father, the surgeon Mr Paul Houghton. It is an extraordinary story of faith, of medical affairs, and of the Royal Navy in wartime. Mark writes with love and conviction drawing on an unusually complete archive of material from an age which is now gone. Not only is Through Fire and Water a valuable social history of the twentieth century, but Paul Houghton saved the lives of two famous admirals in the Second World War, Edward Syfret and Philip Vian. To save one altered the course of the war, but saving both puts Paul Houghton into a unique niche in medical a naval history.

Captain Peter Hore RN, Naval historian and the author of Paul Houghton's Daily Telegraph obituary

Contents

Foreword by Mr John Black PRCS   9
Author's Introduction   11

Part One: Surgeon, 1911-37

1. 'Save the Ship!'   19
2. Long Long Ago   29
3. The Piratical Grandfather   37
4. The Great War   41
5. Teenager in the Twenties   49
6. Two Bright Rebels   57
7. Barts by the Meat Market   61
8. Friends and the Gentler Sex   69
9. Sodom by the Sea   75
10. Tide on the Flood   87
11. Love and Life   91
12. A Grim Awakening   95

Part Two: Sailor, 1938-1945

13. A Passage to India   105
14. Here We Go Again Boys   113
15. Called Up by the Navy   119
16. Into Battle   127
17. Deception with Honour   137
18. Enemy Invasion Imminent   141
19. Battle of the Atlantic   153
20. To the North Atlantic Station   169

21.	Flagship Nelson	173
22.	Flash of Inspiration	181
23.	Rock Bottom	185
24.	Happy Isles	191
25.	South to the Heat	203
26.	Into the Fire – Operation Pedestal	211
27.	Saving Admiral Vian	223
28.	Another Fighting Admiral	231
29.	The Courageous Captain	243
30.	Malta and Sicily Saved	269
31.	Hope for Italy	281
32.	Home Is the Sailor	291

Part 3. Senior and Son: 1945-2009

33.	Crisis in England	301
34.	Moored Alongside	305
35.	Work	311
36.	A Reunion of Enemies	317
37.	More Work	321
38.	Worcestershire	331
39.	Africa	347
40.	Caribbean and Israel	351
41.	Season of Mists and Mellow Fruitfulness	359

Postscript	367
Acknowledgements	371
Appendix	375
Glossary	377
People and Nicknames	381

Foreword

*Mr John Black, former Consultant Surgeon
Worcester Royal Infirmary
President of the Royal College of Surgeons 2008-11*

In 1995, a meeting was held in Worcester to mark the passing of fifty years since the end of the Second World War. The highly respected and much-loved local surgeon Mr Paul Houghton spoke of his wartime experiences. He showed a black and white photograph taken at sunset from the battleship HMS *Nelson* of burials at sea from the aircraft carrier HMS *Indomitable*. At this point he broke down in tears and was unable to continue, a moment of unforgettable poignancy for me and everyone else there that day.

Born before the First World War, Paul Houghton had a long and eventful life, combining a distinguished career as a civilian surgeon with a remarkably busy period of service as a naval surgeon in the second great conflict of the twentieth century. He served in a variety of ships, was torpedoed and rescued, was present at one of the most famous convoy battles of the war, and treated successfully two legendary senior officers with conditions potentially fatal at that time. Many who worked with him in his consultant career in Worcester, and indeed in his long and active retirement, knew that he had been in the Royal Navy, but none were aware of everything that had happened to him. Few doctors had such an 'interesting' and perilous period of wartime service.

It is fortunate that he left an archive of journals, letters and photographs that together with personal memories have allowed his son, Mark, to author this book, which will appeal not only to doctors, surgeons and readers of the history of the times, but to those interested in how normal people are swept up in great events, sustained in Paul Houghton's case by his steadfast Christian faith.

Author's Introduction

Among my earliest memories is seeing this tall man, striding in through the kitchen door from work, with dark, wavy hair and a side parting.

Tossing his trilby on the kitchen table, he sweeps up my sister, Pippy, and me in both arms and holds us in a bear hug that nearly bangs our heads together. Planting himself on Mummy's wicker chair by the Aga – one of us on each knee – he issues orders from the Bridge, 'Steam up on main engines,' and we are heading for the open sea, bobbing up and down on his knees – the wavelets.

It's a Malta convoy and our battleship HMS *Nelson* is butting out of the English Channel towards the heaving Atlantic. Dad's suit and starched collar are scratching my face as we enter the slow roll of the boundless ocean. The remnants of Old Spice and Bay Rum in his hair waft about. The 'crew' shriek with laughter and grin at each other. Suddenly our 'ship' heels over at an impossible angle and Pippa's head swings past the Aga's iron corner; then we are swept up on the Atlantic rollers towards the old meat hooks on the kitchen ceiling, shrieking with excitement.

'Here's a big one,' bellows the captain on the Bridge. 'Hold, hold tight...' We are running downhill, down, down the front of a wave, 'Lord – look at it! She's buried her bows right back to "B" turret.'

Now we are into the calm blue Mediterranean when 'Action stations, whoop, whoop, whoops!' 'Emergency red turn . . . ping-ping . . . ping-ping!' goes the echo sounder locating a submarine, faster and faster, as an air attack comes in: 'Bang-bang-bang!' go the Pom-Poms – then the Oerlikons' ear-splitting 'rat-a-tat-tat' almost simultaneous with four bear hugs as depth charges explode nearly underneath us: 'Look, look, there's the tar oil spreading on the water – showing another U-boat has gone to the bottom.'

'Do the big guns, Daddy . . .' I yell above the din, and the command crackles over the Tannoy: 'All hands below deck! Don flash protection – ' followed by a rumbling roaring whoosh from Dad's chest, an extra hug for the shock wave, a 30° roll to starboard from the recoil, under the eruption of triple 16-inch guns: 'The biggest guns in the navy.' Three tons of 'grapeshot' are hurtling at the incoming planes. (His faded blue all-in-one flash suit hung in our garage for years. A huge sailor's clasp knife lay about and when I could read, I was enthralled by 'Sur. Ltd PW Houghton' engraved on the handle.)

The game ends with a clash of Pip's head on my nose at the top of a wave; the ensuing nosebleed, as Mummy walks in, propels her to us, mopping blood with her apron. 'Oh, Paul, I knew it would end in tears; I just had them settled down for bed, and now look . . .' Mummy's oval face and rosy cheeks framed by black wavy hair look so lovely I can't get my head round it; and I muddle her up in my mind with the young Queen Elizabeth I've seen in photos.

This was Dad with his endless fund of stories. It seemed as real as yesterday – and for the 'grown-ups' it *was* yesterday,

Author's Introduction

just over ten years earlier. At weekends when Dad put on his old navy-blue seaman's jumper and announced for the tenth time, 'This close-knit weave is just wonderful for cutting out cold winds,' we knew he was going to relax and enjoy himself – and so were we.

But other days were clouded, when he wore a face like thunder and marched about dog-tired and distant, as if we were not there. We gathered that the tiredness was from devotion to the patients; devotions that continued into Saturdays and Sundays because, 'Surgery is like war, endless vigilance to catch trouble early.'

But not only tiredness, for I came to believe in later years we were the unknowing victims of post-traumatic stress disorder (PTSD). PTSD can come on years after the terrible traumatic events. It changes the way you think; with feelings of being overwhelmed. Guilt, sadness and anger boil over, along with feelings of fearful entrapment.

Tucked up in bed, we would hear angry shouting downstairs. Mummy would quietly let us know the next morning, 'He is in a mood . . .' – which could last days, with everyone on edge and miserable.

It was the 1980s before the dark heart of the sea war began to surface in my dad – by then, the black moods were fading, and he began to reveal more of the horrors like men swimming in fire.

Now my own children are in their twenties and thirties and I thought, what a waste if this raw experience of the greatest conflict in history was lost. God willing, these stories can steady later generations by looking back to the great works of God and his people through fire and deep waters.

Then there were the letters. After our parents died, we found a huge correspondence between our dad and his friends and family from about 1920 until the love letters and marriage in 1947. And in 2018, Pippa and I began to read them together. Picking one out, I see an envelope stamped MARITIME MAIL FROM H.M. SHIP – PASSED BY CENSOR, annotated in Dad's script '5/1/43 P. Houghton' – he often *was* the ship's censor.

The recipient is 'AJ Houghton Esq., 438 Fulham Rd, London, SW6. England', his father. I am surprised and excited because the envelope appears never opened. I slide the letter out tenderly – was I the first to read it? – and read:

Everyone on board looks ahead to the day when we shall begin the old life again in quietness and peace, with travelling days over. 'We desire a better country . . .'[1] The discipline of uncertainty and restlessness and isolation is quite severe . . . It's good to know one can return to Lingfield village some day and find the things we love as we like to remember them.

These letters, nearly eighty years old, brought me up short. One thing is sure, my father never expected his letters to be put in a book. I shortened and lightly amended some for clarity in today's English.

Furthermore, a charismatic naval character shone in our lives as we grew up. Tall, lanky and charming, 'Uncle' George and his glamorous wife 'Auntie' Marcelle, would have us over to Christmas lunch at their house in Warwickshire which I remember (mistakenly) as a castle. I can see George beaming before the Christmas turkey, unbuttoning his jacket with a 'time to shake out a reef from the main sail'. Then,

---

1. See Hebrews 11:16.

Author's Introduction

brandishing a carving knife like the cutlass of a boarding party, he commanded us to 'dig in the gun room for the stuffing'.

After lunch, he would show his silent cine films taken at the height of combat. This was our dad's great companion in war, Captain George Blundell of HMS *Nelson* who has featured in recent BBC television accounts and Sir Max Hastings' 2021 book, *Operation Pedestal: The Fleet That Battled to Malta, 1942.*

We children gazed rapt at cheerful faces and admirals in their tropical 'whites'. There spread the sea beyond the mighty guns, and seagulls wheeling past, and men covered in lather before being 'shaved' by 'King Neptune' at a Crossing the Line ceremony.

Then the enemy planes were wheeling about amid enormous waterspouts from near misses. 'George really should not have been filming at the height of action,' smiled my father privately. After the show, oiled by a fine wine, Dad would begin, 'George, do you remember the time the admiral sat on your cacti, leaping up clutching his backside and roaring, "Throw them overboard"?' Both rolled backwards roaring with laughter and wiping the tears away.

Another shipmate, Lieutenant Commander Geoffrey Bullock, with his wife, Joan, were near neighbours in Worcestershire. 'Uncle' Geoffrey was made my godfather and many was the time we walked to their lovely house with its lawn stretching away to a fenceless 'Ha ha' and the oil painting of a square-rigged man-of-war at sea.

For more than fifty years, my father and I pondered these tales together. As ship's doctor he attended the lowliest sailors and the highest admirals. This is my attempt to convey the ways of ordinary men and women under supreme pressure. It began as fun – but at times tears of the trauma welled up – in reliving his life. I hope it helps us dig and find for ourselves the roots of resilience in war and peace.

Poetry bubbled out of his inner wells, so some are in here; the ones that Paul loved.

Dad, this is my long 'Thank you'.

Part One

Surgeon, 1911-37

CHAPTER ONE

'Save the Ship!'

1941: Operation Halberd, convoy to Malta in the Mediterranean

No captain can do very wrong if he places his ship alongside that of an enemy.

Admiral Lord Nelson, before the Battle of Trafalgar, 9 October 1805[2]

Just before the torpedo struck, thirty-year-old Surgeon Lieutenant Paul Houghton and two medical orderlies sat sweating in their 'action station', the forward sick bay of HMS *Nelson* under the main deck. She was one of the most famous ships in the British Navy and flagship of the Mediterranean fleet. It was 1.31 p.m. on 27 September 1941. They had been pushed out of their rear sick bay by the admiral coming aboard. There in that cabin, they had heard a *thrum* and looked at each other in horror – an enemy torpedo had passed underneath.

---

2. The British Library, www.bl.uk/learning/timeline/item106127.html#:~:text=Captains%20are%20to%20look%20to,alongside%20that%20of%20an%20Enemy (accessed 29.6.22).

Now the roar and clatter of the ship's anti-aircraft guns hit a crescendo and Paul reached for a boiled sweet, trying to focus on the sweetness – or sharpening a pencil – any distraction from the fear. With the crescendo they felt the ship heeling over in a violent emergency turn.

The three had sat in the sick bay some hours, in that peculiar agony of intense fighting, yet having nothing to do. And all three knew the mighty ships, planes and submarines arrayed against them that summer day on the Mediterranean. It was almost impossible not to think of the normal – shipmates and friends frying in fuel oil, toasted in steel ovens or boiled in flooding brine.

Paul pondered how he had come to be posted to the *Nelson*. Was it his outstanding work rate and surgical success at the Royal Naval Patrol Depot in Lowestoft, under a rain of bombs? If so, his reputation for stand-up arguments with the commanding officer made this top job inexplicable.

Yet here he was, and glad to find the *Nelson* a happy ship – nicknamed 'The Nellie' in the fleet. He also liked her First Officer, Torpedo Officer, Lt Commander George Blundell. 'Torps' was an engineer; tall, lanky, energetic and everywhere loved by the crew and charming all with his charismatic smile. He and Paul had got off to a good start together as they discovered a mutual love of cycling – indeed, any exercise to be had anytime.

They also discovered a shared delight in popping pompous balloons – especially among their lordships, the admirals, who they encountered daily aboard ship – which did nothing to help their promotion prospects. The day before, Blundell had recorded in his illegal and secret diary, 'In the morning watch I wore my OBE ribbon for the first time.' A friendly officer mentioning that 'OBE' stood for Other B-----s Efforts.

'Save the Ship!'

A few minutes before the lull, about 1.25 p.m., Blundell had suggested to Captain Jacomb that the crews manning the torpedo tubes, near Paul's sick bay, could be moved towards the stern of the ship because the Italian battleships were no longer threatening. The captain agreed and the men hastened aft just in time – undoubtedly saving their lives.[3]

Despite the ceaseless roar of the guns overhead, Paul felt a nonsensical peace deep inside. This seemed connected to another world beyond this life and, judging by the racket, arriving sooner rather than later.

It was Day Three of a convoy to Malta codenamed *Operation Halberd*, outward bound from Gibraltar and travelling east through the Mediterranean. Gibraltar, the vital British naval base, was a huge rock connected to the Spanish mainland at the narrow gate where the Atlantic met the Mediterranean. Here, a vast array of British warships and merchant ships had gathered, set on bringing life-saving food, fuel and troops to the beleaguered and starving island of Malta.

The island of Malta lay about halfway between Gibraltar in the West and Egypt at the eastern end of the Mediterranean; she was uncomfortably close to the enemy occupied southern border of Sicily, lying off the 'toe' of Italy. Yet she was a keystone for the British hopes, serving as an unsinkable 'aircraft carrier' from which ships, troops and planes could attack occupied Europe to the North, or Africa to her South.

Sicily, Italy and North Africa were packed with German and Italian aircraft, and just after midday, intensive air attacks had begun. Large, three-engine Italian torpedo bombers – Savoia-Marchetti SM.84s – were coming at *Nelson* through a curtain of exploding shells thrown up from the warships all around.

---

3. Ronald Careless, *Battleship Nelson* (London: Weidenfeld Military, 1985), p. 52.

Seconds later a silence made the three men listen intently, wondering: Why?

High up above on the ship's bridge, the officers and crew were watching three Italian torpedo bombers tearing straight at them, like hornets attacking a bull. The captain bellowed down the speaking tube to the helmsman far below, and the behemoth began to turn, agonisingly slowly, towards her tormentors, trying to present her sharp front end as a smaller target for incoming torpedoes. Below deck in his Sick Bay Flat, and unable to see out, Paul knew the calm blue sea was boiling white from the shot and shell falling from the sky.[4] Suddenly with a roar and whoosh their cabin healed over as *Nelson's* broadside of great guns went off — things must be desperate for that comparatively uncommon event.

One plane blew up, falling into the sea in a fountain of spray. The second broke away, buffeted by the shockwaves from the largest aerial shells in the navy. But a third, with incredible courage, pressed on...

All over the ship, sweating gunners, some stripped to the waist in the midday heat, fired and fired. Several saw the splash as a torpedo from the surviving bomber hit the sea to starboard and sped towards them on its underwater journey. Torpedoes, driven by compressed air tanks, left tell-tale tracks of bubbles. Yet something strange was happening; the remaining Italian pilot, streaking ahead of his oncoming 'tin fish', pressed on towards them at wave top height, until he was so close that the guns fell silent, unable to depress their barrels low enough to aim at him.

In an act of supreme skill and daring that would be talked over for decades, the Italian judged his safest hope was flying at water level right up close beside the ship and turn towards her stern. Tearing past at hundreds of miles an hour, Blundell

---

4. PWH to the author.

caught him on film, flying parallel to the port side with his wing tip virtually brushing the hull. Before they could blink, he was vanishing away behind. Incredibly, George, Paul and that Italian would meet again.

As the guns roared again every eye revolved and riveted onto the bubble trails of incoming torpedoes, captured by Blundell:

> The first torpedo to be dropped was clearly going to miss. The ship had turned to starboard towards another plane when to everyone's horror the track suddenly reappeared no more than 200 yards ahead and coming straight for the ship. Then it disappeared under the overhang of the bow. There was an interval in which people thought that, by some miracle, it had missed or run deep beneath the ship's bottom, and just as we began to breathe again there was a sickening underwater thud.[5]

Closest to the explosion were Paul and his two companions, as Paul remembered:

> We were shaken by a great crash, an enormous crash, and the whole ship reared up like a horse, shook like a dog emerging from water, rang like a deep bell and settled down again. We had been hit. The torpedo got us underwater below her belt of steel, 14 inches thick, and blowing a hole in her side that, when I saw it later, you could drive a double-decker bus through.
> We were unharmed but all the lights went out and the three of us sat in the darkness and listened. We

---

5. *GC Blundell Papers*, with kind permission of Imperial War Museum, London SE1 6HZ, and John Blundell, son.

had flashlights but kept them switched off to conserve batteries. So, we sat and sat, and our seats began to tilt, pointing down to the bottom of the sea.[6]

Far above on the Bridge – moments after the hit, Blundell's laborious study of the ship's structure sprang into life. 'I rushed down the ladders to "ginger up" the damage control parties. I went for'ard below the Main Deck as far as the Sick Bay Flat [where Paul and his two orderlies were] and found that from here going for'ard, and down below decks, all lights were out.'

In the darkness, the three men waited. Muffled voices came through the steel as sailors screwed tight the watertight door from the outside. Their cabin was now their coffin. Everyone knew it was essential to secure watertight doors to create floatation air spaces. Paul was thinking, 'They don't dare let us out in case opening the door drops the pressure in the sick bay which bursts the bulkhead.'

Time dragged by and:

I realised we were slowing down, the worst possible situation for a warship under attack. Why could it be? This was bad; we were a 'sitting duck' helpless to evade planes and submarines hungry to finish us off. I turned on the torch and checked my watch. Then feeling my way forwards in the dark with my hands on the steel walls I walked to the front bulkhead of the sick bay. I noticed my journey was a little downhill. The bulkhead felt odd; it was bulging inwards towards me. I flashed the light around and, to my relief, saw no water coming in.[7]

The heat of the summer day deepened the oppressive atmosphere. When the guns paused they could hear footsteps,

---

6. PWH, interviewed 24.11.2000 by Dr Chris Howard Bailey, Royal Naval Museum.
7. Ibid.

'Save the Ship!'

shouts and grunts. Blundell and his men were dragging heavy power cable around in efforts to restore electricity. And what would the Italian fleet do? Would they come at them, slowly sinking and paralysed? No information came from outside their locked door: all Paul knew was that 'we were off Sicily trying to force our way through. This was the most dangerous point, known among the convoy men as 'Bomb Alley' for the massed ranks of aircraft above us and the wolf packs below.

'Fifteen minutes later by my watch, I felt my way forwards again and this time it was downhill without doubt. Under my hands the steel bulged towards me more than the first time. Walking back to my seat felt uphill – more uphill than before.'[8]

High on the Bridge a signal came through that all dreaded. The Italian battle fleet was indeed heading south hunting the merchant ships. At a command from Admiral James Somerville, the main British battle fleet turned north and charged at the danger. A buzz spread through the ship from the officers above, to the cooks passing ammunition, to the bandsmen plotting positions deep in the operations room, to the sweating engineers immersed amid howling steam turbines.

But *Nellie* could charge no more. Blundell, ran for'ard and, standing on the very front of the ship leaned over, trying to see the hole. Gazing back he saw, 'The bow has gone down ... and, looking along the upper deck, the ship looks ... as if she were plunging downhill. It feels as if one could step straight off onto the sea.'[9]

What ran through Paul's mind as they turned to face the Italian battleships? Was he thinking of Admiral Lord Nelson more than a century earlier? Paul had learned to apply to surgery the great sea leader's approach to the enemy – the

---
8. Ibid.
9. Careless, *Battleship Nelson*, quoting Captain Blundell's diary.

leader who had crushed Napoleon's combined French and Spanish fleets at the Battle of Trafalgar. 'Admiral Nelson,' Paul said, 'would go *straight at them* with the command, "A captain can do no better than lay his ship alongside the enemy."' If Paul was thinking of Nelson, he continued to feel – 'as small as a pinhead' – carried here and there in a great conflict of steel and men and water and fire.

'For the third time I walked to the for'ard end of the sick bay and noticed it was even more downhill.' He knew their predicament from Joseph Conrad's awful tale *Lord Jim*. Jim too had been in a ship 'with the light of the lamp falling on a small portion of the bulkhead that had the weight of the ocean on the other side'. Like Jim, Paul glared at the iron, overburdened by the knowledge of an imminent death.[10]

Survivors told of these bulkheads giving way and thousands of tons of water flooding from one compartment to the next. The steel doors would, under the weight of a ship driving towards the bottom, play out a terrible tattoo as they burst. So far no one on *Nelson* was hurt, but it would be better to lose three men and save 2,000 – and a great ship besides.

Nelson was drifting to a halt because she was filling with water at the front end and see-sawing, bows down under the weight; so the rudders at the stern came almost above the water and she was unable to steer. 'That was awful because we couldn't manoeuvre to evade submarines. Meanwhile, hours and hours went by and the air in our compartment was getting rather foul.'[11]

What was to be done? 'Back to the damage ... I [Blundell] went down to the Communications Messdeck. Here water was rushing in through a gash in the deck and bulkhead under the hammock netting ... The whole deck seemed to be

---

10. Joseph Conrad *Lord Jim* p. 62, The Great Writers Library, © 1988, Marshall Cavendish Ltd.
11. PWH, interview with Royal Naval History, 2000.

heaving and through the jagged edges of the hole one could see the blue glistening sea. I organised a party to remove the hammocks and lockers ... to give some space to work in. Then, with not much success, we banged at the torn edges of the plates to try and even them down, stuffing the hole, about four feet square, with hammocks over which we put tarpaulins backed with sawn planks, and shored the whole thing down to form a big 'pudding', the ancient way sailors patched a hole in their ship.'

Even in this extreme danger, Blundell, 'organised a party to remove ditty boxes to save the men's valuables. I inspected a quick-acting door ... and opening it found the room flooded. Thank heavens there was nobody down there. I gave orders that the watertight door in 43 bulkhead was not to be opened as 43's bulkhead didn't appear to be damaged. The door hinged for'ard and had it been opened the water from the Communications Messdeck would have rushed through making it difficult to shut it again. Obviously, there was a damn great hole in the ship's side somewhere. The pressing need was wood for shoring up ceilings and walls'.[12]

Damage control parties began scouring the vessel for lumps of timber, anything they could find, to support the bulging bulkheads keeping the ship afloat ... Eventually the Messdecks came to look like forests with the amount of vertical shoring erected!'

And the flooded refrigeration rooms brought grief for Blundell rushing about: 'I feel heartbroken about my 10lb Cape Town cheese, husbanded all these months in the Cold Room, waiting for the day I go on leave.'

Paul and his companions could only wait and wonder: 'What could mere men do against unyielding steel that was

---

12. Careless, *Battleship Nelson*, quoting Captain Blundell's diary.

fatally fractured? Next came a deafening rumble beginning overhead and rising to a roar; this went on and on and on and on. We had no idea what it was, and no one told us anything.'

Drifting before a hungry enemy in the path of the oncoming Italian battle fleet and wounded underwater – who could save *Nellie* now?

Then came the message that stood their hair on end – 'over the tannoy, "All hands save the ship."'[13]

---

13. Paul Houghton to the author.

CHAPTER TWO

Long Long Ago
1911 to the First World War

I remember, I remember,
The house where I was born.
Thomas Hood (1799-1845)[14]

When little Paulie was a few weeks old in his mother's arms, a young politician was staying as a guest of Prime Minister Asquith in Scotland. The PM asked him:

> whether I would like to go to [lead] the Admiralty? Burning with ambition the young man discovered in Asquith's guest room 'a large Bible lying on a table ... I thought of the peril of Britain, peace-loving, unthinking, little prepared ... Of mighty Germany towering up in her cold, patient, ruthless calculations ... I opened the book at random and saw in the 9th chapter of Deuteronomy, ... a message full of resonance.[15] 'Hear, O Israel: you are now about to ... dispossess nations greater and stronger

---

14. www.poetryfoundation.org/poems/44387/i-remember-i-remember (accessed 7.3.24).
15. Winston S. Churchill, 1911-14, pp 48-49. Quoted in John Scriven, *Beyond the Odds* (London: Wilberforce Publications, 2021), p. 434.

than you ... But be assured today that the LORD your God is the one who goes ahead of you like a devouring fire. He will destroy them; he will subdue them before you....'

(Deuteronomy 9:1-3)

This spoke to the politician how God does not allow evil to continue and may use other nations to judge evil nations. That man would lead Paul and millions on a great endeavour. His name was Winston Churchill.[16] Years later, at a critical hinge in the world struggle, he would exchange coded signals with Surgeon Lt Commander Houghton across the vast ocean.

Paul was born only ten years after the first aeroplane got off the ground and he lived through two world wars and from the Russian Revolution of 1917 to the digital revolution. 'Imagine it, Mark,' he would say, 'when I was a boy there were people alive who had known the Duke of Wellington and survivors of the battle of Waterloo. The Duke would say, "It was a near run thing – a damned near run thing. The finger of God was upon me." I have lived in the century of peace that Waterloo bought.'

Paul survived breech delivery at home – many did not. It was about midnight when a midwife delivered his mother, also a midwife, of a boy at home, whom they named Paul. 'My father was born in 1875, my brother John in 1908, and I followed on 30 September 1911, as one of the hottest summers of the century began to cool. I was born at 434 Fulham Rd, London. It was a pleasant late Regency home with a large garden, backing onto Chelsea Football Club, Stamford Bridge. Friends liked watching matches from our windows.' Coal and milk were delivered by carts to the door. 'The milkman ladled out a pint into the house-maid's jug – after blowing the froth from

---

16. Ibid.

the surface to show it was an honest pint – a habit that kept tuberculosis and other horrors in constant circulation.'

His mother, Edith, had no need to go out to work. She enjoyed their piano, having been taught by a student of Mendelssohn, and was soon teaching simple hymn chords to her boys and music hall tunes for their high spirits.

A shameful event befell Paul's maternal grandmother, and it led to Paul's second name, Winchester: 'I recall my mother's mother living in a pleasant house in the sunny village of Great Bookham. She was formidable but kindly and died in 1918. She had married in youth a character from Wiltshire surnamed Winchester and my mother, Edith, was the only child of the marriage. So her legal name was Edith Winchester. My mother's date of birth was maintained a secret – but she was some years older than my father born in 1875. They married in 1905.' Wandsworth Registry has Edith's birth in 1869 making her forty-two when Paul was born. As Paul would say to us children when we were lagging behind the herd, 'We Houghtons are late developers, but we get there in the end.'

'My maternal grandmother used the new Married Women's Act and Mr Winchester, a house painter, departed after the divorce was granted for "domestic violence". Those were the days when divorce was so rare and shameful it almost needed an act of Parliament to get one! Recalling my grandmother's indomitable, uncompromising character this separation did not surprise anyone.'

Paul continues, 'My father had come up from Broadstairs, on the Kent coast and began a builder's business on the fringe of London's smart estate called Belgravia. He bought number 434 Fulham Road towards the outskirts some three miles away.

'My earliest recollections originate here in Fulham. Father was a man with enormously strong hands. I can see him throwing down a wrench which had failed to turn a large rusty nut on the end of a water pipe. Grasping the pipe in one hand and the nut on the other he tore them apart.'

Those powerful hands were passed on to Paul – great oblong blunt-ended fingers – 'a surgeon's hands,' as he called them.

He would come to admire two giants of the twentieth century, who both had life-changing events in suburban gardens – G.K. Chesterton (1874-1936) and C.S. Lewis (1898-1963). They and Paul glimpsed, while still only small children, another Garden that was from of old, yet for ever new – a place where a Presence of utter delight lived. Paul came to find their writings blazed like lighthouses through two world wars: Chesterton in the First, and Lewis in the Second. After these intense moments of joy, all three men longed for that something that seemed just round the corner – if only it could be found.

In those days, the suburb of Fulham was, Paul remembered, 'a quiet area, and residents recalled green fields towards the Thames near Putney where Charing Cross Hospital now stands. You still saw hansom cabs with their two high wheels and a horse trotting along, mixing with the growing numbers of cars and little double-decker motor buses with open tops – there is one in the Imperial War Museum like I used to go to school on. The summer months were rich with the smell of horse muck.

'My father and his men became masters of the craft of restoring gilded plasterwork, stucco designs, around the ceilings of the great London houses.'

Two generations later, my dad still kept a booklet of that gold leaf in the drawer of his desk. When I was old enough to stand, I would position myself beside Dad's desk, while he tried to invoice his private patients: 'Mr Houghton begs to inform you that his fees for the private consultation are ten guineas.' I said, 'You get about £10 just for talking to someone!' My tiny hands opened the book of gold leaf to find a touch on the gold leaf gilded my finger, followed by, 'Oh Mark, come and wash it off before it poisons you.'

Next, I found a photo: 'Daddy, who is she?' I asked, holding up a little girl with long frizzy hair.

'That's me! It was fashionable in those days for small boys to have their hair long.' (The child looked revolting and I was glad to be born later.)

Years after, amid the loneliness of the sea, he wrote home:

My dear old Dad,

The ship's company is painting ship today... and I can never smell the oily pigment without recalling my childhood days in London, the sight of the stacked paint cans in the 'paint shop' and the odour of the timber in the adjoining workshops.

So also, the sight of men working cement now, recalls some afternoon when I watched, as a very small boy, some of your Great War veterans clearing out the cement under the steps of '434'. The smell, the sight, the colours all remove hundreds of miles of space and ¼ of a century to the days when the world seemed small and responsibilities few.

Your loving son,
Paul

Life was comfortable for the Houghtons and that summer of 1911, young Dad Albert did a railway 'package tour' to Lake Lucerne. He returned home humming the popular *The Maid of Lucerne*. More than six decades later, I got engaged to a Swiss girl, Esther, working in Lucerne.

One day little Paulie and his mother saw a crowd gathering as they walked on a London street. Children were throwing their arms in the air and screaming. Edith elbowed her way in to find a small boy lying on the pavement, blue in the face and silently gasping. 'There's a marble stuck in 'is throat ma'am,' screamed an urchin. Edith promptly held him upside down by his feet and banged him on the back. Out popped the marble and great was the rejoicing as he turned pink.

Her family were Londoners, and we don't know where they met but they were close, and Albert lavished on her a silver tea pot for their silver wedding anniversaries: 'Before their marriage, my mother had qualified in midwifery at Earl Street Hospital in central London. She would go "slumming" as volunteers with her fellow nurses in the frightful Dickensian housing around Seven Dials. Putting on their uniforms and grasping their midwives' bags they saw young women through their home deliveries.' Later, Edith became a 'matron' at the Public School in Guernsey and told how she had to jump into a sailor's arms to make a landing from an open boat.

Edith must have been a merry lady with her twinkling eyes and piano – a counterbalance to Albert's religious scruples. While brought up Church of England, she was happy to attend Albert's nonconformist 'meetings', and her letters reveal a lively faith. Paul came home one day to hear her singing a new 'hit' set to the Londonderry Air.

> I cannot tell why he, whom angels worship,
> should set his love upon the sons of men,
> ... But this I know ... he lived at Nazareth and
> laboured ...[17]

He little knew that half a lifetime later he too would labour in Nazareth.

---

17. William Young Fullerton (1857-1932), 'I Cannot Tell', (https://hymnary.org/text/i_cannot_tell_why_he_whom_angels_worship (accessed 25.10.24).

Edith retained her love of dancing, yet to her sorrow she could never persuade Albert onto the floor – a frustration to be repeated in Paul's own marriage.

There were two emotional anchors in Paul's life. Along with his mother, there was a teenage girl. 'Lucy Vine had joined us as our nurse cum nanny cum housekeeper. I would flee to her kitchen when my father had a severe mood, and she would comfort me. She too became a devout servant of the Lord Jesus, faithful to Him and loyal to us – living on some years after both my parents were dead.

'She had come into the family as a girl of 14 from the hop yards of Kent – born out of wedlock. I remember her singing me to sleep with a lullaby, the first words I committed to memory,' – words which, nearly a century later, re-emerged at the gates of death:

> My sheep know My voice and they follow,
> Yes, they follow Me, they follow me.[18]

Lucy read the boys an illustrated *The Pilgrim's Progress* with an awful illustration – that fascinated Paul – of the fiend Apollyon leaping on the hapless Pilgrim. Unknowingly, Bunyan's writings like his hymn, 'He Who Would Valiant Be', instilled courage for the coming years of conflict and for Paul's inner spiritual wrestling:

> Hobgoblin nor foul fiend
> Can daunt his spirit,
> He knows he at the end
> Shall life inherit.[19]

Little did this humble land girl guess what a harvest she would see from her sowing in such mercurial soil.

---

18. Based on the Bible, John 10:1-16.
19. John Bunyan (1628-88), 'He Who Would Valiant Be', www.hymntime.com/tch/htm/h/e/w/h/hewhowvb.htm (accessed 19.2.22). *The Pilgrim's Progress* was first published 18 February 1678 and has never been out of print. It has been translated into more than 200 languages.

CHAPTER THREE

The Piratical Grandfather
1850s to the twentieth century

Paul's paternal grand-father had a 'distinguished' career in the Royal Navy – but the wrong sort of distinguished. Like generations of Houghtons before him, Aaron had joined the Royal Navy and in the mid-nineteenth century he sailed aboard a privateer – almost an authorised pirate – prowling the American east coast. Gold fever was wafting aboard from ports along the continent and young Houghton became obsessed.

One night he and a friend deserted ship by stealing the captain's boat. Forsaking the Eastern coast they plunged into the Appalachians, the first of countless obstacles to America's vast untamed and often unknown beyond. Round them flourished unknown trees like Fraser firs and new shrubs such as camellia and rhododendron. Snakes, bears and panthers abounded, alongside elk and wolves. The trees rose to dizzy heights, chestnuts of 100ft and white pine more than 200ft. Destiny drove them forward in the vision of gold, an allure so deep they could almost smell it. Any risk was worth taking.

Heading west across the Great Plains, there was no choice but to walk towards California, along with countless others, for the gold discovered in 1849 – a staggering feat of endurance that only dawned on me in 2022 when we flew that way taking many hours. Our son, Daniel, married his American bride, Ella, in Denver at the eastern foothills of the Rockies. And the Rockies were only about half the distance, as they probably took the Oregon Trail. More people died of gunshot accidents than from Native Americans.

West of the Rockies disaster struck in the Painted Desert where water ran out and Aaron's diary recounted agonies of thirst. Paul continues:

> They were rewarded by no gold but – thirsting for more adventure – moved south to the Civil War. Offering his credentials as a sailor, he got command of a Mississippi gunboat. This he adapted with home-made armour made of railroad rails. The craft was now called, 'the Block Tin Ship,' and the innovation was imitated.[20]

During an action on the river, Aaron was leaning with his head against the mast when a cannon ball hit the mast higher up and the impact whipped down the wooden spar and concussed him. Dazed and helpless, he fell into the hands of the Royal Navy again and was clapped in irons on a ship heading for England – and court martial.[21]

As it happened, on the voyage back to England, Aaron was allowed exercise up on deck. Blinking in the sunlight, he noticed a crumpled piece of paper on the deck – a disorder almost unthinkable under Royal Navy standards. Opening the paper, he found a text from the Bible. Instantly his mind turned to God and Christ became alive and real to him.[22]

---

20. Known to PWH from reading Aaron, his grandfather's diary, lost in a house fire in 1984.
21. Told to me by Paul's cousin Tony Houghton in about 2000.
22. A tale told by Paul, based on Aaron's diary which he had read, and confirmed by Tony Houghton, Paul's first cousin.

The ship's chaplain took the doomed man in hand on the long voyage, schooling him in the new life born in his heart through faith in Christ.

Back in England the court martial sat, finding Aaron guilty of desertion and stealing a ship's boat. In the dock his life hung in the balance – naval judges of that era had pardoned capital offenders, but not all. Perhaps the ship's chaplain stood by him pleading on the evidence of a reformed life.

Sentence was passed – a lengthy period in Lewes Prison, Sussex, shifting round-shot from one corner of the prison yard to the other. But somehow, Aaron had 'interest' with the Duke of Devonshire living nearby and this good man secured his release.

Taking to the sea again Houghton's ship stopped in Guernsey and in double quick time he married a local girl living near the seafront in St Peter's Port. Eventually he would receive a pension from the American Confederate forces, a Civil War medal (dispatched to England in the late twentieth century) and even a pension from the British Navy. In Paul's opinion, 'The generations since have followed Christ becoming truly regenerated, born-again children of God. There were exceptions in each generation, but the succession continues.'

Aaron's sea chest found its way to Paul's brother John in Shropshire. There the priceless diaries were consumed in the fire. Paul remarked ruefully of his brother's house full of antiques, 'That's what happens when you set your heart on riches.'

But Paul had read the diaries and knew, 'In this box of family papers going back to the eighteenth century. Each generation had members serving in the Royal Navy. One such was captain of a "privateer," another "pirate" like Aaron. Another, a boy of twelve, was captured in the Napoleonic wars and never heard of again.'

In London, the Edwardian age of the early twentieth century was closing as Paul and his older brother, John, enjoyed their toy soldiers and locomotives that ran on live steam. Yet the wheels of history were grinding out something far worse than the American Civil War.

CHAPTER FOUR

The Great War
1914-18

Only the monstrous thunder of the guns.
Wilfred Owen (1893-1918), Anthem for Doomed Youth

The young Churchill's inklings about Germany came true. Paul's enduring memory of the First World War was walking every day, as a small boy, with his mother to Fulham Town Hall to read long lists of names – the latest casualties from the Western Front – searching for names she knew.

Walter Page, the American ambassador in London, captured the mood: 'How to pull the English off? that's a hard thing to say, as it is a hard thing to say how to pull a bulldog off.' The ambassador, watching the never ceasing procession seeking news of missing sons and husbands, was struck by the stoicism and wrote:

> Not a tear have I seen yet. You guess at their grief only by their reticence. They use as few words as possible and then courteously take themselves away. It isn't an accident that these people own a fifth of the world. Utterly unwarlike they outlast everybody else when war

comes. You don't get a sense of fighting here – only of endurance and of high resolve. I have never seen such grim resolution. [23]

'When the Great War broke out,' wrote Paul, 'my father was called up twice and was twice rejected on medical grounds. The streets were filled with men in uniform and columns of soldiers – marching to Victoria Station for the battlefronts. Then the air raids began, the boom of anti-aircraft guns, and our primitive planes passing over to attack the Zeppelin airships. One night in London we watched a Zeppelin falling in flames like a giant cigar in the sky.'

The opposing armies faced each other across 'no-man's land' – usually a stretch of mud between a network of trenches from the Channel coast to the Swiss border – the infamous Western Front. Supernatural events made a deep impression on the small family at times of overwhelming German attack and peril. In 1914, Britain's 'contemptible little army,' as the Kaiser called it, was in full retreat to Mons and the Channel ports of France. A wife received a letter, 'During the battle I saw the angels all around.' A German prisoner said to an English soldier, 'How could we break through your line when you had all those thousands of troops behind you?' But the soldier replied, 'Thousands of troops! Why, we were just a thin line with nothing behind us.'[24] Christians thanked God for prayers granted.

Paul remembered 'having violent diarrhoea one Sunday, walking in shorts, to the meeting. My father, a strict Sabbatarian, broke every rule to buy a Sunday paper to mop up my bare legs.

---

23. Arthur Bryant, *A History of Britain and the British People*, Volume Three, The Search for Justice (London: HarperCollins, 1990).
24. Scriven, *Beyond the Odds*, pp. 86-91.

On a summer's evening in June 1916, my father looked grave, standing with the newspaper in hand. "Well boys, there's been a great battle in the North Sea off the coast of Jutland. Goodness gracious, it involved 100,000 men on 250 ships. Both we and the Germans are claiming victory . . . Over 6,000 British dead and 14 ships gone to the bottom."

'That year of 1916 the air raids, though trivial by Second World War standards, became sufficiently trying for my father to move my mother and us boys to a rented farm near Haslett in Sussex, just north of the South Downs.'

These Downs are rolling hills of chalk, rising meadows that scrape the sky in arcs of close-cut grass and cropped to a springy turf by centuries of sheep. Wildflowers of summer attracted clouds of butterflies which were a delight to the two brothers. Sunshine and the wide outdoors evoked joy in Paul all his days:

Where the thistle lifts a purple crown
Six foot out of the turf,
And the harebell shakes on the windy hill –
O breath of the distant surf![25]

The boys roamed with their butterfly nets, building up collections of beauties in glass cases. 'Where are they now, Dad?' I asked as a boy.

'Oh mites ate them. When I came home from the war there was nothing left but dust.'

The hills look over on the South,
And southward dreams the sea.[26]

---
25. Francis Thompson (1859-1907), *Daisy*, https://allpoetry.com/poem/8481629-Daisy-by-Francis-Thompson (accessed 25.11.24).
26. Ibid.

The Downs where English land and sea meet. A thousand years before, people on the white cliffs watched King Alfred the Great's tiny ships – the seeds of the Royal Navy – sailing out against the pagan Danes. The Downs from where Elizabethans watched the scattering of the Spanish Armada. From these Downs, Edith and her boys could have seen the grey steel craft limping into Portsmouth as shattered remnants from the Battle of Jutland.

'Do you know?' Paul would say. 'We three, Mother, John and I, were walking one summer day on the Downs and we stopped to listen. We heard the ceaseless rumble of the guns at the Battle of the Somme – not only heard – we could *feel* the rumble under our feet. It was coming from France under the English Channel through the chalk rocks. I will never forget the horror.'

Historian Paul Fussell wrote:

The effect of the war in Britain was catastrophic: a generation was destroyed that might furnish the country's jurists, scholars, administrators, and political leaders. As one soldier wrote of the countless dead lying out in No Man's Land, 'they are England's flower, the men that England can ill afford to spare.'[27]

And Sir Arthur Bryant wrote:

The angel of death beat his wings against the panes of innumerable homes. By the spring of 1917, the German submarine campaign was sinking half a million tons of shipping a month. For a few weeks – though the hideous

---

27. Paul Fussell, *The Great War and Modern Memory* (Oxford: OUP, 1975, 2000, 2013), Kindle edition.

truth was hidden from the multitude – it seemed as though the price would be famine and defeat.[28]

The poverty of wartime diets gnawed at Paul's stomach. 'We were always short of sugar and butter and rationing was primitive compared to the Second War.'

One day little Paulie, clinging to Lucy's apron, was startled when she opened the front door to a soldier standing there, caked in mud from head to foot – it was Albert's brother. Lucy showed him into the living room. Mother appeared and ordered, 'Don't move! Lucy, fetch a sheet for Uncle Herbert to stand on.' There he peeled off his lice-laden uniform and went to a hot bath with unspeakable joy.

Herbert 'came to us straight from the battlefield. He had gone to France with the Canadian volunteers and got some leave in London. In the last week of the war, working as a stretcher bearer, he was blown to pieces, and his remains are buried in Belgium'.[29]

'I attended an "old dame school" where two elderly ladies taught me elements of learning, and devotion to Christ, according to church creeds. Then John and I went to St John's Church of England Training College school. He was a clever boy and got a scholarship to Westminster City School.'

In 1918 the nation held its breath, many praying, as a furious German onslaught threatened to overwhelm the British Army. Again, the Houghton family home was gripped by many witnesses with news of a second cluster of angelic interventions. A soldier reported:

---

28. Bryant, *A History of Britain and the British People*, Volume Three, The Search for Justice.
29. We have directions to a grave in Belgium.

At the focal point of the enemy's advance at Bethune, the Germans concentrated [their fire] on a slight rise beyond the town. The ground here was bare [of our troops] – yet enemy machine guns and shells raked it from end to end with a hail of lead. And as the British watched, they saw the Germans throw down everything they had – and fled in frantic panic...[30]

These angelic armies helped turn defeat into victory for Great Britain. Germany had nothing left. The guns of the First World War fell silent at the eleventh hour of the eleventh month, 11am, 11th of November 1918 – to the unspeakable relief of everyone. But away in Eastern Europe the pogroms flamed amid the Russian Revolution:

Unarmed Jews were thrown off moving trains, drowned in rivers and ponds. They were raped, shot, cudgelled, sliced, burnt alive and mutilated. Old men, young men, women, children, babies, the wealthy and the dirt poor. More than 100,000 Jews were murdered from 1918 to 1921.[31]

And one group was not surprised – the small bands of Plymouth Brethren diligently studying their Bibles. Albert, pointing to chapters like Deuteronomy 32, was saying, 'This is only the beginning. We haven't seen anything yet,' while Paul and John wondered what to make of it.

---

30. Scriven, *Beyond the Odds*, p. 150.
31. David Aaronovitch reviewing the book by Jeffrey Veidlinger, *In the Midst of Civilised Europe* by Jeffrey Veidlinger, The Times Saturday Review, 25 February 2022, www.the-tls.co.uk/history/twentieth-century-onwards-history/in-the-midst-of-civilised-europe-jeffrey-veidlinger-book-review-david-herman?gad_source=1&gclid=Cj0KCQjwsoe5BhD iARIsAOXVoUuXtFQSGQb4IDFJ71BLNOQpCBThzwjt5cNb39O-hb5dej6SXCrLa44aAhnw EALw_wcB (accessed 30.10.24).

Every night, Father left milk for the cat, saying with a twinkle in his eye, 'You know boys, the Lord has promised to come back and get us when we don't expect Him; and Mr Tom may need this if he is left behind.'[32]

The pogroms lay in a pattern of events that put Jews on the path to the Holocaust and a repeat world war that would sweep Paul into its maw. But now, still under twelve, he had to find his own path of life. 'Beside John, I seemed to be always in trouble.'

---

32. Mark 13:32-37, 'You do not know when that time will come . . . whether in the evening, or at midnight'.

CHAPTER FIVE

Teenager in the Twenties
1923-30

Gathering speed at an alarming rate, the two brothers hurtled down a dreamy lane in Surrey on their brand-new bikes. It was Christmas 1924 and Paul was thirteen.

Rounding a bend too fast, they met a loaded dung cart behind a plodding carthorse.

'John in front came off worst with all my weight on top of him, and when we stopped sliding, he looked as if every protuberance on his body had had a coarse file with red paint over it – nose, elbows and knees – and we were plastered with manure and heartbroken to look at our bikes.

'We staggered home and took them to the blacksmith. His face fell like a judge before giving sentence, "They will have to go through the fire." To my horror the paint came peeling off as his great hammer got to work.'

Paul's father received a letter from a local 'brother' Sydney Austin, in the Brethren: 'I am writing to tell you that your ministry on 14 December was most highly appreciated. I feel sure your son would feel free to speak in the evening if the Lord gave him a message.'

Paul and John had other ideas than preaching; so, as the price of new bikes, Albert made them learn the immortal eighth chapter of St Paul's letter to the Romans, a challenge easily met. And like leaven raising dough, through war and peace, the words worked their purpose out.

A generation later I would hear quotations pouring out of my father so I asked, 'How do you remember literature, Dad?'

'Well, I read what I enjoy, and what you enjoy you remember.' (Yes, if only.)

Before Paul arrived, Albert wrestled a tough challenge. 'My father had been brought up as a strict member of the "Exclusive" branch of the Plymouth Brethren. But once he arrived in London he separated to join the "Open" Brethren, an event which pained him.' The elders of the Exclusives assured him of a grave error. He departed feeling guilty – an unnecessary reversal of one of Christianity's unique guarantees, 'There is . . . no condemnation for those who are in Christ Jesus' (Romans 8:1).

In later life, Paul warned of Pharisee-like Christians, 'Woe to . . . you hypocrites! You shut the door of the kingdom of heaven in people's faces . . .' (Matthew 23:3-14). Albert clung to his Saviour and, Paul noticed 'my father kept his good judgement in spiritual and business matters'.

On the streets of London, men hopped past on crutches and the legless begged from wheelchairs. Other veterans seemed to stride as if against the wind, swinging their arms widely with contorted faces. 'Shellshocked,' muttered Albert, and the sheer weight of numbers forced the psychiatrists to study these shattered victims; priceless data for the next war.

At home, something had to be done. 'By 1920 Mother's chest was becoming a winter anxiety and she was apt to be bedridden for weeks at a time in the London smogs. "Fevers" were epidemic among the people. Polio spread paralysis in the hot summers. Crowded homes brought meningitis, diphtheria and scarlet fever. Only diphtheria had an "antitoxin" and antibiotics were unknown.'

Paul never got over one thing: 'You just can't believe the huge improvement in health that vaccinations brought to the population. So much heart-wrenching suffering, as parents watched their child – will she survive or not? – has become a thing of the past. St Paul's Cathedral should hold a service of thanksgiving annually for the blessing of vaccines.' (I am transcribing my father in 2020 as the coronavirus pandemic begins to terrify – and a vaccine may never be found.)

'I passed on from my "old dames" school to St Mark's School. The tuition was excellent, and kind and I recall with gratitude some of the teachers, such as Miss Douglas and the headmaster Mr Nielsen. But the Great War veterans were jumpy and prone to fits of rage in the classroom.

'When I was eight or nine years old, we had a book of excerpts from famous authors and Tennyson's *Sweet and Low* filled a page. So I had discovered a means to be transported into "realms of gold." My brother had a feeling for verse too which led to a source of pleasure which remains as I approach eighty-seven.

'At about ten, [1921] I passed an entrance exam and entered Latymer Upper School in Hammersmith, an ancient foundation with a good record of acceptance into Oxford and Cambridge.'

Little did Paul know that May of 1921, far away and deep in the Shropshire countryside on the Welsh Marches, a girl was born at the Home Farm in Great Bolas. Christened Jean – and arriving a few minutes after her twin, John – she was destined to be the most important woman in his life. She was the darling of 'the men' working the great horses. Carthorse Tommy was steady, and could be ridden. 'Once,' said Jean, 'I was walking ahead and fell down by the pond, but Tommy stopped and did not tread on me.'

Young Paulie noticed, 'Post-war London was changing. Motor cabs had almost completely replaced horse-drawn hansom cabs; but the London of Sherlock Holmes had vanished. The great London houses around Piccadilly became beyond the means of the titled aristocratic country gentry. My mother went to the sale of the superb contents of Devonshire House in Piccadilly, coming home saddened by the downfall of high society. The palm tree nursery next to our house closed and they built a block of flats in its place for the war wounded.'

Long after, when my dad and I were in London, he pointed out the re-built facades on Park Lane. 'Those great houses with their gold leaf plaster work inside had kept the family finances afloat during the Depression in the Hungry Twenties. My father kept faith with God and God never failed to provide work.

'In 1922 the BBC began its daily broadcasts with the call-sign, "2LO calling" and many of us schoolboys made crystal sets for reception. Telephones became numerous in households – our London number, Fulham 3805.

'Mother pined for green fields, and none was easy to access. For short excursions we had to be content with Brompton Cemetery where, among creepy catacombs, we found grassy plots to play on.

'Thus, my father decided the family must live in the country – a sacrifice for him who was happy in the changing scene of London and enjoying the various fine centres of Christian fellowship.

'My mother began house-hunting in south Surrey and went to a village called Lingfield. At the station she chartered a horse and carriage and ordered the cabbie to visit any likely house for sale. The first house observed was St Claire not far from the village centre. My father followed and, doubtless weary of this wild chase, bought it for £1,700.'

'We moved into St Claire in July 1924 and remained there until my father's death in 1962. My father, a conservative character, never learned to drive a car but kept up his business in London with a railway season ticket.

'That summer was warm and exciting as we discovered the lovely country in our new neighbourhood – I remember how we walked up from the station for our first evening through a cornfield and a bean field exhaling the sweet smell of the flowers – pure pleasure.

'Of course, I had to change schools, to Whitgift nearer to London. It was a 400-year-old Elizabethan foundation; closely attached to the Anglican Church.

'I cannot say I enjoyed school life and avoided "games" [sport] when possible – also because my sight was imperfect. I could do cross country because all you had to do was keep plodding at a run and I came thirteenth in the school race [so did I, MH]. I was *not* clever by many standards, and I lagged in school life.'

Turmoil hit the country, with huge unemployment and poverty culminating in the General Strike of May 1926. Fifteen-year-old Paul wished he was old enough to drive a tram to keep the nation moving.

'At home, my father and mother attended the Mission Room where the Open Brethren welcomed us in a segregated, profoundly spiritual society led by the retired village doctor, Sydney Austin MRCS. He led the assembly in the strict ways of "a people dwelling apart".

'In those days we were a group of country folk, farmworkers along with a few middle-class families. My mother kept in touch with the Church [of England] and her friends in that social world with whom she could exchange a quiet social life of morning coffee and afternoon tea. She was utterly satisfied.

'A nearby family, in a pleasant house with a tennis court, attended the Mission Room and soon became our friends because they had a girl and boy about our age. The Whitechesters were agreeable though it is hard to believe now the barriers of custom then. My parents and they always called each other by the family name preceded by "Mr" or "Mrs".'

Patricia St John, born in 1919 and later author of *Treasures of the Snow* and other bestsellers, was a guest of the Houghtons with her parents on their missionary travels.

Up north on South Tyneside, a shipbuilder was laying the keel for an enormous warship to be called HMS *Nelson*. The Admiralty were worried because Japan had an even bigger one. *Nelson* was to carry Paul beyond the horizons to the far side of the world and nations would surrender on her decks.

For now, Paul was thinking over his direction in life – as if he had some choice in the matter. But: 'Mother had one ambition for my brother John and myself. We were to enter the medical profession. John concurred readily and entered the Science Sixth Form at school. He was three years older and quite different in character and temperament – following any seductive influence. At first, he was following the world of young Christian activities, and I followed him.

'Every Sunday in our teens we cycled to a Crusaders Bible Class seven miles away staying on for tea with a pair of elderly Christians, before joining their evening service and then cycling home in summer and winter. We went to some camps and house parties but once qualified and away as a house surgeon John rapidly dropped all such activity and developed an uneasy conscience as he went his own way. He was clever, good-looking, gullible. We always kept in touch and on good brotherly terms.'

Tensions were boiling. How were John and Paul going to survive in this small clique on the margins of the community?

CHAPTER SIX

Two Bright Rebels

'Let's burn it,' agreed the brothers, so John and Paul took their father's cane that had brought them pain, snapped it and crammed it into the living room fire.

Edith took one look at a new portrait of Paulie and exclaimed, 'You look too sad – we can't have that.' He had been beaten that morning. So the portrait was repeated with a smile in place and the cane never replaced.

Nevertheless, it was the sad version which would touch a woman's heart.

Surrey offered plenty of scope for trouble . . . stories which Dad regaled me with as a boy. Wouldn't this, I wondered, make me likely to do the same? (Confidentially, yes.) So, when our own children arrived, I resolved on secrecy about my past – a policy conspicuous by its uselessness.

'As we got older we took to night running and night rides – even reaching Hever Castle. There in the moonlight was the sluice gate on a dam across the River Eden at one end of the great lake. A handle to lift the gate invited immediate use. We wound and wound till the water was roaring through under the stars. Then we vanished into the night.

'Another attraction was a vicarage with a long drive and an enormous dinner gong. It hung by a rope outside the front door for the servants to call the children in for meals.

John, me, and Murray Whitchurch used to dare each other to pick up the hammer and see how many times we could hit it before our nerve broke or the door opened. I did ten and John made twelve.'

On Sundays in the assembly the brethren had, in the boys' eyes, an over weighty seriousness. Seeing an elderly brother heave himself to his feet and ask the little flock to turn to Exodus chapter 3, the two waited for the exquisite moment: 'Now Moses,' intoned the brother, 'led the flock to the backside of the desert...'[33] and no sooner was 'backside' out of the man's mouth than they began to snigger at the black-suited backsides in front of them. 'Several times we were dragged out howling with laughter.'

Another opportunity was the well-known hymn:

As pants the hart for cooling streams,
Though heated in the chase...[34]

Tortured with suppressed laughter they invented more adventures for the hart named Pants.

Family holidays involved 'packing half the house and decamping for a month at a time by train' to a house by the sea in Devon or Cornwall, the luggage going on ahead. Albert often tormented the family by disappearing to buy a newspaper. As the guard's whistle blew, he would reappear dashing through the belching steam to be dragged aboard the moving carriage.

Lucy travelled as the housekeeper and 'made life just too easy for those boys'. This was the view – later in life – of their wives, Jean and Frankie. 'John [or Paul as the case might be] is

---

33. Verse 1, AKJV.
34. N. Tate (1652-1715), N. Brady (1639-1726), 'As Pants the Hart for Cooling Streams', https://www.hymnal.net/en/hymn/h/349 (accessed 25.10.24).

awful. He leaves his towel on the bathroom floor in a pool of water and walks off.'

All his life, Paul's holiday packing was minimal, yet somehow he never forgot his books and bare essentials; then he relaxed in the sun, while the family flew about trying to get ready in time.

Such carefree living left the boys: 'rather bored, so we used to go off exploring. There was a Cornish tin mine nearby with tunnels and little wagons on rails. One of these rested on an incline heading into a tunnel so we got in and pushed off with John in the front. Faster and faster, we plunged into the gloom when John shouted, "Light ahead," and an instant later, "Jump ... jump" and leapt over the side – revealing to me a circle of enlarging whiteness – as if zooming-in. I jumped a second before the wagon launched itself into space and plunged far below into a flooded quarry with a great splash.'

As if that was not enough, they tortured each other by sitting on the luggage rack of a bicycle facing backwards while the other steered fast downhill. This sounds benign until anyone tries it themself on the gentlest incline – torture!

Despite the cynicism the flickering flame of faith flared into a fire. Paul decided as a teenager on full immersion baptism. He was glad to act out the death of his own desires and die with Christ – under the water – so as to share in resurrection with Christ up from the water. The divine 'deal' also delivered the Holy Spirit coming to dwell in Paul as the Comforter. Times of desperation lay ahead that could wrestle him to the ground, yet the Comforter would outlast the desperation.[35]

Clearly, something had to be found for these brothers to do in life.

---

35. 'The Father... will give you another Helper, to be with you for ever, even the Spirit of truth, whom the world cannot receive' (John 14:16-18, ESV UK).

CHAPTER SEVEN

Barts by the Meat Market
1928-34

> There is a divinity that shapes our ends,
> rough-hew them how we will.
>
> *William Shakespeare (1564-1616), Hamlet, Act V, Scene II*

In an effort to harness Paul's energies, Albert had entered Paul into the Merchant Navy as a cadet at the age of thirteen, but he was rejected when the routine Ishihara colour chart showed he was colourblind.

That was not putting Edith off her own plans, despite her son's misgivings about blood: he was unsure whether he could even recognise blood as blood – when it was green. Secretly, Paul fostered a wish to become a lawyer and was in thrall to the Inns of Court and the logic of argument. He imagined himself standing before the judge and running rings round the opposing barrister. Never lost for a facetious word, 'I was confident that, had I been allowed to study Law, I should without difficulty become Lord Chief Justice at least.'[36]

---

36. Handwritten account by Paul in his late eighties.

Having none of this, Edith led him up at eighteen to enrol at the famous 'Barts', St Bartholomew's Teaching Hospital in the City of London next to Smithfield meat market.

Paul felt: '... for my part I was less confident about entering medicine with the disease and suffering as it was in the 1920s. My history master wanted me to study for a scholarship to Cambridge, but my mother was resolute and her ambition for both of us was to enter Barts. I suspect she had some sort of emotional liking for a surgeon there, one Mr Adam with strong Christian beliefs.

'My brother was three years ahead of me and my day came. Mother marched me up to London on a foggy autumn morning – but there I led us on a detour. At Gray's Inn Chapel I bade a last reluctant goodbye to the legal world I thought should be mine. The magnet was the body of the great Lord Birkenhead – known as FE Smith in politics – which lay in state from 1 October to 3 October for the legal and political worlds to pay their last respects.'[37]

Paul's ambitions lingered and I recall my father saying to me as he drove me into Worcester one day, 'You have a logical mind, Mark, and I think you would make a very good lawyer.' No pressure – but it stuck inside me. Even so – better a parent's encouragement than ridicule – and my father's belief in the power of truth continues to inspire me in the defence of our fellow humans who face killing by my profession through abortion and euthanasia.

---

37. 'Lord Birkenhead was a figure of enormous importance. He had a furious debate in Parliament with the brother of the poet GK Chesterton. Afterwards *Chuck it Smith*, GK's poem in support of his brother, rippled merrily around the country. Birkenhead died on 30 September 1930 aged 58 and after a cremation at Golders Green Crematorium his ashes were buried in the graveyard of St James' Church, Charlton-by-Newbottle in Northamptonshire, where his country house was.' (Personal communication from Andrew Mussell, Archivist, The Honourable Society of Gray's Inn, London, WC1R 5ET.)

There was no entrance exam for Barts, 'and it came down to enthusiasm, aptitude and the mysterious world of the Dean at interview.'

Well, Mr Girling Ball FRCS, and I interviewed each other. The blustering Dean was one of five senior general surgeons, of whom – if my memory is accurate – only one had a university degree. Neither he nor I could trace any vocation for the profession; he was explicit, and I was implicit, but the fees were accepted, and I was entered on the college roll.[38]

Who could have guessed that only ten years later, senior naval colleagues would record '. . . Houghton has performed all the operations – more than 300 in number – and all have been most successful . . .'? Paul sometimes muttered Shakespeare's line, 'There's a divinity that shapes our ends, rough-hew them how we will.'[39]

'My brother John initiated me into the Victorian hospital founded in 1123.' As Britain's oldest hospital, offering free care for 900 years, Hogarth had honoured it with vast paintings of biblical scenes on the great stairs. And for eighteen months, Paul pursued the study of human anatomy, physiology and biochemistry, taught by eminent men.

'The dissecting rooms where the bodies lay smelled of carbolic preservative, reminiscent of Robert Louis Stevenson's *The Body Snatchers*. Open coal fires at each end rendered the obese corpses liquid and the skinny ones supple. My first acquaintance with its interior occurred in a dense, though unexceptional, London fog which obscured the interior of the

---

38. Article by PWH, 'Digging up the Past', St Bartholomew's Hospital Journal, Summer 1977, SBHMS/PB/1/85. Used with permission.
39. William Shakespeare, *Hamlet* (1564-1616), Act 5, Scene II.

dismal building. Also here, was a large clinical lecture theatre badly lit so that one could recline in secure ease on the upper benches or carve one's name amid the relics of eminent predecessors.

'Mr Hallet, the Attendant, reigned in Victorian gloom among the dead in his tanks and on the tables. Here one could dissect in amiable conversation. The Attendant to the organic chemistry lab was Mrs Gowcher. She was a Cockney lady of inimitable wit and a great (and illegal) help in the vital "Second MB" [Second Bachelor of Medicine] exam at the end of second year. So was Mr Bridle who checked one in for lectures and would accommodate an absent student for a small gift.

'The second-year exams were surmounted and I had gained Second MB, the key to the excitement of three years with real patients before – hopefully – qualification.'

In the Casualty and out-patients the smelly feet of patients nearly made Paul vomit. He 'entered the wards as a student "surgical dresser" under a bully of a man, the aforementioned Dean, Mr Girling Ball. In 1932 antibiotics and "Sulpha drugs" were still in the future and yet major operations went favourably. The invisible staphylococcus, causing septicaemia was a desperate matter and one young surgeon of great promise died after an accidental needle prick.

'I am confident there was much hardship endured by many students, and of course there were no university grants or loans worth mentioning. These were the Hungry Thirties and the idea of living in student "digs" was avoided if possible. I could live at home and most days came up from my parents by train.

'Men up from the country needing to live in London, often did so in poverty unsuspected by the College authorities, who provided no organised care for their wellbeing. Some of us fell by the wayside; tuberculosis was the death-trap and I lost one or two of my friends. The poet and medical student John Keats had had lodgings beside Bow Church in Cheapside. No one could improve his description of the disease that would kill him too, soon after he left medical school:'

> The weariness, the fever and the fret.
> Where youths grow pale, and spectre thin, and die:
> Where beauty cannot keep her lustrous eyes,
> Or new love pine at them beyond tomorrow.[40]

'The disease in the London hospitals was tragic and too often so little could be done. But medicine was on the move. Surgery was pressing ahead without the benefit of blood transfusion or antibiotics. Mr JH Roberts FRCS[41] developed the new concept of the team – surgeons, nurses and scientists together – pioneering surgery on the lungs for tuberculosis.

'Sir Geoffrey Keynes FRCS was contributing new methods and ideas to breast cancer surgery. How I admired him from afar; he who could operate so superbly and also reach such eminence as a writer.'

Men like Keynes had memories crammed with combat and he said, 'A German shell landed near a British artillery battery and killed five officers, including the major commanding, who were standing in a group. I attended as best I could to each of them, but all were terribly mutilated and were dead or dying.'

He wonders why he remembers 'the small ironic detail of the major's dead dog' that enables him to recall an incident of 26 January 1916.[42]

---

40. John Keats (1795-1821), *Ode to a Nightingale*.
41. Roberts artery forceps are still used for operating.
42. Sir Geoffrey Keynes speaking in 1968, quoted in Fussell, *The Great War and Modern Memory*.

Then Paul observed a revolution. 'As I was qualifying a new star rose in the therapeutic firmament; "Prontosil"[43] heralding the era of the antimicrobial; and Prof Garrod, was at hand to apply these weapons.'

In the numerous academic examinations Paul learned perseverance the hard way. This made him soft towards me. As his son, I wanted to shine, but after one of my exam flops as a junior doctor, I had a letter: 'As a family we are used to failing exams but finally getting what we want. My own father was always decent about it and always confident about the end result. My Ma' never doubted – such faith in her offspring and her Lord's will!'[44]

But calamity crashed in. 'One roasting afternoon we students were feeling rather pent-up in the hospital, so we decided to go up on the roof of the Pathology Wing to have a bit of fun.

'From this vantage point we had acquired great skill with a catapult firing steel ball-bearings. There were tables in the street below outside the White Hart pub where men from the meat market took their beer. We got so good that we could hit a glass pint full of ale with precision – terribly dangerous of course. But it was satisfying to see strong men leap to their feet as a golden tide flooded down over their knees. A very fat man stood up and bent over to tie his shoelace, with his enormous bottom stretched like a drum skin towards us. Irresistible. I took aim and got him on the backside . . . He jumped up with a roar clutching his behind, whipped around and looked up. Spotted! The enraged bloodhounds set off as

---

43. 'Prontosil was the first drug to successfully treat bacterial infections and the first of many sulpha drugs –forerunners of antibiotics. Gerhard Domagk published it in 1935. Among the early patients was Domagk's own six-year-old daughter, Hildegard, who had contracted a severe streptococcal infection from an unsterilized needle. She recovered. Prontosil earned its creator a Nobel prize which the German authorities forced him to reject', www.sciencehistory.org/historical-profile/gerhard-domagk (accessed 15.2.22).
44. PWH letter to Mark 1982.

one, running at the hospital entrance and trapping us on the stairs. We were dragged by the scruff of our necks before the authorities. Up before the Dean matters looked grave indeed and I could see no prospect of forbearance – unless the conversation was kept going by every art of the advocate. His mind was directed away from us, as something unworthy of consideration, to himself and his achievements; the glowing description confirmed his own inklings, and we parted almost as equals. Even so, like a judge about to pass sentence, it looked like open door going only one way. Mother came up and pleaded for me and won him over. He could be a most humane man.'

Paul's confrontations with authorities were set to be repeated in the darkest hours of the Second World War. Looking back, long decades later, Paul decided, 'Times past are a distorting glass through which to look. The hospital – although a little too snobbish – was a fraternity excluding no individual. In accordance with the faith Rahere, the medieval monk and founder, all worked to fulfil his intentions – the relief of suffering and the healing of the sick.'[45]

Yet for young Paul this marvellous society raised tantalising questions as to how to meet his need for people – especially females?

---

45. Rahere the monk was a favourite of King Henry I. He founded the Priory and its Hospital of St Bartholomew in 1123 after falling dangerously ill in Rome. There God met him in a dream about founding a hospital in London.

CHAPTER EIGHT

Friends and the Gentler Sex
1930s

I look into your lovely eyes,
I hear your gentle voice,
You came to me from Paradise
And made my heart rejoice.

For his twenty-first birthday Albert gave Paul an essential: a dinner jacket and trousers in the fashionable Midnight Blue. This remained a good fit for the next seventy years, as he remarked, 'it has been in and out of fashion about five times'.

'For the first time I encountered the other sex in the form of the nursing staff. The nurses lived a life of conventional discipline and interminable hours. There was boundless fun, and "with every goose a swan, and every lass a queen."[46] My friends and I did not starve when one could cook bacon and eggs by midnight in the ward kitchen. Absurd events were always occurring in that wonderful society so old and for ever youthful.'[47]

---

46. Charles Kingsley, nineteenth-century poet and prophet famous for *The Water Babies* – the bestselling novel about child poverty and forced labour.
47. Article by PWH, 'Digging up the Past', in *The Barts Journal*, Summer 1977.

'I was painfully shy with girls, worshipping from far off, but it was a delightful experience and lots of nice girls were charming towards me. At Christmastime I was embarrassed and helpless when many of them invited me to their dances. This was considered a wicked frivolity in the Assembly, most of all by my mother who was envious and shielded the male members of her family from the "gentler sex", as it was called in those remote days.

'However, the attraction was strong, and I became acquainted with a very nice girl. We exchanged letters and a few meetings by way of the letter racks in the students' union. I was foolish enough to leave a few of these in my briefcase, locked; but my mother found a key, opened it, read the letters and was nearly beside herself, seeking support from my father.

'Later, he told me that he instructed his wife not to be stupid and to trust me. This was no comfort to my mother, and she wrote to the Dean who knew her by now. He said nothing to me but gave me lots to do in his operating theatre where I discovered a flare for operative surgery. He wrote to my mother a courteous, wise letter, also telling her not to be stupid.

'A rift between my mother and her younger son occurred which was never fully bridged – we were a close family.[48]

'I made some lasting friends in my student days which have only been interrupted by death. We were Christians. I cannot tell a particular moment when I could say that I trusted in the Lord Jesus. As children we were taught this state of a new being in Christ. And I found one or two others in the student world with whom it was possible to share these hopes – and the fears they brought of being different.

---

48. PWH handwritten life story 1998.

'Dick Prewer was one. A constant friend from 1932 through all the years of war and peace. And Maurice Carpenter whose parents were devout Christians of the Brethren persuasion and knew my mother and father. He was working in the family business. Then when I was a third-year student he came to Barts late. He was very clever and sailed through his exams effortlessly, later gaining the MD London.[49] He was one of those characters to be described as "saintly", having a natural other-worldly spirit who was at home with Christ. He was devoted to his sister, Joan, much younger than himself, and he never married.'

Joan was to appear in astonishing circumstances soon!

This band of brothers held evangelistic camps in the New Forest, under canvas, and their names, along with others like 'Old Brodie', keep cropping up in letters their only forms of communication.

Paul loved London and the life at Barts. More than forty years later he and I were sat by the fire in Worcestershire, and I noticed his glum 'winter' face. I tried a story from the Charing Cross Medical Student Christmas Review which I had just acted in:

'Dad, have you heard this one about the two women in the waiting room?'

He barely reacted.

'Two Cockney women are sitting in the doctor's waiting room, and one says, "Oh 'allo, Lil, and what are you doing 'ere?"' (I paused to check he was listening – yes, the newspaper was lowered.)

'"Well, I took those pessaries and stuck 'em in the back passage like the doctor sez, but for all the good they did, I might just as well have shoved 'em up my bum."'

---

49. MD – Doctor of Medicine is a postgraduate doctorate requiring original research.

The shaft went home and his face cracked into laughter until he grasped his knees with both hands and threw back his head as the tears ran. Then came back one of his own: 'I was the back legs of the horse in the Barts Christmas show and my job was the droppings, dried prunes in a paper bag held between my legs in one hand. These were "evacuated" with "thunder" towards the Dean and his front row guests.'

We moved onto names and I said, 'There was the dermatologist Geoff Cream at Charing Cross.'

'Really! Dr Cream?'

'And Dr Brain on staff, a neurologist; along with Mr Waterfall the urologist and even the rectal surgeon Mr ****. Yes honestly.'

Marriage between students was rare then. Junior doctors might work unpaid for the first six months as it was a 'favour' to work for 'their Lordships,' as Paul and his band called them. 'We never had enough money to think of marrying.'

One wonders, was it the Sister for Bowlby ward or Sister for Heath-Harrison who used to snuggle close to Sir Geoffrey Keynes during surgery? 'As students we could see she was in love with him.'

And always the relentless studies went on. I still have a letter Dad wrote to me at boarding school aged eighteen. I was struggling with school life and A-levels:

> I can understand your feelings. But you are making headway although things may seem boring. One has in life to become like the man, '... Who came to like steep hills and heavy loads and all difficult things, even dull things too.' [50] I used to have that written on a card on my

---

50. Author unknown.

desk when I was a student and it helped – and helped others. Lots of people used to copy it. There's always the soft sky, often a gleam of sun, and even a corner of warm ground to relax in. One wants to make a corner of one's interior life, a sort of shrine where one can rest while no one interferes and where one can escape to.

God bless you, you dear old boy.

Daddy xxxxxx[51]

Those disciplines of habitual dedication were about to be tested beyond Barts.

---

51. PWH to the author.

CHAPTER NINE

Sodom by the Sea
1936-38

Ars longa, vita brevis.
'Art is long, life is short,' on a plaque
outside Sheffield Medical School

At last, after five years' study, Paul passed finals and could call himself 'doctor' – Bachelor of Medicine and Surgery. He was quick to point out this was honorary only. In medieval times the 'real' doctor was the Doctor of Theology in the monastic centres of learning like Oxford and Cambridge. There the friars educated the poor to liberate them from the chains of ignorance.

Rahere, founder of St Bartholomew's Hospital, did the same for the sick. Medieval folk called them 'merry friars' because of their cheerfulness among the destitute of the gutters.

After 'a job of little consequence', Paul was fortunate to be accepted at the Royal Sussex County Hospital, Brighton, a hospital with a fine clinical staff. 'In those days, the "Voluntary Hospitals" – before the NHS – could afford few juniors. One or two of us could afford a car but I did not, but I look back to those days with glowing pleasure.'

His first letter home, hurriedly scrawled on hospital notepaper reports

Royal Sussex County Hospital,
Brighton.

5.1.36

My dear old Mum and Dad,

This is now my fifth day at Brighton and my first day off-duty, that is theoretically; actually, there are many duties to perform in your spare time interfering with pre-planned schemes.

Well, 'night cometh',[52] and I must sleep for the days are tiring and I'm very lazy. I think I may be home for the day next Sunday week if all goes well so keep some breakfast for me won't you Mum.

Ever your loving son
Paulie

Cooped up in the hospital the young men had steam to let off.

'We thought it would be funny to rag up a matron who gave us a tough time. I got down in the bushes outside her bedroom and aimed a firework rocket at the window. It backfired and I got a nasty burn on my finger which went septic. A few days later I had to have it lanced by one of my colleagues – a scar I still have.

'This reminds me of the eminent surgeon who had a case, a boy with a red finger. He incised it too early which provoked a full septicaemia. The lad died two days later.

---

52. John 9:4, AKJV.

'Another matron invited us juniors for afternoon tea. This tested our patience and politeness, so we arranged for a colleague to climb up on the roof ready to put a slate over the chimney pot.

'As conversation stalled and the food ran low, a prearranged signal was sent. The room began to fill with smoke from the grate. We leaped to our feet, "Good heavens, what's going on Matron? Something must have fallen down the chimney . . . We'll fix it . . ." the moment for a general evacuation.'

My dear old Dad and Mum,

I wonder, 'who is my neighbour?' I suppose the answer is '[and a] man went down from Jerusalem to Jericho, and fell among thieves' and he is my neighbour.[53]

Because there are many in Brighton who have fallen among thieves. For here is Vanity Fair, a city consecrated to vanity where you may purchase, and many do, all manner of vanities. Brighton and Hove are like Sodom on Sea, like London's sewer mouth.

Suicides we have here in any number; not folk of unsound mind but just men and women claiming their wages of the devil at the end of the day's work. Last night a woman was brought in half drowned – attempted murder or suicide?

I hope Billy is well.[54] Tell him to expect me and tell Lucy to keep breakfast for me. We live like fighting cocks at this hospital. The day's work is never done, and I must go; remember me in your prayers.[55]

---

53. Quoting Jesus, 'The Good Samaritan' recounted by the biblical doctor and author of Luke 10:25-37, AKJV.
54. Billy the family spaniel.
55. PWH to Edith and Albert Houghton 13 January 1936.

Deep in a corner of their hearts Paul and Jack grew longings for those places far away to the North West along the Welsh Marches:

> Had I been Norman William
> Possessing for my goods,
> Fairy tale thatched cottages
> And fairy haunted woods,
> I would have spent my days
> Far from battle frays,
> Drinking sweet apple cider
> At the inn of the Four Cross Ways.[56]

Jack had set off for those parts with a job in Shrewsbury hospital and his first letter home reported, 'Terribly sad, the House Physician died early this morning of pneumonia. He had been ill for eight days. Poor old Dr Warwick is terribly upset and blames himself.'[57]

As I read this letter in September 2020, an envelope arrives from the NHS inviting me for a pneumococcal vaccination: prevention in one shot – amazing!

Down in Brighton Paul was wrestling:

From the HOUSE PHYSICIAN

The Royal Sussex County Hospital,
Brighton
26.1.36

My dear old Mum and Dad,

I have been inside the hospital for four days in a row, and any reminder of the outside healthy world is welcome.

---
56. Original and author not yet found.
57. Dr John Houghton to Edith and Albert Houghton, 5 May 1936.

Patients have a habit of causing anxiety just as one is putting on an overcoat to go out.

There is precious little 'fellowship of the saints' in the place, although the staff are excellent folk. Only when you dwell among the ungodly do you realise the austere beauty of the Christian message and the creative power of the good news of God. Here only lies the power to give dignity to the wayfaring fools of mankind.

Your two parcels found me, and I now have multitudinous pairs of pants...

On Wednesday, I went to Hove hospital, where my friend is house surgeon. We later embarked on a ward service with the Padre's permission – of a 'hot gospelling type'. It's the most courageous enterprise, because the ward sisters have combined to oppose him at every turn, although the doctors support him against them.

Last night I went to the real fold [the Plymouth Brethren], and I went to sleep. They were the same as ever and moderately glad to see me. So very few have the truth or life, and nearly all think they have it.

And now the day is over, very sunny day and delightful, with the evenings lengthening out. A soft south wind is blowing in shoreward from the English Channel, and the sea is talking quietly, and it is peaceful to sit and listen to it.

Ever your loving son,
Paul

Meanwhile Dick Prewer was fifty miles along the coast at Portsmouth and he wrote:

You will not be surprised to be told that I've become friendly with a member of the nursing staff of this place.

Before asking her out I pointed out that there was 'nothing doing'! So that put things on the level. However, to get out in the lanes once or twice a week has done us both a lot of good.

There's nothing more in it, of course: like you, my few affections are locked away and doled out only on rare occasions.

Paul's policy was what he called keeping his affections in cold storage, yet

When all the world is young, lad,
And all the trees are green;
And every goose a swan, lad,
And every lass a queen;
Then hey for boot and horse, lad . . .[58]

Boot and horse could be hired. So Paul invested in some twill riding breeches, taking to the chalk Downs rising in white cliffs and planting some Thomas Hardy lines in his heart forever:

Oh the opal and the sapphire
of that wandering Western sea,
And the woman riding high above
Who nobly loved me.[59]

As to medicines, Paul and Dick knew that the drugs they had were mostly useless. Dick was enjoying his new freedom.

---

58. Charles Kingsley (1819-75), 'The Old Song', www.bartleby.com/336/247.html (accessed 12.9.20).
59. Thomas Hardy, 'Beeny Cliff', 1870.

Prescribing has become a joy. I can baffle the pharmacists and the poor patients of the Workhouse. Sleeping draughts are my specialty, with morphine, hyoscine, omnopom.

Ever yours
Dick

Many of Paul's circle of Christian friends had survived the undergraduate years with their faith intact. Now, money and status began to chip away at this faith. Paul knew what he must do, while maintaining a facetious distance as he wrote to his parents:

> I have just returned from the goodly fellowship of the saints and the Bible reading. A message was given that dealt with St Peter's denials which made me sit up and take notice. I also heard from John yesterday. He is full of the deceitfulness of riches, coining money![60]

Dick wrote about their dreams of missionary work:

> I long for the caresses of a Barts Blue Belt – I'm not particular which one at present, as long as she isn't a missionary in embryo.
> Medicine in England seems to demand almost everything a man has, but what it can be like in Timbuktu or B'nana, one doesn't like to think. Dishonest locals – heat – flies – no whisky – bandits, who demand the very pants you stand up in – your wife's hair falling out – the children with jaundice and diarrhoea – blunt scalpels – the long grass – elephants who break down the Mission Hospital – vertical sun – snakes in your slippers – still no

---

60. Letter PWH to parents, 26 February 1936.

whisky – a consignment of 100,000 *Hymns Ancient and Modern*, when you were hoping for a machine gun or a Ford car. How I recall all our own foolishness – and say, 'No thank you'.

PS Don't follow the 'devices and desires of your own heart' with those nice nurses, will you.

Paul tried to go further: 'I applied to serve overseas with the Church Missionary Society and never got a reply.'

Since there were no specialists in anaesthetics 'putting the patient to sleep' was left to the untrained junior doctors:

The worst death was a child of seven who died on the operating table. I was anaesthetising with chloroform. The operation was practically finished when she suddenly died. It exemplified the danger of this drug and any amount of care won't prevent these deaths. The surgeon completely exonerated me, but it is most upsetting.

These happenings are not altogether explainable, but I always commit the details of the day's work into Divine hands most definitely, and then if untoward events occur, I have the certainty that they are at least planned and foreknown.

I have received praise from high quarters for my work already, which is at least gratifying, but you always wish more could be done.

A patient developed meningitis and I was up all Saturday night and doing all I could for him on Sunday – without avail. He's only one of 4 deaths, and I believe more to follow. These bad patches are very depressing, and one feels helpless.[61]

---

61. PWH to parents 23 January 1936.

Dick wrote from Southsea:

> My dear Paul,
>
> It was pleasant indeed to read your letter, each is a treasured classic to me.
> The medical men here, are not given to wine – but filthy talk – albeit better doctors than I. One loses all sense of shame here and talk openly of VD to the nurses without a blush.
> If you don't take your female friends to dances at least do the decent thing and take them out for a walk. You can take 2 at a time to prevent any mischief.

However, Paul decided the best policy was 'to keep my feelings in cold storage'. One incident only surfaced in 1990 when my father was driving my wife, Esther, and her older sister, Regina. These pretty girls laughing at his stories seemed to oil a readiness to divulge:

> A curious event happened in the fine summer of 1936. I received a letter from an unnamed correspondent signed 'Mrs – – – –,' asking me to come to her home near South Croydon because she wished to disclose a matter of immense importance. The consensus of my colleagues was on acceptance, curiosity overwhelming us.
> So on my first free Saturday afternoon I climbed the long, steep hill to their address and knocked at the door of a small modern house. A grey-haired lady admitted me and reached for my hand. I nearly fled – but entered the trap.
> She then, in the hall, made a statement at high speed that she 'rejoiced at my appearing and that prayer had been answered'. I could not assent but could see no escape.

I tried to say that we were strangers and that I was mystified. She said that I must know Joan . . . And still I looked blank and said, 'Who is Joan and who are you?'

'Oh,' said she, 'I am Maurice Carpenter's mother and our prayers are answered.' Then the penny dropped; the Carpenters were old family friends from Brethren circles.

'What prayers?' said I, and the reply came that, 'That you should marry our daughter Joan.'

I replied that I did not want to marry, that my profession was all I could cope with, and anyway that I had no money.

She replied that Joan had plenty – and that Joan was upstairs anxious to be summoned.

She offered no tea or lemonade on that hot afternoon. All I could say was, 'No, no I must catch my train.' I was led into the Presence. I could feel the heat of the room multiplying my waistcoat warmth and building, under my starched collar, to be almost overwhelming.

Sweat broke out all over me and I thought I might faint and sink like a fly stuck in a pot of runny honey. How could I escape? The terror of being ensnared for ever! Just as I began to make my excuses a huge tray of tea and sandwiches was brought in.

I sat speechless in front of the girl and her parents. How could I tell them that the thought of being stuck with her for life was a fate worse than death? Being plied with more and more tea and sandwiches I began to mumble, 'Look here – you might have heard from God but I certainly have not,' – and declining the offer to pray together I began to back out of the room, turned and rushed for the door and down the stairs.

Never was the fresh air on the street and the throng of people so welcome.[62]

And back in Brighton he was astonished by an incident which turned the tide into a flood.

---

62. Paul's oral and written accounts.

CHAPTER TEN

Tide on the Flood

There is a tide in the affairs of men.
Which, taken at the flood, leads on to fortune.
Forsaken and all their days are bound in shadows.

*William Shakespeare (1564-1616), Julius Caesar,
Act IV, Scene II*

The virgin abdomen lay before Paul's eyes – a white square cleaned and waiting, framed by the surgical drapes. The senior surgeon paused, facing Paul across the patient, and paused to operate. Then the Chief said, 'Houghton, swap places.' So, they changed sides and Paul stood by the scrub nurse, thinking the surgeon wanted a better angle on the abdomen. But the scrub nurse placed the scalpel firmly in Paul's palm. And his heart beat faster.

His hands hovered above the skin. Then, stretching it tight with his right hand he cut with the left. (Secretly, he had been training himself to be ambidextrous.) After the final sutures were in place, the Chief said, 'You almost did that operation yourself didn't you.' His next letter home bubbles, 'I did my first appendix, and soon I hope to have plenty of emergency work.'[63]

---

63. PWH to Albert and Edith Houghton, 29 May 1936.

Something else watered the green shoot of a surgical career. My father and I discussed this.

'When I qualified,' he said, 'I knew the Pharmacopoeia cover-to-cover – a book the size of a family Bible. And I reckoned there were only five or six drugs that were any use at all.'

'Oh really,' I said. 'Let's work out what they were.'

'The sulpha antibiotics had not arrived in useful amounts.'

'I suppose you had aspirin – and for severe pain morphine.'

'Yes and – see that foxglove there by the kitchen garden – the leaf gave us digoxin for heart failure.'

'And you had chloroform as anaesthetic,' I said. 'Queen Victoria popularised this by having it for childbirth – did you know she named her child Anaesthesia? That helped women because if the great queen could have pain relief in childbirth why shouldn't all women? Up to that time the view was that painful birth was just part of life; and unchangeable consequence the curse of Eve's original sin.'

'Yes,' my father replied. 'Adam and Eve made a terrible mistake, but all that about women needing pain in childbirth – it's stuff and nonsense. So you see, with few drugs of any use, I liked surgery because you could help the patient.'

And in Brighton another force was surging Paul forwards. He wrote home in spring 1936:

> My chiefs are quite extraordinary men. One is senior surgeon and a man of great clinical judgement and operating skill and most conscientious. He told me when I 'came on' as a houseman in the hospital that he always puts his patients first, implying that he expects me to do the same. He considers each individual with the greatest care, more care than most men treat their private

patients, knowing them all by name. He is also a first-rate teacher.

I have been very, very busy, working 16 and 18 hours on one or two days, and tired to death in my spare time. I have 60 beds more or less and they cannot be left for many hours.

And yet the big decision hung in the air: 'I should like to get an MD. For I do not expect to become a practising surgeon. My interests lie still in the physician's activities.' And he never wavered from believing a good surgeon is a physician who operates.

Furthermore, their community was inspiring: 'Living in the hospital, designed for the relief of the effects of a grotesquely fallen nature, I wonder and wonder at the happiness of this institution. It is one of the nicest places I have lived in, and beyond all the abnormalities of body and mind found in the walls, everyone finds more to laugh at than those who live in a world of normality.

'So many glorious things are here, noble and right; often we marvel at the amount of good in other people and of evil in ourselves. God is very good to us. Much of his creation is still as he saw it, "very good".'[64]

Lastly, Paul updated his parents on the essential for his waistcoat pocket:

The gold watches are too expensive I'm afraid and the rolled gold watches savour of make-believe. Of the silver watches the Hunters are attractive, and I'm in a position to contribute from my earnings![65]

---

64. 'God saw all that he had made, and it was very good' (Genesis 1:31).
65. PWH to parents 12 April 1936.

On the wards new joys welled up:

> That girl of suicidal intentions is still with us and not doing at all badly.
> I had the pleasure of rescuing from the jaws of death, a patient – gravely shocked – by blood transfusion, three times on Friday night. He was practically dead when I gave him the first transfusion and slowly he improved as the blood passed into his veins. Quite spectacular, I assure you. I took a pint and ½ of blood from the donor and stored it in ice for use during the night.
> The surgeons allow me the appendicectomies now, and already I have quite a collection of my own cases. On Tuesday night I removed the gangrenous appendix from a patient at midnight and next day he was reading his paper and looking very fit.

By the time he left Brighton he had learned to get down on his knees to the patient's level, focusing on the surface of the abdomen and seeking swellings or writhings of the bowels and feeling that 'a blockage in the bowels must be one of the most awful pains we can experience'.

Then he stood and extended a great hand to land on the abdomen, as an insect on a flower. 'Lord Horder taught us at Barts that an examination of the abdomen must be a caress.'

He strove to embody the teaching of William Osler, 'the father of modern medicine'. 'The good physician treats the disease; the great physician treats the patient with the disease.' Paul was learning the power of touch to communicate compassion and healing to the vulnerable. And the cost: 'I began a letter in bed and was overcome with weariness, my pen refused to write and I slept.'

Recharging the batteries became a 'must' – but how?

CHAPTER ELEVEN

Love and Life

Where the thistle lifts a purple crown
Six foot out of the turf,
And the harebell shakes on the windy hill –
O breath of the distant surf!'
Francis Thompson (1859-1907), Daisy

Yesterday evening I sought the solitude of the Downs. I climbed onto the ridge, the southern limit of the Weald, and walked west with a keen east wind blowing me hither and thither. Then I climbed to a high beacon, Blackcap, by ancient hut circles and weird tumuli; and as night fell and the Western sky dimmed, I watched the tiny farmhouse lights appear 300 feet below.

Home I came, along the Wealden road below the Downs, very close to that old chalk pit where you, Mum, would bring me to play and collect the snail shells.

When I was 5 years old and playing carefree on the chalk hills I well remember you bidding me listen to the boom of the guns across the hill and water [the Battle of the Somme].[66] And now alone, I come by that old playground, a medical man from Brighton.

---
66. Several times my father referred to that memory of the trembling chalk under his feet as the 'monstrous thunder of the guns' travelled under the English Channel from France.

And springtime was coming.

Back at the hospital the wards and countryside are colourful with scented stocks and lilac. The hospital is devoutly celebrating Eastertide. I think the strong religious element in the institution makes for a very happy unencumbered spirit. The acts of worship remind folk of the things which are not seen; the staff become, by some degree, spiritually minded and in that degree enjoy the resultant life and peace. It is largely subconscious but nonetheless active and fruitful.[67]

Dick replied to a letter from Paul which sounds so like junior doctors today. After a rant at corrupt drug companies, he added: 'I agree with you absolutely; it is a shame . . . we can't sign X-ray forms or make transfers to other departments but must spend our time seeking people to put their names to our instructions.'

And beyond the patients:

Our famous Stethoscopes Club is looking forward to appearing before you in Brighton one Saturday.

Glad to hear of [brother] John's wedding date. How my spirit faints with hope to see you in the same glad plight. Maurice Carpenter told me that what I need is 'a good Christian girl'.

Fish is on the Medical Unit and our dear Hutt, a new and efficient Hutt, is a very good casualty house surgeon. Brodie, having failed his pharmacology exam again is going to be put through his paces by me.

Ever yours and hoping to see you shortly
Dick

---

67. PWH letter to parents 9 April 1936.

PS Don't follow the devices and desires of your own heart with those nurses, will you.

More than once the band drove an open Bugatti to North Wales for mountaineering, amused to find they had scooped up a sheep on the front suspension somewhere, none the worse under its shock-absorbing wool.

But the need for solitude after work was insistent so, 'Yesterday afternoon,' he told his parents, 'I walked to Stanmer via Falmer and there on the hillside, I read and slept in shade above the tiny village after a long night's work.'

The hungry thirties meant others had solitude thrust upon them and Paul encountered '... that host of unemployed who wandered aimlessly about England at that time,' as Laurie Lee had observed.[68] On one bitter winter evening, Paul passed a tramp settling down to sleep under a hedge. The next day, only a body lay there, frozen stiff.

By June 'as the Sussex sun set, I made my way down the hill to the cottages, and after buying some ginger beer I asked the good woman of the house if the mansion was occupied and she told me that "My Lord, the Earl of Chichester" was in residence and usually spent the summer there'.

Dick reported:

Brodie has passed Pharmacology at the fifth attempt! Yes, the old man is through at last, after many weary hours of grinding away in teaching him. He appeared this morning with a huge pharmacology book under his arm and has shaken the dispensary with new and fearful prescriptions.

---

68. Laurie Lee, *As I Walked Out One Midsummer Morning* (London: Penguin, 1969), p. 62. Quoted in Robert Macfarlane, *The Old Ways* (London: Penguin Books, 2013).

And the nurses! What of them? There is one fairy in the surgery, so delicious and so desirable – but how can even my susceptible soul find access to one so exalted and discreet?

That Blue Belt with whom you were rather friendly asked me if you had gone abroad to a mission hospital yet. When I replied in the negative, she said, 'Oh! They all get like that.'

But in all seriousness, much as I feel the need of feminine interest, a time must come when we shall all have drifted many miles apart.

Within four years those young men were standing amid the tottering towers of shattered cities or being hunted on the high seas. But now Paul was enjoying life:

My dear old Mum and Dad,

I found your letters with the magic Cornwall postmark on them, recalling those happy bygone holidays. I hope Dad that you are sunbathing and sea bathing. I have been doing both . . . It increases the vital activity of the body . . .

This evening I went to St George's church here in Brighton and heard a fine address from Zechariah 3. This royal church is a burning and shining light in the town and is packed out.[69]

Now it was time to find 'cutting experience'. So he headed north to Grimsby and a fright to awaken the dead.

---

69. PWH to his parents 27 June 1936.

CHAPTER TWELVE

A Grim Awakening
1937

> Four ducks on a pond,
> A grass-bank beyond,
> A blue sky of spring,
> White clouds on the wing;
> What a little thing
> To remember for years – to remember with tears!
>
> *William Allingham (1824-89), Four Ducks on a Pond*

How Paul came to work at Grimsby is not known; but there is no evidence he battered God's door about his fate. Like many southern exiles he was surprised to find the locals kindly, and the countryside glorious for cycling. Paul did not agonise over 'knowing God's will' but got busy at work believing, 'if you are uncertain what to do, then duty is a reliable guiding star.'[70]

'I find I'm paid £225 per annum,' [about £12,000 in 2024] he wrote, 'so I shall be able to work my way home one weekend. For a bus ride I can get out to the coast.'

---

70. PWH to the author.

And the flat Grimsby coast was the setting for a story which had us children gripping our seats on a car journey in the 1960s. 'It was a dark and windy night,' he began:[71]

TB was rife on surgical units but radical new methods urged a few of us to enter the battle line to deal with an enemy bent on destruction. Unremitting work and wretched food had left me weary and dispirited, but I was imbued with ambition for new surgical horizons. We had all cared for a young lady in her twenties on our ward. She knew – we all knew – she had TB and was doomed. Yet we all refused to believe it, especially when she began to glow with life and vivacious talk -- the sinister signs the disease was about to win.

The mortuary lay away from town near the sea and I had got permission from the mortician to practise my surgical skills on a fresh body – not allowed now. People today just cannot believe what tuberculosis was like. The 'Captain of the Men of Death' as John Bunyan called it in the seventeenth century.

Surgical pioneers were studying TB of the lung and developing surgical treatments to rest the lung, to collapse it by removal of the upper ribs, and it was effective in some cases, but a very big operation.

'Here you are, sir,' said the mortician, handing me the key, 'she will be waiting for you; have a lovely time.'

Gathering some surgical instruments, I cycled out towards the sea at about 10 p.m. Near the mortuary the tide was high and the thump of the waves carried up from the beach. I let myself in, dripping with damp

---
71. With excerpts from PWH, *The Progress of Surgery*, 1989, unpublished.

and cold. Several corpses lay out in various stages of preparation. The smell cannot be forgotten.

The body lay turned towards the moon coming through the window, a beautiful young woman carried away in the prime of life. Her blue eyes were wide open and looking into mine. Pale lips were parted as if she wished to speak. I was penetrated by horror and a profound sadness – it was our patient.

Unrolling my instruments, I laid out a scalpel and forceps for the first incision. Then I began to shiver. Behind me was a brazier with sticks and coal ready, so I swiveled round and soon had a fire going. I sat staring at the flames a while, hands held up to get warm. The surf was thumping rhythmically, and my heart too and the wind rattling the windows. An unearthly horror overwhelmed me, and I was yielding to terror.

I must have sat watching the firelight for some minutes when a rustle made me stiffen and glance over my shoulder. I looked back at the fire, unthinking, then leapt to my feet with indescribable horror.

She was turning her head and staring – and her arms were widening to embrace me . . . I froze. Her eyes were expressing some hopeless appeal. Her lips were parted as if she would whisper words from another world . . . I swept up my instruments and fled into the night.

In the back of Dad's car twenty little fingers gripped the seat in silence before squeaking, 'Well – she was alive!'

'Oh no, she was dead all right,' replied Dad. 'When I had recovered, I realised it was the warmth of the fire that relaxed some muscles while others tightened causing false signs of life. I never went back.'

I awoke next morning when the sky was changing to splendour and would be gilding the sea to the water's edge – there the girl's body lay face to the window so she would catch the sunny light of a new day – the glory of resurrection.

Nearly half a century of war and peace has done no more than smooth my etched memory. I have often wondered, when winter surrenders to spring, what the truant years would have given her, had her springtime passed into the summer of life. It's pointless to speculate on this life, though we can be confident about Eternity.

The gossamer veil between this life and the next may be drawn back any time. In those days, successful resuscitation from cardiac arrest was rare. But Paul recounted one success. 'My resuscitated pregnant patient is doing well, and her unborn infant is alive.'

Afterwards, 'I questioned her to see if she has any memory of the other world. But her mind is a blank so far as these peculiar experiences are concerned. Since her heart had stopped for ten minutes at least and her breathing for more than ninety minutes, I imagine she was dead and so her spirit must have left its body.'[72]

Paul's openness to the working of God was rewarded by an occasional split-second vision. It would happen in daytime: a magnificent city glowing with golden light. Doors opened and closed, and people were walking back and forth on streets of gold. Paul repeatedly had to refill his needy soul with the treasures of heaven – a place, as Teresa of Avila saw: 'a most splendid palace built entirely of gold.'[73]

---

72. Near Death Experiences are documented by many clinicians. See John Burke, *Imagine Heaven* (Ada, MI: Baker Books, 2015).
73. Quoted in Pete Greig, *How to Hear God* (London: Hodder & Stoughton, 2022).

When helping people in spiritual need – like me at times – he might suggest:

> I give you the end of a golden string;
> Only wind it into a ball,
> It will lead you in at Heaven's gate,
> Built in Jerusalem's wall.[74]

Paul had discovered that the golden string was a Man – Jesus of Nazareth. Indeed, people awakening from Near Death Experiences (NDEs) often speak of a golden city, and beautiful mountains. Paul loved, in sympathetic company, to speak of the 'Delectable Mountains' which Christian saw afar off in *The Pilgrim's Progress*.

Bunyan's *The Pilgrim's Progress* was written from prison – his 'den' – with the opening words, 'While in the wilderness of this world I alighted upon a den...' The tale rescued Paul again and again from the 'dens' of his volatile personality when he found himself climbing the Hill Difficulty or clogged up in the Slough of Despond.

His childhood *Pilgrim* lived on in characters like Mr Faithful and Mr Greatheart. There was the terrible Doubting Castle, home to a brute Paul was acquainted with, Mr Giant Despair who wielded a 'crab-tree cudgel'. It took time, but he learned to remember the key called 'Promise' to escape the giant's dungeon – the key which the feckless Christian had forgotten was in his chest pocket, rusty from disuse. Imitating Christian,

---

74. William Blake (1757-1827), 'To the Christians', a chapter in his book, *Jerusalem*, www.goodreads.com/book/show/350754.Jerusalem (accessed 17.12.24). Note by MH: Having heard this verse several times, it was not surprising that the night before making my first journey to Jerusalem I was too excited to sleep. I made straight for the Old City walls and walked along outside the great East wall facing the Mount of Olives. I stopped outside the enigmatic Golden Gate which has been blocked up for centuries; I was looking up at it and was surprised by joy: suddenly a man wearing an Arab headdress appeared and leaned over the wall above the gateway. He waved to me cheerfully and I waved back. It was the very event I had seen in a vision before leaving England.

Paul found the key – the treasury of Bible promises – would, with difficulty, turn the lock so the dungeon door swung open. For example, when he was afraid he chose the key, 'Even though I walk through the valley of the shadow of death, I will fear no evil, for you are with me' (Psalm 23:4, ESV).

Paul sat the 'FRCS Part One' examination on 30 November 1937. He had to answer four out of six questions in three hours; and he chose, 'Give an account of the metabolism of sulphur in the body.' Two weeks later a laconic telegram arrived in Lingfield, 'Passed'.

Christmas came: 'I have been frightfully busy and jolly tired, but we had a very good time. The matrons do know how to entertain. I have operated on acute cases practically every evening and often until three in the morning. A small boy with a strangulated hernia – not much more than two – and he is alive to tell the tale.'[75]

By now Paul could open a trapdoor in the skull with a brace and bit to let out blood. Without the benefit of an operating microscope – not yet invented – he could clean the delicate mastoid cavity of a child's ear.

He enjoyed 'tiger country' – like the neck, where a slip of the scalpel could render someone speechless. Breast surgery, bowel surgery and 're-plumbing the waterworks' were every day, along with prostate cancer and high amputations for cancer. Back surgery, bones and joints and trauma to any body parts along with peptic ulcers belching blood were all in a day's work. Only 'midwifery' and 'eyes' remained a mystery.

Added to the growing experience came a priceless secret blurted out by a hospital porter at Paul's funeral: 'Mr 'oughton,' he said in the vernacular, "e was the only one who always prayed before operating.'

---

75. Letter PWH to parents, January 1938.

Meanwhile the Spanish Civil War was sweeping into its maw half a million dead by the time it ended in 1939. Thousands of idealistic men and women flocked in from Europe eager to fight. Paul and his medical mates were drawn to put hard-won skills to use in battle.

But seafaring was in the blood, so it must have been a relief to Edith and Albert when, in early 1938:

> I took a trip as a ship's doctor in the merchant service where the pay was quite good, enough to take a course before sitting the Final FRCS. So I accepted an offer from the British Steam Navigation Co and sailed from London Docks to Kolkata with 200 passengers and a big cargo.

The seed sown had sprouted; what could possibly go wrong?

Part Two

Sailor, 1938-45

The Second World War

Unless a grain of wheat falls into
the earth and dies,
it remains alone; but if it dies,
it bears much fruit.

John 12:24, ESV

CHAPTER THIRTEEN

A Passage to India
1938

> But it's hot – too hot – off Suez
> For the likes of you and me
> Ever to go in a P. & O.
> To call on the Cape Parsee.
>
> *Rudyard Kipling (1865-1936),*
> *How the Rhinoceros Got His Skin*[76]

In early 1938, Paul departed from London Docks for his first voyage as a ship's doctor aboard the SS *Mashobra*. He carried along a secret confided to me decades later: 'I find patients get better in my hands.'[77]

At sea his feelings bubble over to his brother:

> I find seafaring suits me down to the ground.[78] Sunday morning I inspected the crew for a chickenpox outbreak near old Brighton with the ship rolling head over heels.

---

76. Rudyard Kipling, *Just So Stories: How the Rhinoceros Got His Skin* (Bardfield End Green: Miles Kelly Publishing Ltd, 2016).
77. PWH to the author.
78. PWH to brother John and his wife, Frankie – 7 March 1938.

Across the Bay of Biscay – the wind blowing half a gale force – gave me one day of seasickness but it did not prevent me enjoying a good dinner.

Portugal and southern Spain were a dream. The Levanter blew at 80 miles an hour and then with the sunset, Cape Trafalgar and Cape St Vincent, just as Browning described it.

'Nobly nobly Cape St Vincent . . .'[79]

We made Gibraltar at night, and at once, within the Straits, a great calm fell. In the morning came the icy pinnacles of the Atlas Mountains. Oh John, I wish you were here! Especially yesterday when the Mediterranean fleet went past in full battle array while the aircraft from HMS *Glorious* circled round the *Mashobra*, pilots waving madly.

Today we passed Carthage, think of it – the actual place!

The officers are great fellows, and we have plenty of good talk.[80]

Doubtless, with the romance of the sea and rising temperatures, the bachelor surgeon standing 6ft2in must have raised hopes of talks among the ladies also.

One morning, Paul reported a small island approaching, lying between southern Italy and North Africa.

Malta at 6.30 on a crystal-clear morning came floating 'like a cloud as small as a man's hand'.[81] As the distance

---

79. Robert Browning, (1812-1889), *Home-Thoughts, from the Sea*, https://allpoetry.com/Home-Thoughts,-from-the-Sea (accessed 5.11.24) © by owner. Provided at no charge for educational purposes.
80. Letter on headed paper, British India line, SS Mashobra, in the Malta channel, 7 March 1938.
81. See 1 Kings 18:44, AKJV.

lessened, we could make out golden walled townships on the hillsides.[82]

Valetta lies on the east side and we anchored in the harbour at 9 a.m. It is very beautiful. The climate was like a fine day in England. The town is very old, with houses walls and aqueducts dating from every century since the Roman Empire.

Here you have daffodils growing between orange bushes bearing their early fruit and you can never miss a sight of the blue Mediterranean. It is an island of fat priests and wealthy churches and I inspected both. Then I went to the English cathedral to read your letters. The English chaplain was so good as to ask me to lunch. So you see the 'barbarous people showed Paul no little kindness.'[83]

Then ordering me his car, I made first for St Paul's Bay and in about 30 minutes I stood where the apostle to the Gentiles, to whom I owe my very name, must have come ashore from his shipwreck and made a fire.

Under a crystal-clear moon, the Mashobra set her poop to the sunset and glided slowly beyond the harbour lights – all the world seem young and St Paul still setting the West aflame with the gospel of Christ.

Now we voyage East under a Mediterranean night with stars as brilliant as they can be; Crete lies to the north. These waters have carried triremes of the Romans cruising down to Antioch, Phoenician merchants, tall gleaming carousels and the trade of almost every civilisation.

---

82. Letter to Mum and Dad, headed paper of 'British India line, *SS Mashobra*', in the Malta channel, 8 March 1938.
83. 'And the barbarous people shewed us no little kindness: for they kindled a fire, and received us every one, because of the present rain, and because of the cold' Acts 28:2, AKJV.

Aboard ship you feel the gospel is the only merchandise worth carrying and I believe it is good trade, if you are a good merchant, if you can display your wares to advantage, but it is remarkably difficult.

He wrote home next, 24 March 1938, fifty miles north-west of Colombo, Ceylon:

Our course brings us alongside Socotra in the Arabian Sea, the British island still inhabited by cannibals; and indeed there is a skipper with us, whose wife and mother were eaten on the island from a wrecked ship.

Now listen to this. I was playing ping-pong when the Chief Officer crashed in. He had an SOS from a ship lying two hours ahead of us and on our course. The distressed ship had a man aboard with acute appendicitis – could we help?

At midnight we sighted her lights from the bridge. Meanwhile I had had my operating things rigged and the cabin prepared. Of course the whole ship's company – passengers and crew – were thrilled, lining the rail.

We steamed into position and the captain brought the ship round to shelter our rowing boat because a heavy monsoon swell was running.

The first officer and I entered the stern sheets as she lay in the davits, and we swung out 50 feet above the oily swell. And within five minutes we were rowing away from Mashobra, upon the Indian Ocean by night.

The Greek ship rigged a filthy wooden ladder for us. It gave way as we set foot on it and the sharks seemed very near.

Finally, we leapt on the decks and made our way to the sick man. I concluded that he probably had a tropical liver abscess and found him extremely ill. We transferred him in a stretcher to our boat, everyone heaving at the oars on a 6-foot swell and with great difficulty got him aboard.

We were today at Columbo, Ceylon, and the Greek has been put ashore much fitter. He made a miraculous recovery – I resisted the advice of another doctor to operate and I'm very glad.

Your loving son
Paul

Every clinician uses a precision instrument wryly termed the 'Retro-spectroscope' – that 'Ah ha!' moment when the best decision becomes obvious – *in retrospect*. Much kicking of one's shins happens after using it. Yet this surgeon, only twenty-seven, on a heaving sea, at night, had the assurance to say 'No' under pressure from a colleague to operate. Paul had an enviable advantage far away in his Surrey village – there his father's 'old biddies' (as Albert called them) were pleading in prayer for their Paul to save lives on the waves.

Connemara Hotel, Madras.
13 March 1938

Today we are in Madras, departing after two delightful days holiday in Colombo – bathing on a coral reef with palms stretching along the coast for miles.

With love in haste
Paul

Then it was on to the Port of Calcutta.

6 April 1938

My dear Mum and Dad,

Since we arrived I have spent every day in the city visiting acquaintances from the ship at their hotels. I dined with Mr Cameron Kerr in his bachelor flat. He is a pillar of the town and the Brethren Meeting and a very fine type with a very beneficent influence on this great city of the Empire.

Do you know the voyage gains more than £50,000 carrying 8000 tons of various cargoes loaded to the very limit. The British India company is fabulously wealthy, owning their own coalmines, manganese ore mines and half the oil depots. Their ships arrive each day from Australia – Japan – Singapore – East Africa – Burma – Rangoon and Europe loaded to the waterline with an enormously rich cargo for a thousand ports.

But it was time to head back to the wet westerly isles.

We sail tomorrow (15.4.38) after an incredibly hot fortnight but it has been wonderful, and I have spent lots of money enjoying myself. Passengers have had me out to meals on the town.

At home you can have no idea of the vastness of our Empire, but for 6000 miles we have seen no flag flying in the ports but the Union Jack and the White Ensign of the Royal Navy.

The city is filthy, and vice is the rule of the day. I could take you to places where you would feel tainted for life. There is a Chinese quarter here and you recognise it first by the lack of stink, and then by the pleasant smell of the teakwood and sandalwood, because John [Chinaman] is a talented carpenter. You mother would fall for the Chinese with their shaven heads. They never beg and scorn to barter.

These are the people for whom Christ died and to whom William Carey (1761-1834) came with the gospel. They think a great deal of Carey here. I can see his Botanical Gardens and I went to see his church. He beautified the town with parks and avenues of mahogany trees.[84]

The gospel is at a low ebb in Bengal. The Bishop is a fool and the European town is concerned only with whiskey and 'the pride of life'.[85]

Tell Lucy that I have bought her a real Kashmere silk dressing gown.

Despite the heat I feel like a battleship after a refit.

With love
Paul

By early May they were homeward bound up the Gulf of Suez where he writes from the Bitter Lakes leading into the Suez Canal: 'We could distinguish "the land of Midian [Saudi Arabia now] which did tremble at the break of day".[86] We could see where the Children of Israel, made the crossing and it's wonderful to think that under our keel we may have passed over the remains of Pharaoh's army of chariots.'

Back in European waters they headed up the Elbe to dock in Hamburg – a window on the precarious agony of the German people.

The head stevedore came aboard for a drink in the mess. He was wounded five times in the First World War; he has two children of 10 and 12, who have been pressed

---

84. William Carey, became known as 'the father of modern missionary work'.
85. 'For everything in the world – the lust of the flesh, the lust of the eyes, and the pride of life – comes not from the Father but from the world' (1 John 2:16).
86. '. . . the land of Midian did tremble . . .' (Habakkuk 3:7, AKJV).

into the Hitler Youth Corps for indoctrination in the arts of war. Safe on board a British ship he could express his loathing of Hitler and the Nazi regime who have stolen their 400 years of freedom in this free state.

Nevertheless, Paul's normal foresight seems blind to the gathering storm because he writes home, 'In a year or two I shall take to the sea again in the merchant service. I had a wander round Hamburg where Nazi propaganda was everywhere and people saluting.'

CHAPTER FOURTEEN

Here We Go Again Boys
1938

> I used to wonder how long my nerves could stand the strain ... There's always the soft sky, often a gleam of sun, and even a corner of warm ground to relax in. One must make a corner of one's interior life, a sort of shrine, where one can rest while no one interferes and where one can escape to be with God.
>
> *Paul Houghton, letter to his son, Mark, 1990*

It was just twenty-two years after the Battle of Jutland and Albert was – once again – standing with the newspaper open, looking gravely at Paul and John over his gold-rimmed spectacles: 'Here we go again, boys. This Hitler fellow is not going to back down and it's going to be war. You had better join up.'

Fresh back from India, Paul took the hint from his father and enrolled with the Royal Naval Volunteer Reserve – the RNVR – along with several of his friends.

The RNVR were civilians, affectionately known as the 'Wavy Navy', for their wavy gold lace on their sleeves. Dick reports to Paul in June, 'You remark on the navigational abilities of the merchant service. But I think you would have to feel the magnificent preparedness of Her Majesty's ships to realise that seamanship is only a part of an officer's job: navigation, gunnery, torpedoes, landing ashore . . . But, as you say, lying tied up to a buoy begets gin drinking and slackness.

'To hear that you too are a secret drinker: it should open up a whole lot more pubs to visit. We must meet, and we will upset old Brodie by ordering pints together!! Brodie, has failed finals again.'

Paul returned to Grimsby and, after a seventeen-mile bike ride through the Wolds to unwind, warned his parents in the summer of 1938, 'The Final FRCS course, begins February 7th at Barts. So I want to come down. I badly want a week free, chiefly to sleep. There is more very hard work ahead for this exam.' Workaholic he now was, but ever prone to quote Toplady's lines:

Not the labour of my hands
Can fulfil Thy law's demands;
Could my zeal no respite no,
Could my tears for ever flow,
All for sin could not atone:
Thou must save, and Thou alone.[87]

By the autumn they were all watching and weighing the looming clouds to the East and Dick wrote from London:

---

87. Augustus Toplady (1740-1778), 'Rock of Ages'.

My dear Paul,

I have often been minded to write or visit to discover your plans should our worst fears become facts. I was up at St Barts Hospital and it all seemed the same as ever, a good thing in 'these dangerous times'. Brodie of course no nearer to qualifying.

I think I shall need your assistance as Best Man, but should the worst come – war – we shall get our wedding over quickly and quietly.

All my naval uniform is packed up and I now await orders. Our cause seems entirely just and . . . I feel confident that we shall prevail in the passage of arms. Which reminds me to urge you to put your scalpel at the disposal of their Lordships in the Admiralty.

I would much like to have heard your father's views in the light of Scripture prophecy. Several times I have been stricken with a great fear these may be literally the 'last days;' and then weighed down with sin as we are, we should 'lift up our heads' as we are told to.[88] The ridiculously poor leadership that the organised churches – Anglican and Roman Catholic – are giving at present only tends to make me feel we are now 'even at the doors'[89] of the return of Christ.

Hoping to hear from you and trusting you are happy in your job.

Ever yours,
Dick

PS. Don't forget to 'follow the sea'.[90]

---

88. 'And when these things begin to come to pass, then look up, and lift up your heads; for your redemption draweth nigh' (Luke 21:28, AKJV).
89. 'so likewise ye, when ye shall see all these things, know that it is near, even at the doors' (Matthew 24:33, AKJV).
90. Letter, 26 September 1938, from Dr R. Prewer to PWH.

Dick's longing to hear Albert's analysis events was fired by the years these young men had listened to Brethren elders. They would unroll paper charts with timelines and try to match the writings of prophets, such as Daniel, with contemporary events. When Hitler's Nazis began to crush and humiliate the Jews in events like *Kristallnacht* in November 1938, Albert was not surprised, saying to Paul and John: 'this is nothing, it's going to get much worse.'[91] This may only be the beginnings of the birth pangs heralding the return of Messiah to earth.' Ginger Jim, got a saucer of milk left out each night in case the family were 'caught up together ... in the clouds, to meet the Lord in the air'.[92]

That October Dick was indeed getting the wedding over quickly. Afterwards he informed his best man, 'I enclose a cheque for the money you laid out on the church: One pound, seven shillings and sixpence [£1.40].' Seventy years later Pippa and I found the cheque still in the envelope to Paul, suggesting he was too busy or generous to redeem it. 'The whole thing,' Dick continued, 'went off reasonably well and I am extremely grateful for your powerful moral support.'

'We spent the night – in great discomfort – at the Kenilworth Hotel in London. A double bed was new to me and in my efforts to sleep and yet not be a nuisance I was awake most of the night.'[93]

The wedding tugged on the fridge door of Paul's feelings still 'kept in cold storage', and he confided to his parents, 'Dick has written to me and I understand he is already settling down in great happiness. It must be very pleasant. I often get overwhelmed with the imperious demands and constant need for vigilance required by acute disease. So much energy

---

91. 'Alas! for that day is great, so that none is like it: it is even the time of Jacob's trouble; but he shall be saved out of it' (Jeremiah 30:7, AKJV).
92. See 1 Thessalonians 4:17 (AKJV).
93. Letter, 24 October 1938. Dr R Prewer to PWH.

is needed, and a man should have super brawn to wrestle with effect in this battle.'[94] Letters reveal the nursing Sister from Brighton was still in touch – the first love of Paul's life – in a relationship as yet unresolved.

That July of 1938, Paul and his father accompanied by Albert's brother Uncle George visited the Channel Island of Guernsey. George and Albert wanted to look up their mother's family on Guernsey. Their father had snatched her away to be his wife when his ship called in there in the 1870s.

Edith missed the trip, keeping up her sick visiting and tapping the optimism of Christians undaunted by global clouds. 'I hear they had 300 young people offering themselves for mission work abroad – at the Keswick Convention last week.'[95]

The Guernsey party returned home – it would be many years before such carefree trips were possible again.

---

94. Letter PWH to parents, 30 October 1938, Grimsby and District Hospital (headed paper), President: The Earl of Yarborough MC (Military Cross)
95. 23 July 1939, letter Edith to PWH and Albert in Guernsey. The Keswick Convention is still going strong, sustaining a reputation for excellent preaching in person and online the world over.

CHAPTER FIFTEEN

Called Up by the Navy
1939

Hitler's tanks smashed their way into Poland on 1 September 1939, provoking Britain and France to declare war on Germany to honour their treaty to defend Poland.

Paul badgered the Admiralty in October: 'I am anxious and ready for any sort of service.' Soon he was having a medical and the colour-blind obstacle was solved when the examining doctor said, 'I will tell you the answers.' He was 6ft2in and 13 stone 10lb.[96]

Then, Paul was called up to the famous Royal Naval Hospital Haslar in Portsmouth – founded in 1754 to treat injured seamen.

By 1939 the Royal Navy was a superb – arguably the supreme – fighting force on the high seas. Employing more than half a million men and women, they were inspired by the traditions of Admiral Lord Nelson's navy – the 'iron men in wooden ships'. Every sailor knew that these forebears had sealed the fate of the man who would rule the world, Napoleon Bonaparte.

---

96. Confidential Naval Service Record on PWH, 30 October 1939.

The navy which Paul entered called its greatest battleships, HMS *Nelson* and HMS *Rodney*, after the fighting admirals who had destroyed Napoleon's combined fleets at the Battle of Trafalgar in 1805. Churchill called them the 'Guardians of the Gates'.

Back in the 1920s the government had laid down the keels to build these two sister ships of 38,000 tons each, and now they were ready for anything – or should have been – as Paul was to find out. She would become Paul's home through the valley of supreme threat – the battles of the Atlantic and the Malta convoys.

In mid-September, Stalin, encouraged by his August treaty with Germany's Hitler, marched in and took over eastern Poland for Russia, and the two nations divided the country between them.

By November Stalin had attacked Finland and on 11 November Lieutenant Houghton sent a mischievous note to his father from Haslar:

I have arrived and everything is remarkably strange . . .
I was given a 'cabin' and a very helpful surgeon-lieutenant showed me how to 'get things' – uniform and a gas mask. There is no work, but the new intake consoled themselves with unstinting gin and 'things in wartime' could be much worse.

The eerie calm – which came to be called the Phoney War – inched along towards Christmas. German battleships sank the British cruiser HMS *Rawalpindi* near the Faroe Islands and 270 crew died. Dick reported, 'We had an enemy plane over us this afternoon while my colleagues went on with their drinking in blissful ignorance.'

While things looked grim for an ill-prepared Britain, the Royal Navy fought the Battle of the River Plate off Montevideo on 13 December 1939. Three smaller British cruisers attacked the mighty *Graf Spee*, one of Hitler's 'Grey Wolves'. She had sunk thousands of tons of merchant shipping in the South Atlantic and, with her lean hungry profile bristling with guns, had been a terrible foretaste of Germany's efforts to grip the British Isles by the throat and starve the islands into submission.

Paul reported, 'The officers mess is occupied with the glorious victory of La Plata. Here is the "Nelson touch" independent of armour plate, high explosive and gun ranges, victory from sheer skill and seamanship and courage worthy of Trafalgar's frigates.'[97] The navy had chalked up a much-needed victory.

Then Paul met reality when 'the first casualty of the war I saw at Haslar hospital was my old captain of the *Marshobra* – and he was dead. He had been machine-gunned on the Bridge of his ship in the English Channel'.[98]

These early alarms set a mother's love boiling over

My dear, dear Paulie,

We were pleased to get your first letter from Haslar. Old Bill followed me in your room and looked on your bed and under – then down again into your study – looking at me as much as to say, 'Where has my young master gone to?' I miss you very much, my son.

Paul 'found an absolute mob of doctors most of them without uniform. They were posting them to Destroyers at sea as fast as they could. No one even told me how to salute'.

---
97. Paul Houghton letter to his mother and father, 18 December 1939.
98. Paul Houghton, interview by the *Royal Navy History Museum*, November 2000, track 14.

It was an odd situation, because in peace time the Navy had medical consultants who had become Surgeon Rear-Admirals on condition that, if war broke out, they would give their whole time to the navy. Well, most of them wanted the title Surgeon Rear-Admiral but never thought that war would break out. So, at Haslar there was Sir Cecil Wakely who was to become President of the Royal College of Surgeons and used to nip off to London to earn some money. There was one well-known London surgeon who in peacetime always wore a carnation in his buttonhole and insisted on wearing one in uniform which really isn't done. And there was a dear old physician from The London Hospital who insisted on carrying an umbrella. Those of us who wanted to go on and become surgical specialists were horrified at the standard of the regular naval specialists. None of them had a higher degree, like FRCS, and it was very embarrassing to work with them. A senior one, got sent to HMS *Hood* and was blown up and lost with about 1,400 men.

The effortless sinking of the unsinkable 'mighty *Hood*' by the *Bismark* stunned not only the Navy but the nation.

For uniforms, I had one from my merchant service days, that had belonged to an admiral. I wanted to keep the admiral's gold lace on the cuffs but thought I'd better not. I kept the admiral's waistcoat and wore it in winter. Everyone noticed this and said it was from when I was working on the Mississippi gunboat in the American Civil War. I got permission to go up to London and re-take the Final FRCS papers. Anatomy and detailed physiology were keystones of the whole test, along with biochemistry. Arriving at the examination hall I had a burning need – I was in doubt about the pathway of the Recurrent Laryngeal Nerve. On the steps in I saw a well-known anatomist and asked him my question. He clarified it in a few words, and we parted; I am sure he was sent from above.

'The college gave you the result on the same day – I was so pleased with myself that I walked in uniform past the guards in Buckingham Palace and made them salute me!' From here on the 'Dr' was dropped and he reverted to Mr P.W. Houghton FRCS – a qualified surgeon. *'Et teneo. Et teneor*, I hold. I am held', ran the college motto, summing up the only hope in a world on the brink of terror like nothing seen before.

Dick wrote he 'was delighted and you richly deserve your success' – a success that Paul considered of little eternal value because Dick adds, 'I hope that yet another parchment to your collection [of medical qualifications] may not increase the heap of "dust and ashes" which you claim to have built up. It's the just reward of your last two years.'[99]

One more item was needed to complete the outfit of a true seaman. I can imagine him at a ship's chandler in Portsmouth saying, 'One of those – yes, the big one.'

Of course it needed engraving, 'P.W. HOUGHTON SUR LT.' The maker's name on the blade, was 'J Rogers & Son, 6 Norfolk St, Sheffield'. Every blade was 'Sheffield' then but Paul could not foresee that his own son would one day include Norfolk Street in his patch as a GP in Sheffield. On the other side of the blade, strangely prescient, was the regulation Maltese cross.

Edith dug out the FRCS success from the *Lancet* and *British Medical Journal* and added an annoying reminder, '. . . my child not to delay sending £1 and 3d for the advert as we are

---

99. Letter from Dr R Prewer to PWH, 20 November 1939.

not well off.' Paul responded, 'The Fellowship results were published in *The Times* on Saturday: 31 passed the test from 206 candidates and I was placed fourth.'

He added, 'You do well to modify upwards the wages of your workmen, Dad. I have a bad feeling when I picture the unrivalled comforts of my present life compared with the unspeakable conditions in Eastern Europe.

'PS. Lucy shall be sent a photo but it may be after Christmas. Frankly, I'm scared stiff of having it taken and its distribution is equally scaring.' Never in his wildest dreams could he imagine the picture and story would be the most popular obituary in the *Daily Telegraph*.

Edith cooed over the fruits of her sowing:

> The most wonderful certificates I ever saw have come ... the dreams of my life – that I should have a son who has by *sheer hard study* and continued perseverance, become a Fellow of the Royal College of Surgeons.

She rounds off with, 'I do admire the pluck of little Finland – the Great Bear will have his talons cut soon.' Russia had pounced on Finland but would be humiliated and halted in the bitter White Winter War. A favourite Finnish tactic was to descend by skis from the forests in the night, put out the Russian campfires and scatter the soldiers who soon froze to death. Edith reported the coldest British winter since 1885 and heavy snow falls followed in January.[100] But who could have predicted the shocking cut to the bear's talons just a year or two hence when they grappled with Hitler?

Edith's PS reminded him, 'Be steadfast, immovable, always abounding in the love of the LORD.'[101]

---

100. Letter from Edith to PWH, 13 January 1939.
101. See 1 Corinthians 15:58.

Dick reports, 'a letter from Brodie also arrived today – and he has also had success in undergraduate exams and hopes to be on the Medical Register ere Christmas.'[102]

Shortly before Christmas Paul wrote home: 'I'm glad that all goes well in Lingfield, that Ginger Jim pursues his lawful affairs upon the Atlantic unchecked and that Old Bill passes to his old age severe and bright.' He could not resist being facetious about a pillar of the village Assembly: 'I'm sorry to hear that old Pearson should leave us for heaven but surely he is now occupied with those joys which he was *conterperlating* so long.

'Maurice Carpenter is appointed to the naval barracks here and we both look forward to some good times together. I have lunched on two occasions at Whale Island gunnery school – the Navy's most exclusive mess.'

Unknown to Paul a Wren, Jean Swift – by now a qualified orthoptist – was based at Whale Island teaching naval gunners how to use rangefinders. 'We used to find some very interesting men through our range-finders.'[103] One day she would find Paul even more keen to find her.

Albert wrote, 'Last Saturday's London *Times* proclaimed your success, and we had a warm letter of congratulations from Mr Harland the bank manager.'[104]

'Gordon Scott [Paul's cousin] seems to be getting known and is doing a portrait of a duchess who has introduced him to Sir Kenneth Clark, secretary or something of the National Gallery.' Albert and Edith persuaded Paul to sit still for once in Albert's study while Gordon painted him in uniform.[105]

---

102. Letter from Dr R Prewer to PWH 20 November 1939.
103. Jean (Houghton) as told to MH.
104. Albert Houghton, letter to PWH, from St Claire Lingfield, 21 December 1939.
105. Gordon Scott, letter to Pippa Houghton, 6 February 2013: 'Dear Pippa, it was so kind of you to send a copy of Paul's portrait. I always thought it was my best picture. The books in the background of the portrait were in Paul's father's study at St Claire where I painted it. I heard from Mark [Houghton] at Christmas and Fiona [Mark's daughter] sent me a lovely letter. It is excellent that Daniel [Mark's son] is developing his artwork.'

Just after Christmas the Minister of Food, Morrison announced rationing would be expanded to include butter, bacon, ham and sugar. The Houghtons, seared by the gnawing memory of the First World War, dug up their tennis court to grow vegetables and reared rabbits for meat. There was much snow and frost – the weather that would stir Paul to rub his hands gleefully saying:

When icicles hang by the wall,
And Dick the shepherd blows his nail,
And Tom bears logs into the hall,
And milk comes frozen home in pail,
When blood is nipp'd and ways be foul,
Then nightly sings the staring owl,
'Tu-who;
Tu-whit, Tu-who' – A merry note,
While greasy Joan doth keel the pot.[106]

Then suddenly the Admiralty posted Paul to Lowestoft, on the East Coast, north of London. The Phoney War, with little offensive action by France or Britain, lulled everyone. Little did Paul know he was heading for the fight of his life.

---

106. William Shakespeare (1564-1616), *Love's Labour's Lost*, Act V, Scene II.

CHAPTER SIXTEEN

Into Battle

1940-41

The naked earth is warm with Spring,
And with green grass and bursting trees
Leans to the sun's gaze glorying ...
And he is dead who will not fight,
And who dies fighting has increase.

Julian Grenfell (1888-1915), 'Into Battle'

Paul headed north for Lowestoft to find a huge naval shore depot, where the Navy were converting fishing boats for war, and training up their crews. They called this land-based 'ship' HMS *Europa*.

On arrival, he took a look round and was appalled at the unreadiness to protect some 2,000 men:

> I was young but I had a word with the Principal Medical Officer (PMO) and we went to see the naval Commodore commanding the base. He was a silly old man – he had been called up from the reserves – and the PMO was very polite to him while I said, 'Where are you going to put your dead?'

He had embarked on a long career informing the right people of the right thing to do.

> 'There are not going to be any dead here, don't be a fool,' said the Commodore.
> He got awfully rude, and I was rude back to him, I didn't spare my words, and he put me on probation awaiting a Court of Enquiry – I didn't care.[107]

The battle lines between the upstart surgeon and naval power were drawn. Although the base was as near to the enemy as could be he found, 'the authorities had settled down to an easy life unwilling to face the coming violence. We had a medical staff and there was a very nice Irish Surgeon Commander'.[108]

Once aboard 'ship' Paul was immersed in the naval language, punctuated by the f – expletive in almost every sentence. He treated it as a cultural habit like a parrot speaks without any understanding. (Nevertheless, some twenty years later, when I swore mildly during a tantrum at my mother, he promptly picked up my best homemade arrow and applied it to my backside – and quite right too.)

Harry, an older man and a London friend wrote:

> If you have any sense of disappointment in being retained at a base hospital ashore, I do not share it. The ruthless sea warfare that is now being waged makes many apprehensive for the safety of our friends who go down to the sea in ships ... Having a deep desire that your life may be preserved for many years of fruitful service ... yet the Lord is able to preserve amid great dangers.

---

107. PWH Royal Naval Museum interview 2000.
108. Ibid.

The letter shows signs of being re-read many times:

> So the really important concern is to seek guidance and the place of His will and then abide in that will. But if you are assigned to a ship – go confidently. Either way, perhaps your example and influence will be a help to your colleagues in their drinking habits. A special leaflet has been prepared, 'Manhood', for men in the forces, and I can obtain further copies.

Many decades later my father confessed his weakness as a verbal witness of Christ and I doubt he took up that suggestion of pamphlets – yet a Worcestershire nurse, Marina Dixon, still speaks of his 'clinical excellence – a shining witness to a higher Person.'
Harry finished off:

> Mr Shaw was giving talks in North Kensington . . . and very interested in your appointment in the Navy. He took Habakkuk, 'How long, LORD, must I call for help . . . Or cry out to you, "Violence!" but you do not save?' Then the Lord answers, 'I am raising up the Babylonians . . . ruthless and impetuous . . ., who sweep across the whole earth to seize dwelling places not their own.'

Such ordinary Christians were not as surprised as some when Russia fought back Germany with a ruthless impetuosity. But there is a glorious finish when Harry quotes Habakkuk:

> LORD, I stand in awe . . . You uncovered your bow . . . In wrath you strode through the earth . . . to deliver your people. You crushed the leader of the land of wickedness

... The sovereign LORD is my strength; he makes my feet like the feet of a deer ... on the heights. [109]

As you say Paul – the suffering in Europe today is appalling and one has to be careful that it does not get one down. As children of God I certainly feel that one would do wrong to be uncaring of it.
Lord 'Someone or other,' speaking on the radio was asking what can we do – we who are too old or infirm to take part in the war? I feel strongly the great service of prayer. Where are these praying people today? I suppose there are thousands if we only knew of them.

Countless public responded to Days of Prayer for the nation while 'specialists' like Rees Howells, leading the Bible College of Wales, were beginning to battle in heavenly realms for the nation's very survival.[110]

In February, Edith relayed Albert's preaching from the book of Amos regarding war. 'When we as a nation turn to the Lord and confess our cold hearts towards Him, then he will intervene for us.'[111] And more down-to-earth Albert reported:

Outside your Old Dame School, I saw Miss Vermouth and her sister; poor old things now and bent over, the younger one always a pert little cock Robin (or hen Robin I suppose), went into raptures when I told her you were a 'Fellow'. I suppose she thinks you owe it to her.
Well, do write and thank them for your early tuition. I am sure they are good Christian women.

109. Selections from Habakkuk 1-3.
110. Rees Howells (1879 – 1950) prayed especially for Sir Winston Churchill at key turning points in the war. https://en.wikipedia.org/wiki/Rees_Howells (accessed 10.2.21).
111. Letter, Edith to PWH from Ottery St Mary, East Devon, 15 January 1940.

Heaps of love from home,
Your affectionate Dad.[112]

In March 1940, Finland was forced to sign a peace treaty with the Soviet Union after 105 days of conflict and had to give up significant territory in exchange for peace. England emerged from the coldest winter since 1895 – in later life Paul loved to hear George Knight, the neighbouring farmer, remembering that nineteenth century winter: 'Ahgg-rrh, they roasted an ox on the River Severn at Worcester.'

By mid-March a German air raid on the naval base at Scapa Flow on the Orkney Islands caused the first civilian casualties leaving the public in no doubt now that in this war, violence was coming wherever they were. Dick writing from Chatham noted, 'One by one the old gang have been sent to sea, and now there are only four of us.'[113]

That April Paul squeezed in a few days at home and wrote back: 'those very happy days spoiled me and I have got back with serious outbursts of criticism . . . the inadequacy of our medical supplies is more than I can endure in silence. *Do not talk* of this in or out of the house.'

Just as emotions were about to boil over a safety valve appeared again:

> I had a look round Yarmouth and came on a low brick room. The door was ajar and two elderly otherworldly dames were entering. I saw a notice, 'The gospel of the grace of God' would be preached on Sunday. So as ever, my star has led me to dear Christian society.
>
> I wonder if you have any idea of the utter worldliness of this life, where your friendliness is assessed on your

---
112. Letter, Albert to Paul, 2 February 1940.
113. Letter, Dick Prewer to PWH, 7 March 1940

ability to gin-up three times a day and play bridge. I confess to the appeal of this little fisherman's hut and humble folk.

It's early to talk of summer holidays but I can count on eight days in September ... If these calamities do not otherwise involve us.

And Edith's birthday elicited some surprise:

My dear Paulie, your kind gift has just arrived. Thank you; because we certainly haven't much money to spare.

The Scandinavians will soon be restored to their rightful heritage again – Satan always oversteps himself: He that is for right and justice will prevail for *His power is dynamic*.

Lucy is anxious to have a photo. She says, you are a very naughty boy not to have sent it.

Edith's prediction would arrive – but years later. Soon British troops began withdrawing from Norway with great suffering and Paul's naval depot provided vital transport for the evacuation.

On 8 May Prime Minister Neville Chamberlain barely survived the Norway debate in the House of Commons and two days later German armies were pouring into Belgium, France, Luxembourg and the Netherlands over the same ground that they had been removed from – at a cost of millions of lives – only twenty-two years earlier.

That same day Winston Churchill took the helm of state, called a cabinet meeting and said:

If this long island story of ours is to end at last, let it end only when each one of us lies choking in his own blood upon the ground.[114]

---

114. Winston Churchill, 22 May 1940, recorded by Hugh Dalton, Labour MP, Minister of Economic Warfare, https://winstonchurchill.org/publications/finest-hour/finest-hour-113/wit-wisdom-14/ (accessed 16.12.24).

Paul said, 'the relief was indescribable to have him in charge at last.' Back in Lowestoft, he met:

> the inevitable at about 10.30 in the morning. I stopped in my walk across the parade ground to watch two dark planes circling overhead. Thankfully the parade ground had just emptied of hundreds of men. We had no defences, no anti-aircraft guns and no fighter planes.
>
> After a brief interval, each plane delivered a number of dark objects and the machines turned away over the sea. A moment later I seemed to be in the centre of violent explosions and assaulted by noise. The incident was brief, and I felt astonishment that I was still standing and looking up.
>
> And then I saw the planes return, nose down towards the base spluttering fire. Once more the episode was brief and again the enemy turned out to sea, not to return on that occasion.
>
> I looked around and found a little boy of ten or eleven who had been selling newspapers, lying almost at my feet; both his legs were shattered, and he died as I sought to comfort him. A nearby building was pock-marked with bullets and later I extracted one from the door frame as a souvenir.
>
> This episode was the beginning of sorrows. Before many weeks ahead I should be occupied day and night in the operating theatre with the casualties – working under a glass roof like a greenhouse. There was no defence during the remainder of my time at the base.[115]

---

115. Composite story based on Paul's RN Museum interview, and his typed 'Deception'.

Probably his parents never caught wind of this brush with death – or did they? Albert wrote with homely innocence, 'The frightful cost of victory, the doubts that any Christian has of any true peace ever being established for long along with the lusts and ambitions and selfishness of men make one wonder if the cost is justified? But then again I think of the deliverance of the oppressed and what may happen if no action is taken.'[116]

Paul while 'walking down to the hospital one night, heard a big bang somewhere and a piece of corrugated iron came by, and took a very tall naval rating ahead of me, and cut off his leg at the hip, and of course he fell flat and died within minutes'.

On the continent, the French army were defeated, and the British Army almost surrounded.

They made a fighting retreat towards the port of Dunkirk while Churchill instructed the British troops up the coast in Calais to fight to the death so as to divert German troops.

In Lowestoft Paul's stretched nerves and the battle with 'officialdom' became volcanic, and a hurriedly scratched letter in pencil begins innocently:

Sunday 12.5.40

My dear old Mum and Dad,

Old Maurice Carpenter has spent a pleasant weekend with me in the most glorious weather, and we have eaten and drunk and walked in air delightful beyond description. He has told you tales of his adventures on the Western Ocean, and it is for us to be grateful that we are so far whole in life and limb.

And while the spring comes to its full beauty, that bloody [blood-stained] race is crucifying the world afresh.

---

116. Letter from Albert Houghton to PWH, 19 March 1940.

Bombs falling on township and village 'old in story' and Christian culture. We have been watching the evening shadows across the seascape and the minefields in the North Sea towards the Low Countries where the blood is flowing deeper red than the Western sky tonight.

'Principalities and powers', mustering their unseen army, must populate the very atmosphere.[117] You may almost feel the beat of their darkening wings; let the eyes of the young men of the services be opened to see the un-fallen angels[118] are more than those who fight against us. Let us live for the day when Germany is bombed without mercy, abject in defeat.

Never again did Paul speak so sternly of the enemy. His feelings in that letter came true for German civilians as never before in history. Occasionally, in years to come, he would take that bullet out of the glass cabinet in the drawing room in Worcestershire and tell its story.

Yet Paul's confessional to home shrouded double threats, 'Now – in secrecy – I have been wrestling with officialdom for the bare necessities of medical supplies.

'It came to a crisis, and I took the Senior Medical Officer to the Commodore, sat down at his desk and spared no words in my criticism.

'"No flag officer should ever be spoken to in such a manner by a junior,"' he replied.

'I retorted, "I am a surgeon first and an officer afterwards, and the war is not a gin drinking competition" – and finally got what I wanted.

'The commander has been teetotal for a week! It had its funny side, but I can't write about it.'

---
117. See Ephesians 6:12.
118. Based on Revelation 12:4.

Paul's career was on a knife edge because centuries of naval Top Brass were habitually furious at insubordination and prone to tip court decisions their way.

After an anxious few weeks, 'just as the Court of Enquiry was due to sit the naval Commodore was removed and sent home. We were given a very effective Commodore to take his place and all that nonsense stopped.'[119]

In the furnace the realisation was growing in Paul that, 'real faith is not so much seeing God, as knowing that one is seen. Only this kind of faith is resilient enough to embrace trouble from God. As King George VI said in his famous 1940 radio talk, "Go out into the darkness and put thine hand into the hand of God. That shall be to thee better than a light, and safer than a known way."'

Maurice Carpenter wrote, 'at times we have been in mountainous seas. One washed the Chief Petty Officer hard against the rail and broke his left malleolus [ankle] – a mercy he was not washed overboard. I had to put the leg in plaster.'

That first May of the war Lord Gort became a household name for the worst of reasons: leading the British Army in retreat to the beach at Dunkirk. Paul admired this godly man with the Victoria Cross, Military Cross and bar for bravery. One day the two would meet amid stark starvation on the island of Malta.

Back in Lowestoft a different case of wartime courage fell at Paul's feet in mysterious circumstances.

---

119. Royal Naval Museum interview, November 2000, and letter from PWH at Crown Hotel, Lowestoft to parents, Sunday 12 May 1940.

CHAPTER SEVENTEEN

Deception with Honour
1940-1941

'*Deception*', as Paul headed it, came to light on yellowing paper in 2020:

> Our mess had been placed in a large property on the sandy cliffs above the North Sea. Here, officers could live, as secure from enemy action as if we were living in a hen house.
> One day a regular naval officer joined us. He was married, but for some reason he was unaccompanied. He wore the ribbon of the DSO (Distinguished Service Order), rarely seen at that early period of the war, so clearly he had acted valiantly in a recent sea action. His manner was reserved but one needed little insight to decide he was disturbed. I sought to cultivate some sort of confidence hoping to help him but he responded only with cultured politeness and rarely remained in the wardroom.
> For a time he was a focus of interest for others curious about his exploits – a curiosity enhanced by his reticence.
> From that time the naval lieutenant became more withdrawn; a fine tremor was noticeable in his hands,

and he retired early to his room. I was aware of these grave alterations, but I noted them as a sailor may observe a menacing decline in the weather and remain inactive – until he is overtaken by disaster.

I returned to the mess one night from the hospital refreshed by the onshore breeze and the walk. I stood awhile in the empty wardroom wondering how long my nerves could sustain me in my duties in the glass roofed operating theatre – through which we could watch the German bombers. At that point the duty steward entered.

He was urgent. He was glad to find me because he was alarmed about the state of the lieutenant. On his rounds at midnight the light was still on, which was unusual. So he knocked, and, on receiving no reply, opened the door. The officer was lying prone on his bed, and his right arm hanging over the side. A whiskey bottle stood on the floor half empty, and the officer was dead.

We went to the officer's cabin and attempts at resuscitation failed. He covered the body and crossing the room we stood in silence in great distress.

We concurred about the immediate cause of death and the steward observed he had been aware of the man's unhappiness and that he now regretted he had not opened his mind to me in time to prevent this disaster.

I assured him that the responsibility could not be his and that I myself and others had been aware that all was not right and that we might have rescued the dead man from disaster. After locking the room we proceeded to the Principal Medical Officer and awakened him. He received my report with dismay, requiring me to make a full report next day.

I thanked the steward for his care and concern and we both knew that his misery flowed from some overwhelming experience of war which he dreaded to contemplate or repeat. Without a word, we resolved to keep silence if possible about the manner of his death.

The episode was a matter for the Coroner, a GP in the town, and I called on him that morning. He was friendly and I unfolded the history of the case telling him what little I knew about his family, war record, his condition since the air raid and the final event. He listened in silence and then questioned me almost sternly about the steward, our conversation, our report to the PMO and finally about the character of the steward, the PMO and the Commodore.

The Coroner sat in silence for some minutes and then looked up at me bright-eyed and decisive. He said that he understood courage in the battle line and battle shock.

We met at the mortuary for the post-mortem and I assisted him as he made a thorough external examination of the body followed by an equally thorough internal examination after he had directed the attendant to busy himself some way away.

The skull contents appeared normal and the thoracic organs were healthy. But the stomach was dilated, and the Coroner removed it and opened it after tying off its extremities.

He opened the stomach and discharged its contents into a basin; the contents were entirely liquid which smelled powerfully of whiskey. Neither of us commented but my companion paused and reflected; he then grasped the heart, separated this structure from the lungs, and stepped towards the window though the bright light above the corpse was sufficient. He opened the cavities of the heart, and I could see that he was slitting up the coronary vessels; then suddenly from his rather remote position he exclaimed triumphantly, 'There we are – a clear case of coronary thrombosis, immediate death.' He held up the heart like a trophy without stepping to his side of the table and I was delighted to confirm his statement in a loud voice.

The attendant was instructed to replace the organs and close the body over them, and the Coroner did not move until the stitching was completed and the body sponged down.

Then the Coroner signed the forms and death certificate and requested me to do likewise which I did with great pleasure and profound respect for this most humane doctor. The Coroner had in fact done uncommonly well; the officer's family were bereaved indeed but their memory of this gallant man was unclouded by any knowledge of his suffering or the reason for his death.

I'm confident that the secret remained in the minds of the Coroner, the steward and myself. The resolution of the Coroner was remarkable, and his decision was immediate and preceded the autopsy. The steward behaved throughout with memorable discretion and sympathy. I believe that he was a man of exceptional character.

Stress – and Post-Traumatic Stress Disorder as this brave sailor suffered – were making millions wonder how much they could take. And now, the storm clouds boiled ever higher over France, East of the Coroner's quiet rooms.

CHAPTER EIGHTEEN

Enemy Invasion Imminent
Summer 1940

The onslaught of stormtroopers running up the English beaches and heading north – even through the Houghtons' back garden – edged closer.

By late May 1940, the land war seemed finished for the British and French armies, virtually encircled in France. Paul forced a light-hearted comment that he had begun to learn golf:

> I could not have a more lovely setting, level greens just inside the sandhills and beyond is the sea.
>
> I'm sorry your days may make for depression in the face of the daily news. It is of the utmost importance for each individual to maintain a countenance of reasonable optimism and a spirit of great heartedness at this time. A long face is the best propaganda for the foul enemy and nothing pleases him better and assists him more usefully. Of course, there is no question of failure and do not put up with defeatist conversation. Meanwhile, realise that the battle must sway to and fro, that reversals must come from time to time, and then realise that already our victories by sea and air are

immense, and that morally we are fighting for eternal values with, and not against, the Divine will. Yesterday, I went to Evensong in a most glorious East Anglian 'wool church' and found a congregation of 300 or 400 people. The sermon was superb.[120]

Not far away, and much to Hitler's delight, Britain's army in France – her only army – was now hounded onto the beach at Dunkirk where more than 100,000 men were pounded by the Luftwaffe's dive bombers. Death or captivity awaited all.

On 23 May 1940 King George VI called for a National Day of Prayer the following Sunday; that the nation should turn their faces to the Lord God Almighty: 'If my people who are called by my name will humble themselves and pray and seek my face and turn from their wicked ways, then I will hear from heaven...' (2 Chronicles 7:14).

Long queues formed outside cathedrals and churches and a further call went out for rescue boats. Two events immediately followed prayers. A violent storm arose over the Dunkirk region grounding the Luftwaffe. And, in an event which still confounds the historians – Hitler halted his advance! as a great calm descended on the sea allowing about 800 little ships to crossover into legend.

A retired naval officer had scraped these together – Paul watched the frantic activity as his depot dispatched fishing boats and civilian pleasure craft – announcing defiantly to his parents, 'I shall look forward to our September holiday, war or no war – mind you do the same. Here on the naval base I find numbers of Guernsey men to remind me of our holiday there last summer.' And so from 26 May till 4 June more than 338,000 British and French troops were safely evacuated from

---

120   PWH to his parents, 6 May 1940.

Dunkirk to England.[121] Sunday 9 June was officially appointed as a day of National Thanksgiving.[122] A month later the Nazis occupied Guernsey and Paul's aunt's house on the seafront was requisitioned by the Commandant. Now, with the Commodore removed, Paul looked around: 'I was doing no surgery with the Navy – just general practice and VD clinics. The treatment for syphilis was prolonged and often no cure since we didn't have penicillin yet. So I went to "make my number" with the local civilian surgeon in the Lowestoft hospital. His juniors had been called up and he was only too pleased to have some help. Quite frequently we were working 24 hours at a time. Lowestoft got fairly bombed about and I began to feel very tired from the lack of sleep.'

'I do hope you have read the *Daily Telegraph*', wrote Paul:

The centre sheets describe a page of miracles willingly admitted by the High Command, fantastic protection against sprays of bullets, amazing combinations of favourable weather conditions by sea and land. Sometime I will tell you stories of the Great Deliverance because our patrol service played the leading part in the ship transports to get the troops back to England.

There lies our most vital duty, in prayer to the Most High unceasingly. I am a confirmed believer with John Henry Newman[123] in the individual protection from the angelic hosts, in the personal presence of the Redeemer beside our men, guiding the commanding officers and outwitting the hosts of darkness and powers of hell who have incarnated in the Axis peoples. The men of

---

121. www.google.com/search?q=Dunkirk+troops+saved&rlz=1C1GCEA_enGB963GB963&oq=Dunkirk+troops+saved&aqs=chrome..69i57.562j0j15&sourceid=chrome&ie=UTF-8 (accessed 22.4.22).
122. Letter, Paul to his parents, 7 June 1940.
123. John Henry Newman, influential churchman and writer, 1801-90.

this naval service are sure of these things whatever the sophisticated theologians imagine. America will ease our economic relations and finally join us in arms. The war centre will shift to the Near East, and who knows, it may finish on that great day around Jerusalem. There should be some wine on the way soon and remember war or no war, the fields are still green.

After Dunkirk, Paul and almost everyone felt they now stood alone. Germany would invade. The *Führer* was furious because, once more, the islanders had spoilt his best designs. Only one thing could retrieve his plan to rule the world. The Royal Air Force must be destroyed. And this prompted Churchill's 'Finest Hour' speech, 'The Battle of France is over. I expect the Battle of Britain is about to begin. Upon this battle depends the survival of Christian civilization.'[124]

In Italy, the imminent collapse of France emboldened Mussolini, the Italian dictator, and on 10 June 1940, Italy declared war against France and Great Britain.

Paul hurried off a letter in pencil: 'Today adds another tragedy to this drama of blood, Italy has defamed her ancient name and cursed her future. Our aircraft carrier HMS *Glorious* has been wrecked [by German battleships] and Hell is opening its mouth in the fair land of France.'

Then, aware his family and Lucy were in the line of advance for troops who had raped and ruined Holland, Paul wrote:

You probably feel downcast, yet this is a time and a season when your duty is more significant than it has ever been. Your hope and courage may turn to resignation at the prospect ahead, yet I believe there has

---

124. www.goodreads.com/quotes/938848-what-general-weygand-called-the-battle-of-france-is-over (accessed 17.12.24).

been no better time when we should lift up our hearts and rejoice in our position and our prospects. Why? Because we are Christians, and our nation, even in its failings and forgetfulness, is Christian and we are nationally, consciously, fighting for God and His Redeemer. And if God be for us who can be against us?

Those last words, absorbed from Romans 8:31 as a thirteen-year-old for a new bike – were bearing fruit.

And as the Luftwaffe crossed the English Channel, Paul found in Lowestoft that, 'the regular air raids really began. The operating theatre had a glass roof and I felt rather vulnerable and didn't like it. But all the young nurses were scuttling about getting on with their job, so I thought I had better do the same.'

Someone noted in his Confidential Naval Record:

This officer has performed all the operations – more than 300 – and all have been most successful, a first-class surgeon. He has been able to tackle with conspicuous success all the problems which have confronted him. Very popular with those who know him well – but inclined to be somewhat intolerant. Most earnest over his duties, given to study and as a consequence he did not frequent the mess. Slim build keeps himself fit by cycling & walking. Recommended for accelerated promotion.

Waves and waves of German bombers throbbed over the Houghtons in Surrey, also passing over two other families destined to shape Paul's life – the Swifts and the Whites. Though he had no idea of it, the (other) love of his life was living not far from his family home, at a village called Chaldon in Surrey.

There Jean Swift, nineteen, stood with her mother, Alice, in the cornfields looking up as Spitfires and Hurricanes tore into the massed German planes. 'Dogfights drew vapour trails in the sky, wheeling and diving, and, plunging with trailing fire while we wondered, longed and prayed – would the pilot bail out . . .?' And another fireball was smoking in a summer field.

Nearby lived the Whites – 'or the Granville Whites on high days and holidays' – a family of accountants with two teenage sons, Brian and Pat, and a daughter, June. The Swifts had just moved to Gilston, a rented farm. When the children were tiny the Swifts had been farming in Paul and John's dreamland, the village of Great Bolas, Shropshire where they lived in the Georgian 'home farm'. In the stables were seven or eight enormous carthorses, and nearby the carters, ploughmen and stable hands.

Jean was the youngest of four children, half an hour younger than her twin John, who she called Twinny. John and his older brother, Peter, had been squeezed into Malvern College on money from their grandfather, the cotton mill owner from Oldham. Eight-year-old Jean wrote to Malvern:

Bolas House,
Wellington,
6 July 1929

Dear Peter,

O-O-oh! Peter we have a young sparrow-hawk – We caught two dace with a net by the mill. They were in a shoal . . .

love from Jean Swift
xxxxxxxxxxxxxxxxxxx

Then the Depression demanded moving first to Gilston, near Talybont in Wales where survival meant keeping hens in the sitting room – a horror for their mother, Alice, from a well-to-do Manchester mill owner's home.

Then it was on again to Surrey. As usual the Swifts were hospitable and happy and were welcomed in Chaldon as farmers at the Allt. During a drinks party at the Whites, Jean 'heard the racket from above getting closer and closer and then the whine of bombs – so I hid behind the sofa. The windows blew in – but no one was hurt so we got on with the party'. Was that the party where Alice, brought up Methodist and teetotal (at that stage), famously replied to, 'Would you like a drink?'

'No thanks, I'm not thirsty.'

On 20 August as the Battle of Britain reached its crisis, with every remaining British fighter in the skies, Churchill launched his words, 'Never in the field of human conflict has so much been owed by so many to so few.'

About then, Alice and her older daughter, Muff, were driving a pony and trap when 'a helpful German aeroplane strafed us with machine guns, so we dived underneath the trap – crawling out unharmed to find the pony grazing in contentment'.[125]

Another German parachuted into a field where Alice was turning hay. She went to assess the damage to the pilot holding a pitchfork in front of her. He found himself being addressed in fluent German – Alice had spent a gap year in Germany before the First World War.

Brian White and Muff Swift, sharing a love of horses, fell in love and married. He joined the Royal Marines and 45 Commando. Before long these seven children of the

---

125. Jennifer White to the author.

Whites and Swifts and would be immersed in war – and oncoming tragedy.

Failing to break the RAF, the German strategy switched to something never before experienced: total civilian destruction. On 7 September 1940, came: 'One of those beautiful early autumn days that feel like spring. At 4.40 p.m. the sirens wailed in London and all trooped to the shelters. I looked up and saw a large V shaped formation of planes flying over. More and more followed.' The London Blitz had begun.

That September Paul's longing for the sea was unfulfilled and he experienced 'very disturbed nights. None passes without a downfall [of bombs] in our half mile perimeter. Monday night produced some fractures, a fractured skull and a broken back when a small ship was hit. The owner of the back is straightened out and in a plaster jacket and the others have survived too'.

Albert, sensing change, wrote: 'we are very thankful that you are kept safe from "the arrow" and "pestilence".'[126] 'Should you find yourself in the water, old boy, don't give in and make good use of anything you can get hold of.'[127]

Invasion overshadowed all, prompting Dick to write:

The crisis may come to a head by the time this reaches you, but I do not doubt the outcome. I very much question whether one of the enemy would set foot on our soil, except perhaps as a prisoner. For between us and them 'there is a great gulf fixed'[128] and between lie

---

126. 'You will not fear the terror of the night, nor the arrow that flies by day, nor the pestilence that stalks in darkness, nor the destruction that wastes at noonday' (Psalm 91:5-6, ESV).
127. Letter to Paul from Albert Houghton, 10 September 1940.
128. Luke 16:26, AKJV.

the ships of the Senior Service which we have the honour to belong to, manned by the men who have passed under our own hands; and I know that they will not fail us. It is a privilege to be taking some part, however small, in the conflict. I'm sure our old friends the PB's are watching the moves in Syria, where no doubt the conflagration will spread and overflow into Palestine. The Governor of Malta, one General Dobbie, is a great Plymouth Brother. He is the right man for the job – wish we had some more PB's at the head of affairs.[129]

The government prepared the nation for death and destruction on a scale never seen before. Some civilians had one week's training as Auxiliary Nurses and immediately encountered horrific trauma on and under the streets of London under fallen buildings. Gas masks were issued for adults and children.

'Keep Calm and Carry on' – the wartime poster – was produced in millions but never used. Possibly invented by Churchill for use in an invasion, the iconic saying only came to light in the year 2000. A million children were evacuated from the cities and 80,000 water hand pumps distributed for fire control. Papier mâché coffins were mass produced along with self-assembly air-raid shelters. The Houghtons had one in their garden.

For pets the government advised, 'it really is kindest to have them destroyed' and 750,000 died. Billy and Ginger Jim were – of course – spared.

Dick told Paul, 'I hope your parents are both well . . . The rain of bombs has descended on districts near them. My old home at Southsea was hit so the roof and side wall collapsed – some half ton of bombs in that show and our church was hit.'

---

129. Letter to PWH, 15 September, 1940.

On the Allt farm, Jean Swift's brother John came home from boarding school and, with their father Harry, took out the shotguns and showed Alice and Jean how to defend themselves – no longer from rabbits – but Germans.

Then one day 'a signal came through'. Paul was to report to Glasgow naval headquarters. And in early September a flurry of letters reveals that – at last – he is heading for the sea. Medical cases, letters and emotions followed him north:

> Dear Houghton,
>
> You have left a gap here [in Lowestoft] which cannot be filled. I don't imagine they will get another man to do the surgery plus the crabs [medical slang for STIs] with a similar ubiquity and aplomb.
> That case of the Wren with abdominal pain – well I did another vaginal examination – she was three months pregnant, despite all her denials and history of regular periods!
> With my very best wishes from us both and don't get bombed or sunk.
>
> Yours
> Edward Taylor

And Edith wades in:

> My own precious Paulie,
>
> Needless to say, how I have thought and prayed about my precious son – day in and day out. Trusting that my letter will have a good voyage and reach you my precious, precious Paulie safely.
>
> Your ever loving and devoted
> Mother XXXX.[130]

---

130. Letter to Paul from Albert Houghton, 10 September 1941.

So he boarded the night train north. For luggage he carried his stethoscope and a change of uniform packed into a government issue holdall stencilled 'PWH' on the outside ... A holdall that would be part of our family holidays for a generation.

He also packed the *The Oxford Book of English Verse*, a Bible and a letter-writing pad. Perhaps his mother's last letter with, 'Lord, teach us to pray ...' (Luke 11:1) scrawled on top prompted Paul to pen this prayer.

My Prayer

Use my hands for selfless service
Through the day to be
I do like to take my ease
So find a job for me.
Use my hands for some good deed
To help a fellow man;
Here, Lord, are my idle hands
Please USE them if You can.[131]

---

131. Author unknown but it may be by Paul himself. It reflects his struggles with his own choleric and melancholic personality. There are two more verses on typed paper:

> Use my lips this day, dear Lord,
> To speak some word of cheer,
> For my lips are all too apt
> To voice despair and fear.
> Often I am angry Lord,
> Oh, curb my tongue this day.
> May I speak wise words and true,
> As I go my way.

> Use my heart – and fill it
> With a love that never tires.
> Cleanse it of all foolish pride,
> And little vain desires.
> Breathe into this human clay
> and mould it to thy will
> Here, Lord, is my wayward heart,
> Oh make it quiet and still.

Next morning the steam engine puffed into the small port of Gourock on the south bank of the River Clyde and the Battle of the Atlantic.

CHAPTER NINETEEN

Battle of the Atlantic

September-December 1940

> I tell you naught for your comfort,
> Yea, naught for your desire,
> Save that the sky grows darker yet
> And the sea rises higher.
>
> G.K. Chesterton (1874-1936),
> *The Ballad of the White Horse, 1911*[132]

The tang of salt spray tasted brisk after the all-night train ride. He was amazed to be expected at Gourock, a few miles down the long estuary from Glasgow, and welcomed aboard from the tiny motorboat of HMS *Zulu*.

As they approached, the ship lay waiting in wartime grey camouflage in grey drizzle on grey water.

'Up you go, sir,' urged the boatswain as he glided the pram along the hull. With the adrenaline coursing through his veins,

---

132. *The Ballad of the White Horse* by G.K. Chesterton first appeared in the year of Paul's birth in 1911. Paul quoted this once or twice when a gale was raging outside our house in Worcestershire or when we were leaning into the wind along a clifftop in Wales. *The Times* printed it during the war when things were going very badly. Chesterton based it on the struggle for survival by King Alfred and the English against the Danish invaders in the tenth century.

Paul smelt the pungent marine oil fumes and through his hand on her hull, felt the thrum of steam turbines – foretastes of countless burning ships and planes and pillars of smoke. As the steel side rolled towards them, Paul grasped the dangling ladder and climbed; and all these years later I can imagine him clambering awkwardly on deck, eyes glinting because, 'Nothing can equal the excitement of boarding a warship getting up steam for sea!'[133] And up through the deck via his feet came the lift and flow of the boundless ocean.

'On arrival, I saluted the quarterdeck because in the days before the Reformation there was always a crucifix there – and so one was really saluting the cross.'[134]

HMS *Zulu*, 1,891 tons, was one of the 'Tribals', a class of destroyer with sister ships like HMS *Ashanti*. She was known as a happy ship – a great prize. Looking about him, Paul realised *Zulu* was moored near the port of Greenock, where the Atlantic convoys gathered before setting sail for America and the site of a recent terror.

A few months before, a Free French destroyer called *Maillé Brézé* had caught fire and blown up on 30 April 1940. What happened next moved Paul deeply to say:

> She did not sink, and men could be seen through the port holes being roasted alive. Despite the great danger of more explosions, a naval surgeon went alongside in a small boat. The men put their arms through the porthole and the doctor gave each a large dose of morphine – large enough to render them comatose beyond caring. Afterwards the surgeon was awarded the DSO.

---

133. Remark to MH about 1990, aged eighty-nine.
134. PWH, Royal Naval Museum interview November 2000, track 26.

Paul illustrated two things from this: The courage of the doctor of course, but also how to compassionately relieve suffering in imminent death. Medics knew that morphine in the correct dosage did not kill but rather it induced a wonderful painless euphoria. My father knew perfectly well the difference between actively killing someone (euthanasia) for any reason – and administering medication to relieve suffering without killing (palliative care). He abhorred the former at all times.[135]

The destroyer *Zulu*, 377ft long, was a tiny cog in the grinding nightmare known as the Battle of the Atlantic. Below the grey sea wastes, German submarines waited in wolf packs hungry to sink every ship they could. The noose on food imports into Britain was tightening. It would take years for the Herculean efforts of her farmers to virtually double the volume of home-produced wheat, oats and barley.

Destroyers, small, unarmoured ships called 'tin-cans' in the US navy, worked beside the mighty battleships and cruisers like HMS *Belfast*, hunting and destroying submarines that were trying to break through to the merchant ships.

'We were about to sail with a huge convoy to North America crossing over to Halifax and return with another convoy. My father had begged me, "Buy yourself an inflatable waistcoat before you go." So, I said to the officer in charge on deck, "Can I go ashore and buy a few things?"'

'"You had better hurry up because we are leaving soon." I bought this inflatable waistcoat for £5, which was a lot of money then. But when I tried it on it was so heavy that I thought I would sooner drown; I shoved it away and told my father I bought it, and he was satisfied.'

Paul discovered the ship felt surprisingly small. The gun turrets were open to the wind and weather, as was the Bridge

---

135. Incident reported to the author by PWH, www.greenocktelegraph.co.uk/news/ 13992471.wartime-tragedy-on-river/ (accessed 2.11.24).

for the commanding officers. 'My abiding memories are that I was never dry and never warm, but it was quite good fun. With her two steam turbines she could surge ahead at over forty miles an hour and would lean far over when cornering at speed.'

Going below, Paul found living quarters so cramped he made the tiny sick bay his cabin. Freshwater was only for drinking. 'They gave us "seawater soap" which was next to useless, and everyone became sticky from the salt water.' The men – surrounded by pet cats – slung their hammocks wherever they could and looked forward to their daily 'tot of Rum' as a highlight.[136]

The convoy departed from Greenock in a double line of ships and turned north between Scotland and Ireland. 'I was all right until we were into deep water when I was so seasick I wanted to go home – I nearly told the captain – in fact. I could not think properly. A Maltese steward saved my life, "I know the treatment for you, sir: it's hard cheese, dry biscuits and Crème de Menthe." In no time I had got my sea legs.

'In a gale of wind we were like toy boats tossed around in the bathtub. Up on the Bridge I felt the heave and roll as she began to slide down, down towards the grey belly of the oncoming wave. Then she seemed to just keep on going with the bow burrowing deeper and deeper and you wondered, "Will we ever come up?" Grey water flew down the foredeck leaping the breakwaters until the forward gun-turret was half submerged by snowy brine. You saw great holes appear in the sea surface and I'd say to myself, "We will miss that – yes – but another is here . . . and in we go." Somehow we would

---

136. Virtual tour of a Tribal class destroyer on YouTube at 'War Thunder – Ist Person Walkthrough on Tribal Class Destroyer', www.youtube.com/watch?v=jTqEmXkXFWg (accessed 5.11.24).

corkscrew upwards to "see-saw" on the next wave crest where the propellers raced in fresh air.

'And in the storms we were glad because the U-boats lay low leaving us in peace. Below decks, water was pouring and trickling from every nook and cranny and the bilge pumps were churning ceaselessly.'[137] And north of Iceland, some merchant ships just could not progress against the winds of 80 knots or more and the whole convoy stopped in the water. Crockery was smashed, inch thick steel guard rails bent flat by the waves and broken bones ensued.

But in calmer days they wallowed along sinisterly watched by enemy eyes through periscopes. The destroyers and corvettes rushed about shepherding the slow merchant vessels to keep going and keep in order. Strays were all too quickly picked off. A puff of smoke signalled a hit by a torpedo and while small ships ran to pick up survivors, others circled the area with their Asdic echo sounders pinging in the hunt for the responsible U-boat. When a ship was sinking, or rolling over, men leapt for the sea and struck out with insane strength to escape the propellers. Paul was appalled to find 'as ships rolled over, the men began to slide down the hull and the barnacles tore their flesh as if flayed alive'.

Depth charges to shatter submarines flashed under water, and Paul saw near misses from bombs putting out fires on deck by the drenching downfalls of seawater.

If the men managed to get into lifeboats some would set sail for home – often never to be seen again, or 'we found them drifting as starved skeletons'. The wounded and swimmers were pulled up onto *Zulu* if possible. Paul and his sick bay orderlies dealt as best they could with blast injury, burns, half-drowned men – and women too – nurses from the

---

137. PWH conversation with MH.

troop ships, often with their flesh torn by shrapnel along with cold water shock and traumatic amputations of limbs. The tender care of the male orderlies for their shattered patients touched Paul.

In his own exhaustion Paul observed the captain. 'I believe he had been at sea since the outbreak of war and I used to wonder how he continued. He never seemed to sleep – and he was always on the Bridge – an open Bridge – endlessly battered by wind, rain and salt spray. He was always ready to attend to any call, never lost his temper, always cool; what sort of character a man has to stand up to the strain like that? – I just don't know.'[138]

As a boy in the 1960s I listened rapt to these stories and I would sneak away to the library and books like *The Cape Horn Breed* with the tales of great steel sailing ships and photos of seamen laying out along the yardarms high above the waves. In 2019, I sought the Atlantic my father knew. So, I signed on the tall sailing ship *Tenacious*, 500 tons, with square rigged sails on three masts rising to a hundred feet. We were headed for Portugal from Portland on England's south coast.

Two days before departure my telephone rang – it was the esteemed relative. 'Mark!' she began – and I held the phone 6 inches away to protect my hearing. 'You are stark raving mad! Sailing the Bay of Biscay in *November* – don't you know what that Bay can be like?' I said, 'Goodbye,' in the secret excitement about my treasure: a super storm was forecast.

Once on board, I was excited to discover I was the ship's doctor and soon had to take a sick crew member to a doctor ashore. On my return *Tenacious* was out in the bay and

---

138. Royal Naval Museum interview, November 2000. This was probably Commander John Stuart Crawford or possibly Commander Harry Robert Graham, DSO, https://uboat.net/allies/warships/ship/4428.html (accessed 26.5.23).

heading for the open sea; only the harbour pilot boat got me to the ship in a squall of rain. The dark blue sides and shrouds of *Tenacious* towered above us, 'Jump when I say,' roared the pilot above the wind, and – as the curve of her *tumblehome* rolled our way – I jumped and grabbed and willing hands hauled me over the rail into her waist: Yes, Dad, nothing can equal the excitement of boarding a ship heading for the open Atlantic.

The day before, I had a 'handover' trauma masterclass by the departing army paramedic. Fresh from the war in Afghanistan, she began: 'Supposing a man stepped on an IED [improvised explosive device], it usually takes his legs off, bollocks and other bits nearby . . .' She picked up a needle of brutal thickness: 'So you've got these traumatic amputations – this needle is for forcing saline in through a long bone fast.' I thought of my father at sea: how he would have pounced on such simple lifesavers. He had seen a mooring wire snap and recoil like a bullwhip 'taking the legs off the officer beside me, who bled to death where he fell'.[139]

As *Tenacious* met the open sea the first wave roared along the lee deck in a rush of foam and a young woman turned her face, searched my eyes and asked, 'Is this normal?' I paused – mentally surveying my twenty minutes of experience on tall ships – 'Oh yes, quite normal.'

On watch at night, the mountains threw themselves on us from the North roaring by with bared teeth. 'What about man overboard drill?' I asked my watch leader – a cheery ex-sergeant major. 'Well, if you fall in, don't hold your breath, because we're not going to find you,' he replied. At the helm I tried the redoubtable mate: 'If someone falls over, should I hand the wheel to you?'

---

139. PWH to the author.

'Don't you let go of that b------y wheel for a moment!' she shouted. 'Stay at your post and do exactly what I tell you.'

Down below the round of three cooked meals continued, while cooks and kettles, food and people were flung about. No wonder all those long bone splints lay ready in the sick bay.

Outside the spectacle was spellbinding and at last – after sixty years of reading about the sea – I was ready to 'spring into the rigging'. Wearing eight warm layers under my oilskins I waddled over to the rail and, heart pounding, grasped the shrouds to spring like Admiral Nelson boarding a Frenchman in my Ladybird children's book.

Alas, trussed up like a Christmas turkey I could hardly get my foot off the ground. (Confidentially: I lifted my knee by hand to stand on the rail.) Then I climbed – the vast spreading canvas carving ovals in the sky and the wind pressing me onto the shrouds.

The deck below shrank, and the crunch came before stepping out onto the 'yardarm'. *Tenacious* was designed for disabled people, and I dithered about stepping into space onto the dancing foot rope but, glancing back at the huddle on the high platform, I was amazed to see one man, who was totally blind, waiting to follow me out. 'Get a grip, Houghton, you've done trees and cliffs,' I muttered and, clinging to the Jackstay (a grab rail to help Jacktar stay on the yard), I edged towards the lonely end of the spar . . . Why does the end hanging over the sea feel *less* safe than a 60ft fall onto a hard deck? I wondered.

No photograph can capture great waves in a gale. But Eric Newby's *The Last Grain Race*, describes:

The seas approached very deliberately, black and shiny, with smoking white crests . . . hissing as they came.

I went aloft . . . the noise was an unearthly scream . . . and above all the pale blue sky . . . made me deeply afraid . . .

I felt . . . the existence of an infinitely powerful and at the same time merciful God. Nearly everyone in the ship felt this . . . awed . . . beyond the common experience of men.[140]

Our gale was less ferocious but I was astonished by the violence of the ship and tried to imagine my father working on an injured patient in our little sick bay – just as cramped as in his destroyer. Even carrying the casualty down ladders would be a feat. Simple skin stitching would mean wedging yourself at 45 degrees against the patient's couch with your feet on the opposite cupboard and the patient lashed down.

The *Zulu* and her crew were floundering as 'we got into a terrible storm, going down waves of 50ft, then crawling up the other side. I went below and the steel bulkheads – water-tight internal walls giving the ship stiffness – were buckling and bonging like tin trays. The hull was see-sawing on the crests and bending in the troughs until I began to think she would break in two like the American Liberty ships SS *John P. Gaines* had done.

'So I went to the engineer, who I had got to know, and said, "This ship must be supported." And together we got beams of timber with which we shored up the bulkheads; it was a terrible time – but great fun!

'They rigged lifelines outside, and you hung on and didn't use the deck unless you really had to. I found my Action Station was near the sick bay. I used to get about holding

---

140. Eric Newby, *The Last Grain Race* (London: HarperCollins, 2014).

onto lifelines, and it felt like we were at "action stations" all the time.

'The surgical instruments aboard were very primitive, and you couldn't do much in a destroyer. You could sew up wounds, but we could not put people to sleep for surgery. People came to you with coughs and colds and perhaps a pneumonia – we put those in the sick bay; but there again we have no specific antibiotics to treat them.

'We stoked the men up with tinned milk. Of course, once we got into port we could put a man ashore in better care and leave them behind; but this was the last thing they wanted because their ship was their home.

'Medically we carried a good supply of dressings and some splints; syringes with very blunt needles – not like the beautiful disposables of today. We had many injuries from people banging their heads and being thrown about.

'Basic medicines on board were cough mixtures and diarrhoea mixtures. Dysentery was always raising its head and was awful in a crowded ship. The men's bottoms looked like a red-hot poker had seared them. We treated it with "chalk and opium" which was effective.

'I got to know as many men as I could; one had to look out for men breaking down under the strain and try and get them some time ashore. If you had a case of appendicitis, you would be in real trouble; surgically it was a dead loss to try to operate in a destroyer.'

Dr Chris Howard Bailey from the Royal Naval Museum, interviewing Paul in hushed tones, asked 'What about counselling the crew members?'

'Counselling!' he snorted with a smile. 'Counselling – they didn't want counselling! I talked to them; we talked about their homes and got to know them and that did a lot of good. The thing was to "join the crew" because the crew was a unit.

The navy men fight for their ship; it's the ship that must fight and go on together.'
At HMS *Europa* (Lowestoft) Paul noticed:

Courage is expendable. Courage is like a petrol tank in the car which can drain out. But it can be refilled. I came to know that one must move men out of the line of fire and give them a break to top up the tank – there is no disgrace, it is just treatment.
Many of the men were very worried about their families at home in the air raids – desperately worried. As for the merchant service seamen we dragged from the sea – they were treated disgracefully by the government – I don't think they even got a pension later. I can't think why they joined up because the losses were appalling.[141]

Men and women survived improbable odds. When Lord Louis Mountbatten's HMS *Javelin* was torpedoed at night, the Medical Officer was killed at his post. HMS *Jackal* came back and 'found a number blown overboard by the explosions. One man in the ammunition magazine had the extraordinary experience of seeing the ship's steel side disintegrate in front of him as he was blown towards it allowing him to fetch up in the sea unharmed'.[142]

The challenge was to do what they could:

At sea, we were dealing with dying men (and women rescued from liners and troop ships) who had been appallingly burned, sliced by flying steel or choked

---

141. It seems they did get a pension during wartime – at least from 1943, https://en.wikipedia.org/wiki/Ratings_in_the_Merchant_Navy_(United_Kingdom) (accessed 6.6.22).
142. Rear-Admiral A.F. Pugsley and Captain Donald Macintyre, *Destroyer Man* (London: Weidenfeld & Nicolson, 1957), p. 61.

by smoke and oil. People ask if we used euthanasia to relieve their suffering? The answer lay in copious amounts of morphine and heroin.

We did not hasten death as that is the province of God not man, but we did not hold back on these wonderful agents of relief inducing a sense of pain-free peace and euphoria. Indeed, the oral version in its bottle, proved too much temptation for some doctors who became secretly dependent. The medical orderlies assisting me were tender with their wounded comrades. I grew to depend on their skills and admire the love they showed to the end.

The striking aspect for a surgeon at sea in the Battle of the Atlantic and major events like *Operation Pedestal* was how little you could do. Every ship was insulated from its neighbour in action. And when the crews were hit on other ships, you knew they were in trouble – but you couldn't communicate well across the water. Sometimes we went back to the old system of signal flags conveying short messages, just like Admiral Lord Nelson sent at the battle of Trafalgar: 'England expects that every man will do his duty'.

It was surprising how much loss of life happened that we could not deal with in the turmoil of battle at sea. You see we didn't have even that elementary item of resuscitation the intravenous drip and say line. Blood transfusions were rare anywhere and on ship we had no means of storing blood or cross matching from a donor even if one could be spared from essential duties of fighting the ship.[143]

---

143. PWH interview with Naval History Museum, November 2000.

By December 1940, the bombing was even threatening brother Jack and his family in the quiet cathedral city of Shrewsbury far away in his dreamland on the Welsh Marches. Frankie updated the family:

> After the raids we are all very bright, merry and well. Thursday we had an eight-hour raid and a big raid on Liverpool; the ack-ack fire was terrific and livened the night up for us. We all slept partly clad on the ground floor except the children; we carried them down asleep in their cots and they never woke up. The flames were terrific. If we have a direct hit, well, we are with our babies and will go to our Heavenly home – rather we go together.
> Peter [Frankie's brother] was over on Saturday. They are full of beans despite shrapnel through their roof and bomb splinters and are completely unshaken.
>
> Yours with all love
> Frankie[144]

On 8 December Edith wrote:

> How I long to see you. Your portrait looks splendid in the frame, and we are going to hang it in the Drawing Room. Planes and guns are very busy here tonight – we have been having some good nights and peaceful sleep. So grateful, but one does so long for the end of this nerve tingling time.

In London hundreds, often thousands, were dying every night.

---
144. Frances 'Frankie' Houghton, letter 3 December 1940 from Drapers Hall Shrewsbury to her in laws, Albert and Edith Houghton.

One has need of much patience and we have our Friend and Saviour who undertakes for us and He will do the best for us as He knows best. Dick called in the other morning with his wife and wee son Carl. Judging by what he said, he has been kept from danger in a marvellous way and appears to me to be much softened towards God's things. He thinks the world may end soon.

Mother

Zulu returned from sea and Paul managed a week's leave at home in December. Afterwards, from Lowestoft, he confesses to his parents by letter:

I'm afraid I was very irritable, forgive me; I was so tired.
I see the war is spreading. The Admiralty will not send me to sea again for two months at least. The captain [of HMS *Zulu*] was very kind, very complimentary and promised me a good ship later if I possessed my soul in patience. I should be very grateful because few juniors in temporary rank like me are so favoured.

Paul was pleased they had a new Anderson bomb shelter in the garden; these hoops of corrugated steel looked like pig styes but saved many lives. 'As well as the cellar shelter you should use the stronghold because it is particularly secure. I think you are all very brave.'

Paul was back and forth between Lowestoft and *Zulu* in a most frustrating manner. In May 1941 she took part in sinking the giant German battleship *Bismarck* but Paul was ashore. He did meet the biplane pilot who said, 'It was low cloud and hard to get sight of anything when suddenly I saw a window with the *Bismark* framed in it. I dropped down and let go my tin fish which hit her astern and disabled her rudder. From then on she could only go in circles and her fate was sealed.'

Again it was noted confidentially, 'April 1941: A first-class surgeon, extremely keen on work. Has done about 130 operations some of which serious, all results excellent. Spares neither time nor trouble over surgical work. Good messmate, deservedly popular. Recommend for accelerated promotion.'[145]

Paul's medical circle were afloat on large warships and he desperately wanted one too – big enough to put his surgical skills to use. Then one day, far out in the Atlantic in August, Paul heard the captain say, '*Zulu* must leave the convoy and sail independently for the 'North Atlantic station'. So the ship bid farewell and we sailed south having no idea where the North Atlantic station was.'

And a buzz of speculation rippled through the crew.

---

145. PWH, Confidential Naval Service Record.

CHAPTER TWENTY

To the North Atlantic Station
September 1941 to September 1942

Little *Zulu* sailed on alone.

No one liked sailing alone because if your ship was torpedoed you might spend the rest of your life on a raft – which wouldn't be a very long life.

Everyone noticed the weather got warmer and the sea calmer, and the captain ordered 'happy hour' and all the damp bedding to be aired on deck and tidied shipshape and we began to enjoy ourselves.

About midnight, under a full moon in warm balmy air, the lookout suddenly shouted, 'Sail oh.' We didn't expect sails in mid-Atlantic in 1941 and it turned out to be a Portuguese schooner sailing from Lisbon to the Azores. So, we overhauled it, the schooner backed her yards to come to a halt and our boarding party drew cutlasses from their rack – just like in *Treasure Island*, and a full moon all I wanted was a parrot, like Long John Silver – and went aboard armed to the teeth.

The romance of the occasion was not lost on the crew and decades later Paul was still striving to discover the author and the rest of a poem that begins:

There's a schooner in the offing
With her top sails shot with gold . . . [146]

The boarding party came back rather late, having lingered some time. They were rather the worse for wear – having been pressed to sample the Portuguese wine – and laden with fruit to fill our ship. So, we bid them farewell and good luck and *Zulu* had a lot of oranges and good things to eat for some time which was great.

Travelling south and south-east we zigzagged like mad near the danger areas, infested with German submarines, around the entrance to the Mediterranean; and so it dawned on us that the 'North Atlantic Station' was in reality – Gibraltar!

Coming along the north-west coast of Spain these lines sprang to life:

Nobly, nobly Cape St Vincent . . .
Ships were found in grand array.[147]

And there was Cape Trafalgar itself, passing us to port, where Lord Nelson was killed in 1805 in the greatest sea battle the world had ever seen. So we came to the great Rock of Gibraltar and entered the harbor on 10 September 1941.

Gibraltar, attached to the southern tip of Spain, but ceded to Great Britain, had been of immense strategic importance for centuries. It had a deep-water harbour for the Royal Navy and could exert control over every craft passing through the

---

146. Richard Hovey (1864-1900), 'Sea Gypsy', although the word is 'fire' not 'gold'; see www.daypoems.net/poems/1126.html (accessed 21.11.24).
147. Robert Browning (1812-1889), 'Home Thoughts from Sea', www.poetryfoundation.org/poems/43759/home-thoughts-from-the-sea (accessed 2.11.24).

narrows between Europe and Africa just across the Straits. From this fortress, honeycombed with bomb-proof tunnels, the Royal Navy projected authority across the Atlantic Ocean, Mediterranean and, through the Suez Canal, into the Indian and Pacific oceans. And in Lingfield, Albert's old biddies prayed on.

CHAPTER TWENTY-ONE

Flagship Nelson

As *Zulu* tied up in the Royal Dock, Paul took in the sights and sounds from her rail then jumped ashore and dashed to the top of the Rock, for spectacular views of Africa and games with the insolent apes.

Far and wide he could see the machinery of the brutal war of attrition that was being waged in the Mediterranean. In port below lay British ships, planes and submarines determined to sink and kill German and Italian ships, planes, submarines and troops – particularly the convoys crossing from Italy to the Africa Corps on the North African coast. While on the other hand, German and Italian ships, planes and submarines were lurking to pounce on any supplies heading for Malta or the British Army in North Africa.

Gone was the grey Atlantic and there lay the icing on the cake – swimming the warm blue Mediterranean where Paul promptly lost a gold signet ring, a gift from his father. Being in 80ft of water, that was the end of that – or so it seemed.

Paul 'had no idea what lay in store for me. But having got into Gibraltar the signal came almost immediately that I was to join HMS *Nelson*, lying at the South Mole across the harbour – this great big battleship. And the captain said, "You had better hurry up because she is sure to sail, so I will get the pram out."' So out came the pram and we scuttled across the harbour towards this huge ship that made me feel about as big as a pinhead'.

Nelson lay long and low in the water, exuding power. Towards her for'ard end were the three vast gun turrets sprouting her famous triple barrels. The diameter of each barrel was 16 inches – wide enough for a cadet to be pulled through to inspect the inside. She was a household name throughout Britain and also the flagship of the legendary Force H – the battle fleet of the Mediterranean convoys.

Paul, 'went up the gangway, where I saluted the quarterdeck and the officer of the watch who said, "We are expecting you – I'm glad you've come." And I was amazed that some wretched little junior officer like me was always expected'.

'On board this great ship were three of us medical officers. There was the Principal Medical Officer, a very nice man, and two of us juniors. There was a crew of nearly 2,000 men and the numbers increased when the admiral was a-board with his staff; then it became a Flagship as it usually was.' The ship was vast and bewildering with eighty officers in the mess.

Whereas the little *Zulu* had an open bridge, *Nelson* had armoured glass giving protection from the wind and water flying about. In fact, she had separate bridges for the admiral and captain. At sea the captain had final authority for his ship and – to the amusement of the crew – could – if the safety of the ship demanded it – transport the admiral in a different direction from his wishes.

Paul's dream had come true and he looked around. 'I found the sick bay was quite well-equipped. There were even swing beds that used to sway about in a storm while the patient stayed level. I liked to sleep in one if possible.

'There was an operating theatre, which was quite absurd: it had white tiles on the floor! The first time the ship got shaken up, all the tiles came unstuck.

'It had a proper operating table which slid about on the tiles as the ship rolled! And there was a dispensary with racks and racks and racks and racks of utterly useless drugs. Honestly, you can't believe it – sort of fifteenth-century stuff – pills galore and a lot of purgatives, violent purgatives. We did have quinine tablets in case you got malaria, but 90 per cent of the dispensary could have been thrown overboard – and should have been.

'There was a lot of bandages and splints, but almost no Thomas' splints which are so vital for keeping broken legs straight and comfortable.'[148]

Yet it had only needed one sea mine to twist her hull (and lacerate dozens of sailors' bottoms who happened to be on the throne). Everyone knew how vulnerable the great thing was.

Paul knew: 'We had no antibiotics at all aboard ship – although one sort of sulphonamide had been produced and I brought it with me from home. Alexander Fleming had shown the value of penicillin, but this was 1941 – and later when they did produce them in quantity, they went out to Burma and quite right too; the terrible tropical infections there were disabling our troops.

'When it came to surgical instruments – you can't believe it – they were sort of Nelson and Napoleon's era in mahogany brass bound boxes – I used to long to get a box home because they would have looked nice in the house.

'They had sufficient saws that I could have amputated every leg in the navy. Unbelievably there was still tarred string for tying off bleeding arteries; but at least they didn't have any hot tar! – they were very keen on warm tar for applying to stumps in the navy of Nelson's day. Back in those days the

---

[148]. P.M. Robinson, M.J. O'Meara, The Thomas splint, ITS ORIGINS AND USE IN TRAUMA, 1 April 2009. https://doi.org/10.1302/0301-620X.91B4.21962; https://online.boneandjoint.org.uk/doi/full/10.1302/0301-620X.91B4.21962 (accessed 28.7.20).

phrase ran, "The devil to pay and no pitch hot." Well, the "devil" was the seam between the planks of a wooden ship, above and below the waterline, but the caulking was always coming out, which "played the devil" because water came in. 'If that happened they had to beach the ship, "list" her over on her side, repack the cavity with oakum – a rope caulking made from jute – and quickly seal it with hot pitch tar. So, "the devil to pay" meant you paid him with hot tar. However, if there was no pitch hot you couldn't seal it off. The next thing was the tide would come up while the ship was still listing over on her side and anything might happen as the water ran in. Honestly, even in my day in the navy, I think I could have got the tar all right – for surgery – to stop bleeding and sterilise the wound; think of that – the agony of it!

'Then there were a whole set of instruments called Probangs – long whalebones for getting coins and fishbones out of gullets – certain death to use them.'[149]

While *Nelson* was still tied up at Gibraltar, Paul surveyed his tools – about to head for Malta through the most violently contested stretch of sea in the world – and they had equipped him like this!

'I discovered only a few modern instruments for operating. You might have done a very easy procedure – with a very few and rather crude artery forceps – but almost nothing really. Thankfully I had brought out a full set, and I used it too. The situation looked dreadful. I thought of Lord Nelson – wounded and dying at the Battle of Trafalgar in 1805 [not far from Gibraltar] and said to myself, "Here we go again. England expects that every man will do his duty." So I spoke to the PMO about it – and he said, "Well that's what they give us you know."

---

149. A probang is a surgical tool 30 to 40cm long. Its invention is credited to Walter Rumsey (1584-1660).

'As for anaesthetics, they had an old Boyles machine which was quite good, a primitive thing invented by a Bart's anaesthetist called Boyle – he was there in my time. And you could give a mixture of 'gas' [nitrous oxide the 'laughing gas'] and oxygen and ether through it.[150] There were always plenty of oxygen cylinders because the welders wanted it for their oxyacetylene torches.

'When I was at Haslar hospital, Portsmouth, an anaesthetist there killed two patients in quick succession by connecting up carbon dioxide in place of the oxygen line – and that came to a Coroner's inquest. But it was all washed over and hushed up, and that sort of thing happened and doubtless still does.'

But as to the rest of his new ship and her 'family' Paul soon decided, 'the *Nelson* was a happy ship. It was a very good life and I rather enjoyed it', Later telling his parents:

> Don't you think the old 'Nellie' is a magnificent fighting ship. My cabin is on the starboard side, aft of the '6-inch' gun battery. You can see the Bridge structure with the slits in the armour marking the Admiral's Bridge above the captain's compass platform, and, towering above both, the gunnery control and look-out stations. Then, forward of the bridge, the three giant turrets each housing three 16-inch guns. Looking aft, between the funnel and the tripod mast, on each side is the secondary armament of three turrets along each side of the ship. Each gun turret has two '6-inch' guns making twelve guns in all. The anti-aircraft weapons are numerous and the full barrage all going off together, is a sight to be sought-

---

150. 'Gas' was nitrous oxide with quite useful painkilling effect still used to this day – but not sufficient to put the patient fully asleep and pain-free.

after when your faith in our English moat [the English Channel] concerns you. My constant wonder is that such a steel mass can float.[151]

It so happened that *Nelson's* Torpedo Officer, George Blundell (who we met earlier) was laid up with a septic foot when Paul joined – so their first meeting was professional. George, confined to his cabin – garrulous as ever – recorded visitors in his illicit diary. Blundell recorded a Petty Officer called Cocking coming in 'to cut my hair and tell me about his daughter "birthed foot foremost" and "the doctor, he was a woman". The kid, two and a half pounds . . . was perfect to look at. "I could have put her in a pint beer glass," he said.'[152]

And Paul, discovering that George had a bicycle on board, saw a door to many pleasures ahead.

So this was it, the famous – or infamous – Battle of the Mediterranean. Just a month earlier, the merchant ships heading for Malta in the centre of a large convoy, began turning back under withering attacks. Suddenly the admiral sent up a signal flag, '*The convoy must go through.*' Only the day before in Gibraltar a message went personally to each ship's Master from Admiral Sir James Somerville:

The gallantry displayed by the garrison and people of Malta has aroused admiration throughout the world . . . Remember the watchword is THE CONVOY MUST GO THROUGH.[153]

The ships reassembled into their lines and pressed deeper into danger. Paul, awestruck by the merchant crews' courage,

---
151. Letter, PWH to his parents, 9 May 1943.
152. George Blundell diary, Wednesday, 27 August 1941.
153. Malta War Diary, https://maltagc70.wordpress.com/2016/07/21/21-july-1941-malta-supply-ships-captains-told-convoy-must-go-through/ (accessed 19.8.20).

noticed, 'I don't suppose the merchant ships even carried a Medical Officer.'

Now, freshly in from the Atlantic, there was little time for him to rest, or get to know the crew, or do anything about the shortage of surgical instruments. 'All the cats came back aboard – they always seemed to know when we were leaving. Then Admiral Somerville came aboard flying his flag on the foremast and bringing his own staff; so I had to move my sick bay forward into a dressing station under the main deck near the bows; this would almost be the end of me.

'The senior officers were showing signs of stress. They would come and see me saying they couldn't sleep or complaining of this and that and we would have a talk and they would go away again.'

From Gibraltar they sailed East, 27 September 1941, in a convoy codenamed *Operation Halberd*, heading for Malta 1,000 miles away.[154] Halberd was, at that the time, the largest attempt so far to resupply Malta. There were nine merchant ships carrying 81,000 tons of military equipment, fuel and supplies.

Tasked with guarding these vital supplies were the forty warships of Force H, including three battleships – HMS *Nelson*, *Rodney* and *Prince of Wales* and the aircraft carrier HMS *Ark Royal* a ship which would linger long in the nation's memory. Beneath the water were eight allied submarines, and Paul's old home HMS *Zulu* was also coming along.

Paul delighted in the balmy bright climate and found 'I was pretty free to wander round the ship as I liked because as medical officers we did not have "watch keeping duties" like all the other officers did. The officers followed the navy's

---

154. PWH interview with Naval History Museum, November 2020.

time-honoured habit of four hours on and four hours off on a rolling pattern that changed every twenty-four hours.

'I had to organise and check equipment, but I was often delightfully idle, and liked to wander around on the bridge. There the watch keeping officers had their charts rolled out with dividers, compasses, pencils and Admiralty books revealing the tides and hazards. A blue haze of pipe smoke drifted around, and half-finished cigarettes smouldered in the ashtrays.

'Those charts were works of art and prized around the world for their detail and accuracy, annotated with dates such as, "Surveyed by Lieutenant Hornblower," or some such, "1834, revised 1896, 1897" and engravings, in fact anything that might save the hapless navigator from their worst dread – going aground.

'We were travelling in huge parallel columns and it took us about three days to get to Sicily, off the toe of Italy. The merchant ships, battleships and the aircraft carrier were in the middle protected by the smaller ships in front, behind and on both sides. Everything was quiet for the first two days then the "fun" began.' The Italian air force – the Regio Aeronautica, attacked at 1 p.m. on the 27 September with thirty-eight torpedo planes and fighters and the whole ship closed down armoured hatches with everyone at Action Stations.

As we saw in chapter 1, three torpedo bombers pressed through the intense barrage of anti-aircraft fire on the starboard wing of the convoy to launch torpedoes at *Nelson*. She turned to 'comb' the torpedo tracks, and inadvertently steadied on the course of a torpedo which struck the port side of the forecastle, sealing Paul and his two sick berth attendants in the deep darkness of their sick bay where the hours dragged by. Then they heard an alarming announcement: 'All hands save the ship.'

CHAPTER TWENTY-TWO

Flash of Inspiration
September 1941

After the blast *Nelson* slowed to fifteen knots, but maintained position in the convoy at first, before slowing to a stop – a predicament which Paul and the two sick berth attendants could sense with the Italian battleships bearing down.

Apparently sinking by the bows at the front end, *Nelson's* rudders were lifted out of the water at the stern end and she was unable to steer. With the enemy air attacks continuing and submarines hungry to finish her off, the Nelson was in terrible peril. All this in mind, Paul's new friend, Torps, rushed about his damage assessment and harried the ship's first aid teams trying to stem the water and bring electrical power lines forward.

Hours later George Blundell had a flash of inspiration, as Paul recounted. 'After the torpedo struck, what was happening was that Lt Commander George Blundell devised a way to save the stricken vessel. A resourceful man, George had been in HMS *Kent* and nearly killed when she was hit in the steering gear. On that occasion, they lowered George down into the dark machinery to inspect the damage. He landed on softness which turned out to be a body. That's what he had got his OBE for – saving one of her Majesty's warships.

Now, on *Nelson*, he realised that, since she had dropped 40ft lower in the water at the bows, it might work to rebalance her with heavy weights at the rear end. The middle of the ship would be like the middle of a seesaw. That could, just could, lower her rudders back into the water sufficient to get a bite and recover some steering.

So Blundell harnessed men and steam winches to drag hundreds of tons of anchor chain out of its forward locker and pull it towards the rear of the ship by laying it out backwards and forwards in great snakes on the deck. First though, they had to 'cat' the anchors to let them hang free on each bow separated from the chains.

Catting the anchor, by knocking out the securing pins, was the job of the ship's blacksmith – a new one in this case. Three months earlier, off Cape Town, the *Nelly* had dipped her bow under a big sea which swept the cable party 'into the ship's side corners' injuring 20 – the blacksmith was one of the two who drowned.

In the darkened sick bay, the three shipmates could only listen to the inexplicable roar on the deck above their heads as link after link of battleship chain was dragged towards the stern. 'It seemed like we were in the dark a very long time.' Then, to the inexpressible relief of everyone the trick worked. The ship settled lower at the back, the rudders were able to bite on the water again for steering and they could get underway.

'Eventually we were let out into the daylight and it seemed wonderful. They gave us some food and sandwiches. Everyone had had sandwiches during that time.

'Now much lower in the water but at least travelling, we turned around and headed West back on our tracks towards Gibraltar with an escort of warships at the reduced speed of about ten knots. There we went into dry dock on my thirtieth birthday – September 30th.'

Arrived in Gibraltar's naval dockyard he just had time to collect two letters before departing again. Back in England, on that very day, his parents were alarmed to read in the newspapers of damage to HMS *Nelson* – along with the Italian's claim they sank a battleship. Edith had written two days earlier, gushing again, and dropping a hint about his temper:

29 September 1941, England –

My own precious Paulie. This is your birthday – very many happy returns – so I add this verse:

Go with me oh my Saviour;
Go with me every hour,
Control my whole behaviour,
By thy Spirit's power.[155]

Albert wrote too:

My Very Dear Old Paul,

Being away as you are and it being your 30th milestone I would wire congratulations but do not think one should put unnecessary burdens on the postal authorities in these times.

Of course we should like to know more of your whereabouts.

We are all very well including the youthful Ginger Jim, and the aged Billy – the latter has just come upstairs and flopped down on my room here where I am writing. He sends you several wags of his tail.

---

155. Author unknown.

Thank you, in their name, for your kind message to all the saints [local Christians] and I'm sure they all wish me to reciprocate it –

With heaps of love from home.
Your affectionate Dad

All except one of 'Halberd's' merchant ships got through. Malta could eat a little longer. The Italians lost twenty-one aircraft and Admiral Somerville was knighted for his leadership. It was the second time Somerville received that honour, prompting a message from Admiral Cunningham: 'Fancy, twice a knight at your age.'

Nelson tied up at Gibraltar and George Blundell climbed inside the gaping hole to survey the damage. Picking up a piece of the torpedo he read *'Made in England 1934'* and kept it. Years later it resurfaced in a reunion no one could ever have predicted.[156]

---

156. Britain had sold torpedoes to the Italians before the war to earn a pound or two – receive it back with interest.

CHAPTER TWENTY-THREE

Rock Bottom

Autumn 1941 to Spring 1942

> But (when so sad thou canst not sadder)
> Cry – and upon thy so sore loss
> Shall shine the traffic of Jacob's ladder
> Pitched betwixt Heaven and Charing Cross.
>
> Francis Thompson (1859-1907), 'In No Strange Land'[157]

By October Paul had been expecting 'I should get a holiday now on Gib' and have a nice quiet time – but not a bit of it. Within twenty-four hours they had put me on a destroyer and sent me back again to Malta, 'through the wolf packs, minefields and never-ending alarms.

'I got rather fed up and the strain was very tiring. I was expecting to get home to England on a merchant ship for some leave. At the last minute they sent another doctor, who I knew, home in my place. The ship was torpedoed, and he was never seen again.'[158]

---

157. www.theguardian.com/books/booksblog/2017/jun/26/poem-of-the-week-in-no-strange-land-by-francis-thompson (accessed 20.8.22).
158. PWH interview with Naval History Museum, November 2000.

Paul, hoping for some post-traumatic comfort, bared his feelings to Mother. The response was – well – muscular, when her reply reached him:

So my deary, you are needing a little bit of courage today. A writer said, 'Do not be afraid or discouraged no matter how sorely pressed by circumstances. A discouraged soul soon becomes helpless. He can neither resist the wiles of the enemy [Satan] by himself nor can he prevail in being helpful for others.'[159] We must flee from every trick of this deadly foe, as you would flee from a cobra, and be not slow in turning your back on it lest you bite the dust in bitter defeat.

So [God advises] in Joshua 1:9, 'Have I not commanded you, be strong and of good courage,' and I feel sure my precious son, that here lies Britain's great power in resisting this mighty foe, who I fear must have been coined in Hell.'[160]

Yet the trauma drain on his courage tank did not let up.

Coming back from Malta on the *Zulu* in November 1941 we were within 30 miles of Gibraltar, and I was on the Quarterdeck – you could see The Rock only 30 miles ahead – escorting the *Ark Royal* and I watched her turn away out of our destroyer screen: and she was immediately torpedoed. We suddenly noticed she was listing 45 degrees to one side – we didn't hear much of a bang. I saw her go down; she turned over.

Before she sank, their little ship went near the vast hulk to save survivors and Paul feared that she would roll over and

---

159. Source unknown.
160. Edith, letter to Paul, 21 October 1941.

crush them. 'Thankfully, there were only a few men damaged, and we got them off. Then the captain ordered that they were to abandon ship.'

Two stories surfaced from the *Ark Royal* to Paul's delight:

> Some months before the Ark went down, she was ploughing through perfectly impossible sees in heavy Atlantic weather, and most of the company were seasick. The flight deck was devoid of life and even the Bridge ports [windows high up] were closed. Suddenly at sundown, a portly rat was seen to emerge onto the flight deck, walk to the side, preen his whiskers, take one look aft and one forward, and then plunge overboard. He simply could not face the weather any longer and preferred death. He has all my sympathy.
>
> Weeks after, when I saw the ship take her final plunge, all this creature's acquaintances left the ship and were seen swimming in a V-formation to the African coast, but I doubt whether they ever made it. The Ark's cat was found at daylight afloat on a bit of wood and very annoyed. A motorboat rescued him.[161]

Paul watched the great ship go down with a heavy heart, feeling things could hardly get worse for England. It now seemed as if the Royal Navy had no useable aircraft carrier. And while the *Nelson* was out of action, Paul was carried back and forth to Malta in *Zulu* amid the thick of the threats.

He was longing for a break from the sea; to get back to the 'quiet' of Lowestoft, where daily bombing raids would feel easy. Letters to old colleagues held hopes of some surgery there. A reply came back:

---

161. Letter, PWH to parents, c/o GPO, London, 19 August 1942.

My dear Paul,

Thank you for your letter. I see by [sic] the newspapers that the *Nelson* has been in the wars but luckily it appears there were no casualties.

Your successor has not had quite enough experience for this job. Another surgical lieutenant is arriving tomorrow, and he should be all right.[162]

Then in November Paul also got a letter from his vicar of Lowestoft days:

Dear Doctor,

It was very nice to get your charming letter. It must be rather thrilling to be in so great and so mighty a ship. I wonder what opportunities you have for worship.

Did this kindly man conceive how terrifyingly vulnerable even the large ships were? Did he imagine how shattered the young surgeon felt? But he rounds off: 'We have special intercessions on Tuesdays and Thursdays on behalf of the war and all you men at sea.'[163]

Britain plumbed the depths of her fortunes. Alone against the Axis and assailed on every side; her navy stretched beyond all limits of endurance, with terrible and mounting losses from the far Arctic through the Mediterranean to the Far East.

In December came disastrous news from the that quarter, the Far East, of two capital ships, the *Prince of Wales* and the *Repulse*, sunk by torpedo bombers, having been dispatched

---

162. Letter from anon, 6.10.41, *HMS Europa* (Lowestoft naval base).
163. Letter to PWH from R. Whytchead, 3 November 1941, from The Rectory (probably in Lowestoft).

with no aircraft carrier for protection. Paul echoed his crewmates – 'absolute madness'.

But three days earlier the Americans had had a worse wake-up call from the surprise attack by Japanese aircraft on the American fleet at Pearl Harbor in Hawaii. The awful loss of life and ships brought one great dividend for beleaguered Britain – America was now well and truly at war.

At last, the Royal Dockyard at Gibraltar got *Nelson* patched up enough to be watertight and limp home for a full refit to the boundless joy of thousands of crew – and with Paul aboard. They sailed for Scotland, carrying 970 survivors from *Ark Royal*. 'On the way, escorted by my old mess mates in *HMS Zulu* we ran into a terrible Atlantic storm and it seemed touch and go whether we would make it through in our weakened state.'

Having witnessed the horror of the *Ark Royal* sliding helplessly to the bottom, the ship's surgeon was feeling the same about himself and turning in on himself. Such PTSD is better understood now. One can survive conflict but still lose the life you once knew – tormented by flashbacks and nightmares. The depression, anxiety and anger can tear families apart, ruin relationships and devastate lives.

Yet again respite appeared providentially.

Safely back at Rosyth, Scotland, *Nelson*'s scars could be healed while Paul, glad to be on dry land, found an opening at the University Hospital Edinburgh, just across the water. 'The professor there was awfully good to me. I brought him cigarettes which were very bad for him – I knew what he liked and I could buy them in the ship and slip them through the customs with a bottle of gin. Professionally that was a very useful time because I had been feeling that life at sea as a sort of General Practitioner doing little surgery was eating away at my skills.'

In the New Year of 1942 Captain Jacomb noted on Paul's record, that he was 'An able and experienced surgeon, conscientious, keen on his profession. Retiring not easy to know. A little intolerant of weaknesses of others. Irreproachable sense of discipline and loyalty to superior officers'.[164]

Then March brought a hint of brighter days ahead. The ship's purser added £5 for a tropical outfit: several pairs of long white shorts and socks, shoes and shirts and everyone's spirits soared in hopes of a voyage south.

But not quite yet.

---

164. Confidential Naval Service Record on PWH, 3 January 1942.

ABOVE:

HMS *Nelson* fires her main 16-inch guns. Note the fiery flash and the water sucked up by the blast. (PWH collection).

LEFT:

Lt Cmdr Paul Houghton and Commander George Blundell OBE, aboard HMS *Nelson*. (PWH collection).

BELOW:

Surgeon Lt Paul Houghton RNVR, FRCS 1939.

ABOVE:
Edith Houghton (nee King) 1869 to 1943

ABOVE RIGHT:
Paul aged two

RIGHT:
Paul aged ten. Smiling again after being caned the day before.

ABOVE:

Lucy Vine and Paul aged 2.

LEFT:

Paul in London aged 12.

ABOVE: **Edith Houghton**

ABOVE: **Albert Houghton** (1875 to 1961). They married 1905.

BELOW:
New Forest Christian camp for boys run by Paul and friends

LEFT:

Medical student Paul Houghton (top centre) 1936.

Sir Geoffrey Keynes FRCS (lower right), Sister in charge of Bowlby Ward (lower left) – was she the one in love with Sir Geoffrey?

BELOW:

The twins, John and Jean Swift.

BELOW:

House Surgeon Dr P Houghton (extreme right), The Royal Sussex County Hospital Brighton 1936.

ABOVE:
Surgeon Lt Paul Houghton FRCS, RNVR, 1940, in his father's study at Lingfield. Painted by Paul's cousin Gordon Scott.

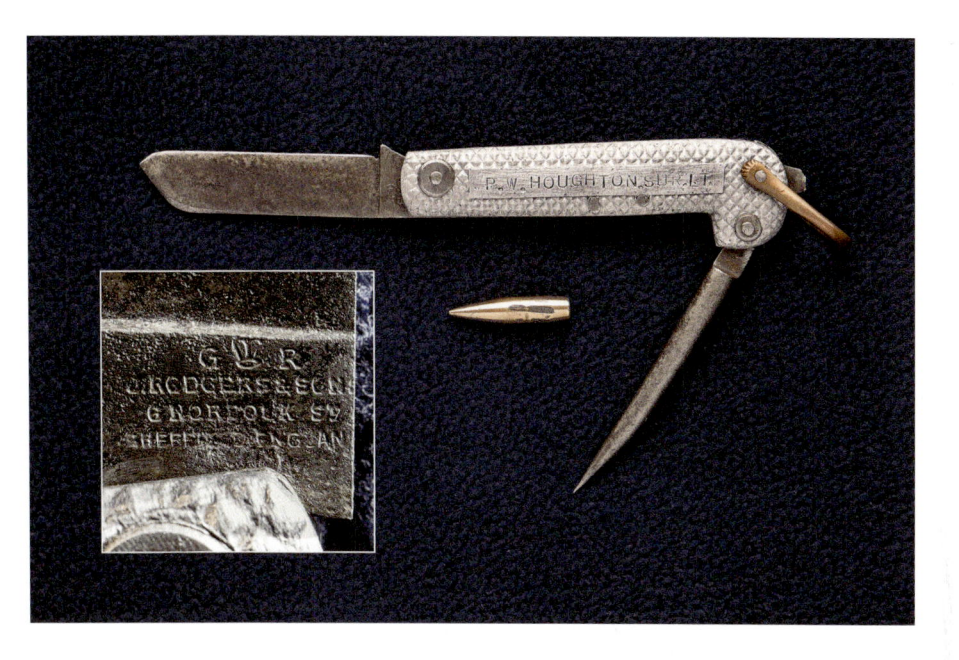

ABOVE: The sailor's knife Paul bought in 1939. The blade is stamped, 'Made in Sheffield 6 Norfolk St.' A German machine gun bullet: one of many that near-missed Paul in Lowestoft, 1940.

BELOW: Paul (centre back) Lowestoft, HMS *Europa* doctors, 1940.

ABOVE:
SS *Tenacious*, crossing the Bay of Biscay 2019. Painted by the author.

ABOVE:
Paul at sea. He labelled this, 'coming up for air, 1941.'

ABOVE:
Dr Richard 'Dick' Prewer, RNVR.

ABOVE: **An aerial view of Gibraltar 2019** (by Adam Cli, https://commons.wikimedia.org/wiki/File:Gibraltar5.jpg#filelinks 25-2-25)

BELOW: **HMS *Nelson*,** (PWH collection).

ABOVE: **Paul, George Blundell and the Salvesen children with their mother Marion. 1941.**

BELOW: **HMS *Ark Royal* about to go down, 14 November 1941.** (PWH collection)

ABOVE: **Pedestal convoy August 1942:** sailors catch sight of the first disaster, HMS *Eagle* rolling over just as Paul saw it. The cargo ship in the foreground is *Dorset*; notice her lifeboats are out ready for a hasty evacuation, as they were on every merchant vessel throughout Pedestal. (©Alamy 2HAR77B).

BELOW: **Operation Pedestal 1942, SS *Brisbane Star* and SS *Rochester Castle* under repeated Luftwaffe attack.** By John Hamilton (IWM). Paul wrote, 'I was there.' on the back.

ABOVE:
Ohio enters Grand Harbour Malta supported by two destroyers.
(© Alamy 2T1MM9G).

BELOW:
Italian torpedo bomber falling at Operation Pedestal. (©Alamy 2HAR76D).

ABOVE:

Operation Pedestal, HMS *Indomitable* under attack. A cruiser is in the foreground.

LEFT:

Admiral Sir Philip Vian, in 1942 (before Paul's surgery.) He joined in the attack on the Bismarck (1941); showed courage and resourcefulness when a Malta convoy engaged the Italian battle fleet (May 1942); took part in the invasion of Sicily (1943); commanded the Eastern Task Force invasion of Normandy (1944); Admiral of the Fleet after the war. (© National Portrait Gallery X76877)

LEFT:

Vice Admiral Sir Neville Syfret, KBE, vice chief of Naval Staff, Admiralty, London, 1944 – two years after Paul's surgery. (© by kind permission of IWM).

ABOVE:
Italian surrender aboard *Nelson* at Malta: General Badoglio (third from left), Eisenhower (fifth) General Alexander (sixth) and Vice Admiral Willis (right). (PWH Collection).

BELOW:
German generals on board HMS *Nelson* as prisoners of war. (PWH Collection).

ABOVE:
Paul in 1945: after 5 years of war.

ABOVE:
First officer Jean Swift, WRNS.

ABOVE:
The wedding of Paul and Jean: 27 September 1947, Leighton parish church, Shropshire.

Left to right, the Bishop of Shrewsbury, best man, groom and bride, Harry Swift, Albert Houghton

LEFT:

Jean and baby Pippa at their first home 1956: the double curved oak trunks supporting the frame for a medieval 'cruck cottage' are visible and the extension Paul built.

RIGHT:

The surgical ward at Ronkswood Hospital, Worcester in the 1960s. Paul Houghton, consultant surgeon, with his wonderful Sister Pullen – she was twice picked out of the sea by Paul's ship in the war.

ABOVE:

Battle of St Vincent; Nelson boarding a Spanish ship.
Painting by John Kenney, in my Ladybird book, The Story of Nelson.
(Penguin Random House.)

ABOVE:

Yardway in 1987, with the lawn, doubling as a tennis court, that Jean made in the 1950s.

RIGHT:

Pippa, Mark and Paul on Gower, South Wales, late 1960s.

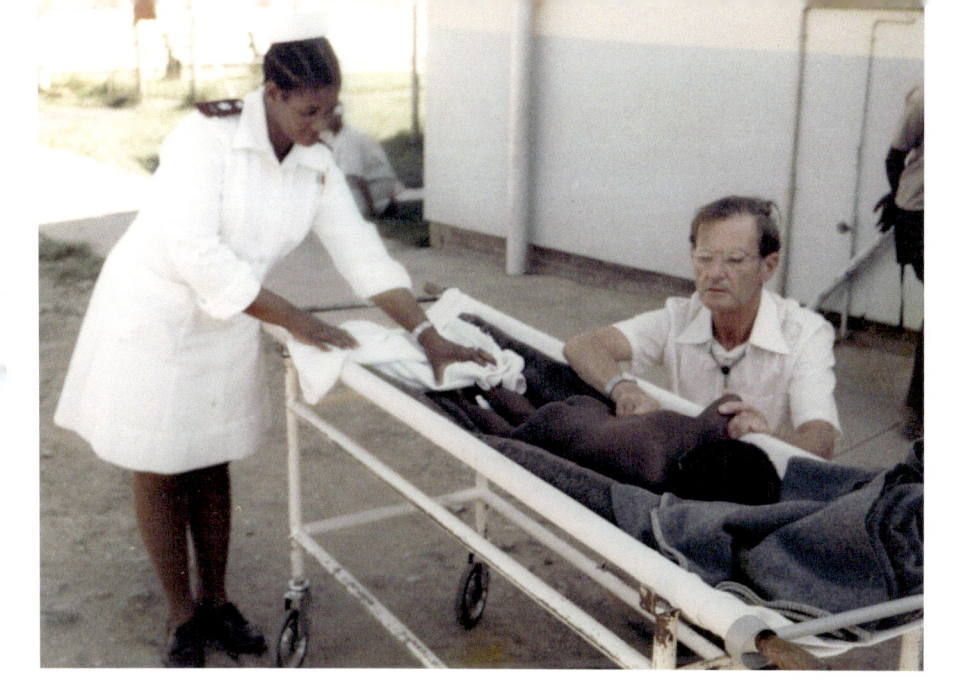

ABOVE:
Paul in Transkei, southern Africa: examining a child with TB.

BELOW:
Paul in retirement at Yardway.

ABOVE: **Paul at 77**

BELOW: **Jean at 68, both in 1987.**

CHAPTER TWENTY-FOUR

Happy Isles
Spring 1942

> There lies the port; the vessel puffs her sail;
> There gloom the dark broad seas. My mariners,
> souls that have toil'd, and wrought,
> and thought with me –
> That ever with a frolic welcome took
> The thunder and the sunshine . . .
>
> *Alfred Lord Tennyson (1809-92), 'Ulysses'*[165]

By April 1942 *Nellie*'s scars were healed and they were ready for sea again. The 'boiler clean' in dry dock had permitted the crew to refill their courage tanks. Paul was boosted by some home leave – but only time would tell whether the pus of post-traumatic stress was lurking deep underneath.

Soon he was on the train from Surrey heading back north; as was George Blundell who spoke for countless sailors: 'Rather sad seeing the little family group waving on the platform: Father always looks at me as if he may never see me again.'

---

165. Alfred, Lord Tennyson (1809-92), 'Ulysses', www.poetryfoundation.org/poems/45392/ulysses (accessed 25.11.24).

That evening as he climbed back aboard, Paul reflected to his parents:

The squalor and heat and dirt of the crowded mess decks are in strong contrast with the spacious cleanliness of home. How quickly the golden hours passed by in the South Country. I should like to bid 'the sun stand still'[166] for a few hours of warm midday, so I could finish the rockery, and explore once more the field ways and valleys we know so well. But the memory of each day can always beautify the picture falling on our mind, and so it becomes a shrine where one may turn aside in all circumstances.

I'm sure that all beauty and goodness is but something of the mind and face of God, revealed to us according to our capacity, the sacrament if you will, of what we shall see face to face sooner or later.

Then he remembers how happy he was that:

Dick and his family should come over. You know they both have you in great regard and I'm sure the feeling returned greatly cheered them up. I will let you hear of his movements in the Service, though I'm sure he will not go to sea. The life puts a constraint on one's endurance, not only because of enemy action, but because of the confinement and disturbances by night, and I do not think he would stand the restless vicissitudes over well.

Well, 'the day is done, it's hours have run'[167] and the daylight is nearly finished. I wonder if you are enjoying the pleasant moist Sou' wester blowing this evening.

---

166. Joshua 10:12.
167. Frederick W. Faber, 1814-63, 'Sweet Savior, Bless Us Ere We Go: Thy Word into our Minds Instill', https://hymnary.org/text/sweet_savior_bless_us_ere_we_go_thy_word (accessed 22 August 2022)

May I hold onto the 10-shilling note [£0.50] until the end of the month when we are paid and then I'll send it back, though I have not used it?

Your loving son,
Paul[168]

He also discovered, 'during refit they had learned some lessons of war and added all number of anti-aircraft guns and their crew on any free surface they could find. I went and examined the sick bay which was almost unchanged except for much better equipment, though still no antibiotics against infection!'

'First, we headed north to Scapa Flow, the huge natural harbour on the Orkney Islands, bristling with defences.'[169] Paul could only reveal by letter:

We are upon our lawful duties, fighting fit and all of us immensely keen. The ship looks superb and we have a grand [new] captain, Humphrey Jacomb. He is the man you would take for the typical British sea captain and to be your ship's commander.

But now Paul felt he had no option but to fight for essentials. Slapping his thighs and rubbing his hands he told the wardroom, 'Look what they've given us – tarred string from the Napoleonic wars. But I can't safely do a simple abdominal operation.'

I got very concerned and spoke to the Principal Medical Officer on board and said, 'This won't do, Sir, really,

---
168. Letter from Paul to parents, HMS *Nelson*, 31 March 1942.
169. Paragraphs above quoting from PWH interview with *Naval History Museum*, November 2000.

because we can't handle anybody who is badly injured or needs an operation.'

He said, 'Well put down what you want, and I will send it away to the captain.'

Regrettably, however, the request went to the Admiralty in Whitehall – not to the offices of the Medical Director General (the MDG) and:

a furious letter came back from the MDG saying I was a troublemaker and all sorts of rude things about me. I didn't care; and almost immediately a huge supply of instruments came out, and we were able to supply an aircraft carrier (before she was sunk) with the surplus of modern equipment.

Meanwhile, I had got one of the engineer officers to make me some simple stainless retractors for operating and a few other things which were very useful.

The next difficulty was how to divide it within the ship. There were three Action Stations and everybody had his own duty post; so we decided to divide them up among the three stations so that if one got blown up the other two would be available.

And seared by his entrapment Paul had learned something else:

We had a very good Chief Petty Officer who I got to know. When the ship was at sea and all the hatches and watertight doors are sealed shut, you want to know how to get from one area to another; it's an absolute rabbit warren below decks. And I used to crawl about the ship with him in dungarees like crawling about in underground catacombs and so you got to know your ship; then you could reach any area that was shut off by damage.

We medics thought we had better pass our time usefully so we tried to take each division of men for a physical examination. Tuberculosis was always about and these had to be got out of the ship as soon as ever they could – they were sleeping at night in hammocks with the ship packed out, never designed to carry the numbers we had – and TB would spread very quickly by droplet. We couldn't X-ray them for TB but we could if we got them to a friendly port.

Young doctors today never see boils, but in those days everybody got them because the staphylococcus skin infections were so rife. Even today the 'staph' can be invincible, but then we had nothing specific to give. They were jolly painful and you just fomented them with a poultice and hoped they would burst; the awful mistake was to cut into them because you would spread the germ round in the bloodstream.

Eye problems were common and, especially after being in port, syphilis and gonorrhoea. There was no treatment for syphilis, except prolonged injections of arsenic – paradoxically – but we had sulphonamides for gonorrhoea although of dubious value. Later on syphilis could be cured with one shot of penicillin, but in those days the late complications of syphilis were dreadful. About one in fifteen got fatal complications.

On one occasion under heavy gunfire we had a man sent below hysterical, who became rapidly unconscious. I found him covered in a rash, so I gave him one of the sulpha drugs we had – I had brought some out with me – and this cured him eventually! But he would have been dead in 12 hours or less without it. I got permission to write up his case in the *British Journal of Surgery*.

The terrible strain of the First World War had produced many cases of what came to be known as shell shock, where men broke down mentally in ways that could leave them affected for life. When I was at school after World War I, some of our masters – many missing an arm or leg – could become explosively bad tempered, and I think these were often victims of the war. But on the *Nelson* we didn't really see it; we did have some men who seem to give way under the strain of these incessant trips in the Mediterranean, but on the whole they bore up very well.

The other dreaded thing was poliomyelitis which was rife in Malta, causing paralysis; and *Ark Royal* had a case – before she sank of course!

We had rats – when you had a bath there were always rats on the pipes overhead looking at you. We had cats on board; I didn't have my own like some surgeons, but we had more than fifty at one time breeding happily. To keep a ship free from rats is very hard indeed, and of course the men fed the cats – so they didn't catch rats. One day the commander said the cats were to be taken ashore through the for'ard gangway and dumped – but while that was happening they were all brought back up the after gangway – so we were back to where we started. We got into difficulty with one admiral, who always came aboard *Nelson* with a canary and a Siamese cat which lived on the Bridge with him; one of his staff being responsible for these creatures. Well the men put his cat ashore on the commander's orders and that put the 'cat among the pigeons' and he was mad! They found it and brought it back and peace was restored. All sorts of silly things went on like that![170]

---

170. Interview with Naval History Museum, November 2000.

When May came along, Paul informed Lingfield:

> We have passed through areas of ocean entirely new to me, but day by day we have seen land and sea of such sublimity that you could not wonder that 'all the sons of God shouted for joy' at the creation.[171]
> Sunset and sunrise over islands and seas of an infinity of colour ranges are pure delight. The weather is glorious and I'm grossly fat, a face sunburned like the rising sun; altogether in rude health.
> This second expedition is a great advance on the last. We are a very keen ships company after a thoroughly good spell at home and ashore and everything is sweet and clean and tight. In fact everybody feels there is no ship in the world quite so sound. Life in these circumstances is quite magnificent.

Finally, Paul's thoughts turned to his little nephew with cerebral palsy who was spending a few weeks with his grandparents. 'I am very glad Timothy is prospering at Lingfield.'

On the Orkney Islands lay the natural harbour of Scapa Flow:

> Today, our company of 'The Three Musketeers,' escaped with bicycles, to an islet and for some hours we explored the rocky boundaries of the land [Blundell's diary reveals it was Hoy].
> Giant cliffs with every sort of bird about them and wide expanses of glory small and great gave us wonderful opportunities to stretch our legs after days at sea in heavy weather and we laughed and sang and rolled on the ground like escaped lunatics.

---

171. Job 38:7.

The happiest event of the glorious day was a minute lamb on the hillside beside a little cottage. He came running up to us, tumbling along, and I picked him up, a heavyweight of not more than six pounds of woolly lamb. He settled very comfortably inside my coat and I felt very tempted to make him a member of the officers' mess as a seagoing lamb, but his small mistress came searching, in great distress for him so, when I had had his photo taken by the torpedo officer [George], we let him go.[172]

George noted too: 'Landed just before lunch with "Doc" Houghton, Peter Douglas and "Dickie" Richards . . . Stroked a newborn lamb.'[173] Paul confessed some tensions with a fellow Christian to his parents:

John T is stationed nearby. The extreme familiarity of his conversation makes any sort of contact most difficult since he allows his theological instincts to override any sense of Service relationships. I feel it is folly in a community where discipline and respect are the governing rules of conduct. I beg of you not to discuss it openly; it would be a thousand pities to unsettle his conviction in divine matters. By night you may hear the swish of the water passing the plating within a few inches of your bunk and by day the light and air are invigorating. And then, if your vessel is lucky enough to make a quiet haven for a few hours. I try to bring a bit of moorland back with me and I have a flowerpot of daffodils and another of sea pinks and bog moss and they relieve the stark steel walls and rivet heads.

---

172. Letter, PWH to parents, HMS *Nelson*, 10 May 1942.
173. Diary of Captain Blundell, Sunday 10 May 1942. Kindly supplied by his son John.

There were rowing races against other ships' boats – all making for 'a happy ship, and we have enjoyed some shore games too'.

Only the new chaplain is a failure. Why is it that the fit, idle, pleasure-loving priests can continue to drag the name of Christ through the dust and crucify Him afresh. I've told him a few home truths lately, until he fairly wriggled! I have a command of my namesake's epistles.
The war pursues its appointed course. There can only be one end, but the way to it seems long and much blood must flow before the sacrifice is sufficient.

Your letters come through regularly. You have but a small idea of the value of 'news from home', and the ship's company wait for it with their tongues hanging out.

Give my love to all the saints and to Lucy.

Your loving son
Paul[174]

Chaplains sailed with *Nelson*, with services in the onboard church of St Peter panelled in light oak.

That May a delightful friendship offered a haven for Paul and his two cycling friends. It came about when the *Nelson* docked on the north bank of the River Clyde next to the famous Forth Railway Bridge.

On a 'Three Musketeers' bike ride they nosed about the castled town of Aberdour and began snowballing the rooks on the church roof. A young mother with children was passing by and they all joined in. The Musketeers, striving to look simultaneously friendly and hungry, got themselves invited

---
174. Letter, PWH to parents, HMS *Nelson*, 19 May 1942 (received 23 May 2023).

in for tea nearby at Aberdour House – spacious amid lovely gardens near to the castle.

The mother, it was discovered, was Mrs Marion Salvesen from the family haulage business, Christian Salvesen which plied goods by road and sea. George told his diary, '"Doc" Houghton, Peter Douglas and I were entertained by Marion Salvesen and her children, John, Robin, Hilary and Alastair. Iver Salvesen, her husband and a member of the Royal Company of Scottish Archers, was away [in Sierra Leone] organizing convoys for the Ministry of Shipping.'

Back at sea Paul told his parents from *Nelson*, 24 May 1942:

> By way of a pleasant Sunday afternoon, we are firing our heavy guns and the occasional irregularity of my ever-irregular script may tell you when a salvo leaves the ship. I should like you to witness the spectacle of our mighty weapons in action. The blast sucks water out of the sea and the fireball requires everyone in anti-flash clothing. My action station is far down in the steel bowels of the ship, clamped under armoured hatches.

While that may have reassured his parents, anyone who has visited HMS *Belfast* moored in London on the River Thames will see these hatches and understand how blast could jam them into deathtraps.

> I escape to the Bridge sometimes to enjoy the sights, and today when our activities are only for practice. But remember to write from your end, giving all the bits of news and pictures of the countryside and so forth. How vividly I remember the old garden paths back at Fulham and the fun we two brothers had there in the succession of vehicles you made us, Dad. The spacious days of

childhood pass so quickly and none of the latter years can alter the feeling of permanence and stability which early recollections retain. It seems, today, that our hopes and expectations must seek an anchorage beyond the mists that blind us here; we must see into that realm of righteousness where the eternal values have their abode. I had a letter from Dick. He has been posted to the Royal Naval penitentiary at Canterbury. I am satisfied that they kept him off the sea. The sea life of today is very often a tragic experience, especially in the smaller craft. And he is happy in the old city [of Canterbury] which has always appealed to him. How it does to me! I depend on books for such satisfaction now.

Paul closed with pinpoint prescience: 'And so, I think we shall have a famous victory soon and the sweat and toil will be justified.'

CHAPTER TWENTY-FIVE

South to the Heat

June 1942

> I must go down to the sea again,
> to the vagrant gypsy life,
> To the gull's way and the whale's way
> where the wind's like a whetted knife;
> And all I ask is a merry yarn from a
> laughing fellow-rover,
> And quiet sleep and a sweet dream
> when the long trick's over.
>
> John Masefield (1878-1967), 'Sea Fever'[175]

By first of June, they set sail south at the centre of convoy WS 19P, a huge and fast stream of great liners and merchant ships. The destination was Suez on the Red Sea to supply the army in North Africa – which meant going down to the Cape of Good Hope and right up the other side of Africa through the Indian Ocean.

---

[175]. John Masefield, *Sea Fever*, www.poetryfoundation.org/poems/54932/sea-fever-56d235e0d871e (accessed 20.8.21).

Stopping in at Freetown, Sierra Leone, they took on freshwater – and some malaria as well, flown in by mosquito, but the only case didn't surface until long afterwards.

George went off to call on Iver Salvesen, husband of Marion. Salvesen's logistical gifts were serving the country in Freetown. 'We asked him to supper [on *Nelson*] for Sunday', recorded Blundell in his diary.[176]

Paul got a letter off homewards on 11 June with a hint on their latitudes: 'I wish I could put myself inside the envelope and come home to the cool ways of the village. For this is a new heaven and a new earth and not a very comfortable one. I am very fit, sweating like a bull, and wondering if we shall ever see the white cliffs of Dover again.'

Nearing the equator Paul was 'captured' by rowdy sailors for a Crossing the Line initiation. King Neptune and his court assembled on the main deck beside a large bath of brine. Commander Hill, standing 6ft2in, was the obvious choice for playing the king, accompanied by the diminutive Amphitrite played by Chief Petty Officer Sadler. The Chief of Police had 'Gestapo' written on his top hat.[177] Paul and other initiates were duly plastered with shaving foam, 'shaved' and 'bathed' in the seawater, whether they wanted it or not.

Paul retired to a quiet corner and told his father:

Books are a great comfort at sea and we interchange all we have. Then, in the cool of the day, usually in the last Dog Watch deck hockey will lose excessive energy and this most violent game is very good fun. But I think the best time is dawn for we are roused to man action stations, and the cool morning breeze and the quietude of the ship are very pleasant.

---

176. Diary of Captain George Blundell. IWM.
177. Careless, *Battleship Nelson*, p. 70.

The postcards of Worth churchyard and Ashdown Forest and the garden are in my cabin and they often make my thoughts truants, wishing for the old ways and the ceasing of this roving life. The lilac must be over by now and I think the chestnut flower must be littering the lawn, but I can imagine the peace of the night-scented air these late June evenings.

Dawn action stations on 13 June, brought tragedy. Stoker Blades had found a comfortable, cool place to sleep on deck beside a gun turret. In the middle of the night the turret swung round to aim at a suspected enemy – and the rear of the turret silently crushed Blades' chest. Paul certified him deceased and at 9 a.m. a sad procession carried the body aft to the quarterdeck. There the chaplain read a short funeral service, rifles fired a salute, the haunting notes of the 'Last Post' rang out by bugle and the body was committed to the sea, sewn up in his hammock. A signalman forgot to hold onto the Union Jack flag and it went too.

Hardly had they got in sight of Cape Town when *Nelson* and *Rodney* and three destroyers, being recalled by London, did an about-turn and headed north through the double lines of the convoy going on – men cheering from each ship. The convoy's commodore signalled, 'We thank you for your protection and our safety . . . Goodbye. Good luck. God speed.'

Stopping in at Freetown once again they picked up Admiral Syfret. Only Syfret and the very senior officers knew the ship was being urgently recalled to literally save Malta. Churchill had asked the Navy for one almighty effort with the biggest convoy ever assembled.

Malta had signalled in June 1942, that she could only survive another fortnight and then would have to surrender – she was running short of fuel, medical supplies and food.

Meanwhile a tale of terror, caught up with Paul at Freetown from Dick in Canterbury:

My dear Paul,

Since my last letter we have had our own 'Blitz'. it was on the Sunday night of 31 May/1 June. For 70 minutes we were perpetually divebombed.

It was the worst hour of my life – except for when 'the black fit was on me,' quoting Dean Inge. There was no time to leave the hotel, and it was as light as day with the flames, fires and full moon. The hotel has no shelter. I stood in the kitchen passage attempting to put a brave face on it (inside, I shook like a jelly) as representing the Royal Navy and encouraging, to some degree, the domestics.

What with breaking glass, dust, and smoke and the terrific impacts which followed each whining dive, it was appalling. When one is used to the disciplined surroundings of the Service to uphold one at critical times; to be among hysterical women and doddering old men is, to say the least, unnerving.

One big bomb fell at the back, smashing the garage in which my car was asleep, and blew a great crater 30 feet across. The car was badly crushed . . . A new bicycle was also crushed. There were only three minor casualties, but we lost a lot of windows and some of the roof.

In the town itself, immense damage was done. But by a very strange Providence, the cathedral was not hit – though bombs fell all round it and all the glass blew in. St Augustine's College was badly knocked about: it's a pity the old Benedictines were not there to solemnly curse the enemy with bell, book and candle; and a good monkish curse is a lot better than barrage balloons to fell the enemy!

Enough of these horrors: it is a depressing town now ... I frequently go and sit in the cloisters of the cathedral to meditate ... I let the Peace of the Church sink into my bones with the jackdaws cawing in the Bell Harry Tower ... A few feet behind where I sat the saintly St Thomas passed to martyrdom. Before me, beneath the grass, lie two archbishops, mingling their dust with generations of humble figures. It has been a great antidote to the nocturnal horrors.

The Old Brodie paid me an unexpected visit two days ago: he had just got his call-up papers and was due at Portsmouth tomorrow. So three of the Brethren have had their names inscribed on the books of Lord Nelson's flagship. [HMS *Victory* in dry dock].

I have to turn my hand to anything – Two men swallowed needles – one was 4 inches long, but both were passed without difficulty.

Ever yours
Dick[178]

Far away in the South Atlantic, in the Nelson's oak-panelled chapel, Paul and some shipmates sang the hymns that had served the nation in war for 200 years.

> When through the deep waters I call thee to go,
> the rivers of sorrow shall not overflow;
> for I will be near thee, thy troubles to bless,
> and sanctify to thee thy deepest distress.
>
> When through fiery trials thy pathway shall lie,
> my grace, all sufficient, shall be thy supply;

---

178. Letter from Dr Dick Prewer 18 June 1942, to PWH, HMS *Nelson*.

the flame shall not hurt thee; I only design
thy dross to consume and thy gold to refine.[179]

Few guessed the fiery trial ahead as they steamed north. And ominously Blundell was summoned to a meeting with the captain. He racked his memory to think what he had done wrong. Captain Jacomb pacing his cabin, smiled broadly and handed over a yellow cipher message, 'Blundell to relieve Hill as Commander of *Nelson*.' Blundell was dumbfounded at this news. From now on he would command the ship's day-to-day running, answerable to the captain. Another excitement was the reappointment of *Nelson* to be the flagship of the legendary 'Force H' again, in the Mediterranean. Admiral Syfret, a South African, would be in command and his staff came aboard in Freetown; allowing Paul and George to covertly size up their new commander-in-chief.

Harmony was not helped when George gave his cabin cacti a bit of fresh air on the bridge. Syfret sat down to enjoy the sunshine and leapt to his feet clutching his backside and roaring, 'Throw them overboard.'

Sunday, 19 July, as they steamed north, was a National Day of Prayer for the Royal Navy and the Merchant Navy, so Paul and everyone who could paraded on the upper deck.

Amazingly, a couple of days later, they came upon twenty-three survivors of the SS *Cortona* drifting in an open boat for the past nine days. The Master was among them, 'all brave, haggard looking fellows after their ordeal in the Atlantic'. Paul and the medics checked them over and fed them well.[180]

Meanwhile, away to their right, as they travelled north, the 'Desert Fox', Erwin Rommel, was pushing the British Eighth

---

179. 'How Firm a Foundation, Ye Saints of the Lord . . .' https://hymnary.org/text/how_firm_a_foundation_ye_saints_of (accessed 21.11.24). Author unknown.
180. Careless, *Battleship Nelson*, p. 75.

Army backwards along the North African coast – threatening to overwhelm British army HQ at Alexandria in Egypt. Things were going badly for the British everywhere.

At this time the legendary SAS – Special Air Service regiment – was born, as the brainchild of David Stirling, a junior infantry officer. This handful caught Churchill's eye by pushing far behind enemy lines and destroying more than 100 enemy aircraft on the ground in one week – an unheard-of success.

But in midsummer 1942 something far greater than the SAS was needed – and Churchill decided to gamble all. Sir Max Hastings sets the scene:

> Malta, the Allies' only surviving bastion in the central Mediterranean, is starving. Repeated efforts to succour the island have failed.
> 'We must have a victory!' Labour giant Ernest Bevin passionately urges on the War Cabinet. 'What the British public wants is a victory!'
> Thus Churchill ordered the Royal Navy to launch *Operation Pedestal*, which became one of the bloodiest sea battles of Britain's war, to save Malta. At any cost.[181]

As *Nelson* and the new armada gathered around the north of Scotland, Paul gazed from the rail at an aircraft carrier called HMS *Indomitable*, herald of an event that would affect him more than any other in the war.

---

181. Reprinted by permission of HarperCollins Publishers Ltd © Max Hastings 2021.

CHAPTER TWENTY-SIX

Into the Fire – Operation Pedestal

August 1942

> When you pass through the waters,
> I will be with you;
> ... When you walk through the fire,
> you will not be burned ...
>
> *Isaiah 43:2*

Half a century after the event, Paul recalled *Operation Pedestal* as if it was yesterday – 'Pedestal' being the codename for the super-large convoy that battled to save Malta in 1942.

'The Admiralty,' Paul recalled, 'scraped together fourteen fast merchantmen. And they got hold of an American tanker called the *Ohio* and filled her up with everything they could find – fuel oil for the submarines, petrol for the planes, and fuel oil on deck – we all carried that in drums and so the fires were terrible.'[182]

---

182. PWH, interview with Naval History Museum, 2000.

The convoy began on the quiet waters of the Clyde estuary in Scotland, with a gathering of the merchant ships' Masters aboard HMS *Nigeria*. It was Sunday 2 August and all dressed in their best. Bluff burly Rear-Admiral Burroughs – tasked with commanding and protecting the merchant ship fleet – began his briefing with, 'Gentlemen, it is our privilege to be chosen to go to Malta.' Tommy Thompson of merchant ship *Santa Elisa* said later: 'The Admiral might have said it was great privilege to commit suicide. But we all nodded our heads . . . and said, "Thank you, sir!"'[183]

Aboard *Nelson*, Paul watched the Orkneys receding as the convoy formed up at sea including two merchant ships with American crews, the *Santa Elisa* and *Almeria Lykes*. Everyone was astonished to see no fewer than five aircraft carriers to provide vital air cover. *Nelson* and *Rodney* were the two battleships along with three cruisers and twelve destroyers, with eight more destroyers and four more cruisers meant to go all the way to Malta with the merchant ships.

Travelling south the medical officers lectured on first aid. Food depots were spread around the ship for use at action stations. Never had *Nelson* been so prepared for battle. Admiral Burroughs commanding the merchant ships had his personal prayer pinned up prominently. 'Once we were into the Mediterranean,' recalled Paul, 'we realised that the Germans and the Italians knew exactly what we were doing. Before he died in 1999 I met Admiral of the Fleet Lord Lewin (a wonderful man who was on Pedestal as gunnery officer of *Ashanti*). He told me, "We now know there were three wolf packs waiting for us beneath the waves."

'And there was the aviation spirit in cans on deck. One of the merchant seamen told me afterwards, "When an officer

---

183. Hastings, *Operation Pedestal*, p. 66.

shook hands as I joined the ship – never had an officer shaken hands with me before – we knew what was coming all right." So we did what we could to prepare for casualties, rigging hoses for putting out flames and preparing anti-flash gear.'[184]

Thus the convoy formed up in the Western Mediterranean. 'We set off,' Paul wrote,[185] 'and sailed through lovely summer seas; all was beautiful like package holiday photos; you just couldn't believe a titanic struggle was going on!

August 9 and 10 passed by quietly with an occasional call to "action stations", but soon after an enemy plane spotted us, and we became very conscious of impending danger.

A call-to-action stations sounded at 11 o'clock on the 11th but by lunchtime we were out on deck again and no attack had been made. At 1.30 p.m., I was on the Quarterdeck and talking to a friend about the walks between Lewes and Alfriston in Sussex, when the aircraft carrier *Eagle*, lying about half a mile from us, lurched as a succession of three gigantic fingers of steam and water spouted up from her.

The wolfpack had found them.

The noise of the explosions was alarming and then followed the shocking spectacle of a sinking warship. She lurched over on her beam-ends', aircraft tumbling like small toys into the sea from her flight deck.[186]

Paul watched 'the fo'c'sl disappear, and she slid under the water. The stern remained above the surface for a minute or

---
184. PWH, interview with Royal Naval Museum, 2000.
185. PWH to his parents, 23 August 1942.
186. Careless, *Battleship Nelson*, p. 81.

so and quickly vanished. 'She was out of sight in six minutes – I timed it.' It was the second aircraft carrier Paul watched sinking – and his heart sank also.

From that time on, for the next 60 hours, we had little respite. The succeeding days may only be described as a flaming hell as we entered a barricade of submarines, mines, bombs and German E boats racing in at terrific speed, raked by close-quarters gunfire with seamen desperately swiveling their weapons from the open decks.

We were sailing through a sea that was literally boiling as shell fragments, planes and bombs fell everywhere, wide patches of oil spread from stricken ships with survivors trying to swim, plastered with black shining liquid over their heads – just the eyes and teeth white. Then, added to it all was the terrible necessity to explode our depth charges on suspected submarines – explosions which heaved skywards thousands of tons of water – in the certain knowledge that the swimmers would die of 'shock lung'. We didn't pick up casualties aboard *Nelson* – you just can't stop [in a capital ship].

But somehow destroyers picked up 929 of *Eagle's* crew out of a complement of 1,160.

The alarm rattlers sounded as thirty Junkers 88s attacked on the port side, and then came the Heinkel torpedo bombers roaring in at mast height. The approaching aircraft were met by a barrage of gunfire unparalleled in the experience of anyone there. Some German pilots veered aside. Torpedoes near-missed the ship and bombs fell all around with a large one exactly between *Nelson* and *Rodney*.[187]

---

187. Ibid.

Commander Blundell recorded:

When it got darkish about 2115 the barrage put up by the fleet . . . was aesthetically one of the weirdest and most wonderful and beautiful sites I have ever seen. People . . . had a look on their faces as if they'd seen a vision – the sort of look a man would have on his face just after he'd looked on the Almighty.

People in other ships close by were equally affected as they watched *Nelson*. She seemed one mass of stabbing flashes from end to end with streams of sparks racing into the sky, and even the 16-inch main guns adding to the barrage.

Paul's 'chief recollection was the noise as our guns opened up and remained firing for so long that I used to wonder how any ship could carry enough ammunition. The scene from the Bridge was tremendous – like the best view from the best box in the theatre. Admiral Syfret was there smoking his pipe.'

Wednesday 12 August, Day Three, the gunners ate at their guns during lulls in action. *Nelson* shot down three torpedo planes that got among the convoy past the British Hurricanes from the carriers. But the aircraft carrier *Indomitable* was caught by twelve dive bombers, hurtling down from the sun and – once the spouts of seawater and steam had dispersed – she emerged blazing from end to end.

Paul discovered, 'we were very close to her. The flight deck blew up and folded back. The pilots on deck and the crew below suffered terrible loss of life; she was absolutely in flames with the Bridge island sticking up in the middle of it.'

Incredibly, by Herculean efforts, 'within half an hour they had the flames out, and she could steer, and she could move

– that's about all she could do.'[188] *Nelson* and *Rodney* closed in to protect her.[189]

Next came hits on the warships *Cairo*, *Nigeria* and the tanker *Ohio*. Then the *Brisbane Star* was hit, and the ammunition ship *Clan Ferguson* exploded with a roar while near misses damaged the *Rochester Castle*.

Surprisingly, Paul felt, 'some of the other convoys were more violent. We had nobody to treat and in that respect, we had a very easy time surgically – most [ships] went down and were lost. At the end of Day Three, we spent the night off Africa, but the cruiser HMS *Manchester* suffered mortal damage with frightful slow deaths in the steam filled boiler room. The destroyers went in to pick up survivors, some of whom were transferred to *Nelson* along with their pet spaniel.' Paul later rejoiced to his parents:

> We now have 'Philly'. She was the first living creature to be loaded onto the rescuing destroyer as it closed with the maimed vessel, and, despite the horror of a night action, and the crash of gunfire she was not in the least alarmed, but only concerned for her mess mates. She is becoming hopelessly spoiled. The cats of course are completely indifferent to her and keep to the 'starboard side' [reserved for the captain].[190]

Increasingly by now, huge areas of sea were on fire from spilt fuel. Paul admired in particular the marvellous captain of *Brisbane Star* who disobeyed orders by creeping along the African coast, then turned north and got into Malta with a full cargo.

---

188. PWH, Royal Naval interview, 2000.
189. Ibid.
190. Letter from PWH to his parents, 'HMS – –, c/o GPO, London', 19 August 1942.

Decades later, my father and I watched the Pedestal documentary on Channel 4. He listened in grim admiration to Captain Hill telling how he took HMS *Ledbury* into the flames rescuing whoever he could. Hill admitted he was mentally unhinged later.[191]

As Paul recalled, '*Indomitable* turned west towards the Atlantic with an escort of three destroyers, while we went on East. Eventually we also turned back,' to Blundell's disgust, 'heading towards Gibraltar with Syfret, we overhauled the roasted ruin of the aircraft carrier *HMS Indomitable*.' Truly she had lived up to her name: 'impossible to defeat'.

That evening, I overheard the admiral mutter on the bridge, 'D—n the Germans and their U-boats, we will do these burials properly.' He posted a screen of circling destroyers with *Indomitable* and *Nelson* in the middle. The *Indom* was charred and blackened from end-to-end, and we were very close as they carried the dead across to us, preceded by the smell of roasted flesh.

Sixty years later my father gripped my arm:

Oh Mark! You never saw anything like it. I . . . I can't bear to think now of that flaming sunset behind *Indomitable*, a blackened hulk on the water. There weren't many survivors of their injuries – those needing treatment – they were either unharmed or dead.[192]

Against that crimson backdrop, seamen sowed forty-six bodies into their hammocks with the last stitch put through

---
191. Hastings, *Operation Pedestal*, p. 359.
192. PWH, personal to the author, 1990.

the nose, 'to make sure they were dead'.[193] The guard of honour assembled with each body draped in the white ensign – prompting one sailor's surprise that someone had thought to stock so many flags. Standing there was Captain Tom Troubridge, of *Indomitable*, whose jovial leadership seemed to sum up the dauntless spirit of the convoy men. George and Paul remembered him for his miniature field glasses resting on an ample stomach.

Silence fell, followed by the haunting notes of the Last Post on the bugle. The band played the Evening Hymn:

The day thou gave us, Lord, is ended,
the darkness falls at your request;
to you our morning hymns ascended,
your praise shall sanctify our rest.[194]

The Chaplain prayed, and one after the other slid over the side, weighted at the feet.

Pregnant with longing, Paul's first letter home, on 19 August ran:

My dear Mum and Dad,

We have been fulfilling our duties in a particularly active way.

It is five months since I was home at Lingfield and . . . it seems a long time since the quiet and peace of the Surrey countryside lay outside my door.

We have been preserved from so many great disasters that one can feel only gratitude to God, and an obligation to the brilliant organisation of the sea services.

---

193. Peter Hore to the author, 2023.
194. John Ellerton (1826-1983), 'The Day Thou Gavest, Lord, is Ended', https://hymnary.org/text/the_day_thou_gavest_lord_is_ended (accessed 21.11.24). Modernised version.

Well, it was worthwhile. The tanker [*Ohio*] with its nightmare cargo was hit twice, burst into flames leaving her out of control and sinking. But her crew got her going again and made the harbour.

Your loving son
Paul

Only five of the fourteen merchantmen reached Malta. *Ohio* was torpedoed, hit by a bomb, set on fire, abandoned, re-boarded, had an enemy plane crash on her decks, and got struck by another. But she lived, and with 'Chattanooga Choo Choo'[195] blasting from loud speakers, she crawled into Malta's Grand Harbour, just afloat, supported by destroyers *Ledbury* on one side and *Penn* on the other – her precious fuel oil intact.

Her master, Captain Mason, richly merited the George Cross for courage. Captain Hill wrote: 'It was the most wonderful moment of my life . . . To see all these people who had suffered so much'.[196] Bands were playing and thousands of cheering waving people welcomed them.

Then they faded into silence, as the people noticed the twisted steel and scarred decks of the surviving ships. Out of the depths of their own suffering from countless air raids, they realised what a terrible gauntlet the convoys had run. More sailors had died than all the casualties on Malta.

To the Maltese it would always be the Santa Mirija Convoy, coinciding with nine days of prayer up to the Feast of the Assumption of the Virgin Mary. Willing hands wrestled the stores ashore before bombers could destroy them. And the daily floor ration went up a fraction.[197] Malta lived.

---

195. Mack Gordon (1904-59); performed by the Glenn Miller Orchestra.
196. Hastings, *Operation Pedestal*.
197. Ibid.

Captain Jacomb glided the Nelson into her birth at Gibraltar to the admiration of a sailor who exclaimed, 'E's a boy that Captain, 'e is.'[198]

Then the postmortems began. Blundell and his colleagues called it *Operation 'M' for Murder* – disgusted by the way they, in the great ships, had been ordered back to Gibraltar while the merchant fleet went up in flames.

Yet Rommel's Afrika Corps, charging down the North African coast at the Eighth Army, was now more vulnerable than ever to attack from Maltese airfields. The hinge of victory, and hope, had turned a fraction and opened a crack.

Admiral Syfret was knighted, but only two American sailors, Fred Larson and Lonnie Dales, received Distinguished Service Medals having survived the sinking of *Santa Elisa* and afterwards boarding and manning guns on *Ohio*.[199]

Paul wrote home:

> Someday, I'll tell you the details, although many are better forgotten. I don't think any of the company wish to go those waters again! One day I suppose it will be all over and I shall be home again.
>
> Your loving son, Paul.[200]

Postscript: In 2019, while I was crewing on the square-rigged sailing ship *Tenacious*, off Cape Trafalgar, two Royal Marine veterans sidled up to me saying, 'Doc, it's Remembrance Sunday tomorrow – could you lead a service?' So I got permission from the captain.

The next day we nine of the starboard watch clapped onto the sheet (a rope as thick as your wrist) and yelling, 'Two –six

---

198. Careless, *Battleship Nelson*.
199. Ibid.
200. Letter from PWH to his parents, on HMS *Nelson* headed paper, 23 August 1942.

heave, two – six *heave,*' because in the vernacular of Nelson's navy (for it was sailors number two and six in a gun crew who hauled the gun's ropes after firing) we set *Tenacious* sailing sweetly on the breeze.

Then everyone gathered in the waist round the mainmast with the captain and officers looking down from the quarterdeck in uniform. I crooked an arm round the pin-rail for steadiness and prayed aloud, prayed for all in trouble on the sea. Then I told the story of the funeral service for the fallen of HMS *Indomitable*.

Six bells tolled for the eleventh hour of the eleventh month – the hour the guns of the First World War fell silent, and the two minutes silence began; a silence broken only by the sloshing of water past her hull, the creak of her timbers on the roll, and the sigh of the wind in the rigging. My thoughts turned to the waste of war, amid the sights and sounds my father and great-grandfather knew, and Lord Nelson, and Sir Francis Drake, and back for more than a thousand years to King Alfred the Great's little navy. I wish now I had known about the Naval Prayer:

> O Eternal Lord God, who alone spreadest out the heavens and rulest the raging of the sea; who hast compassed the waters with bounds until day and night come to an end; Be pleased to receive into thy almighty and most gracious protection the persons of us thy servants and the Fleet in which we serve.[201]

---

201. Forms of Prayer to be used at sea – the Church of England, www.churchofengland. org/node/364/printable/print#:~:text=O%20Eternal%20Lord%20God%2C%20who, Fleet%20in%20which%20we%20serve (accessed 16.10.24).

CHAPTER TWENTY-SEVEN

Saving Admiral Vian

Autumn 1942 to Spring 1943

Rear-Admiral Philip Vian was a commanding presence with eyebrows bristling like gorse bushes. And Paul was writing home in private how: 'The very senior officers approach me for medical treatment behind the senior [doctor's] back.' But Vian was different.

His reputation was fearsome after his daring raid and release of more than 300 captured sailors aboard the German ship *Altmark* deep up a Norwegian fjord. Anyone picking a fight with Vian chose a fight to the death. So, he required a lure, as an innocent fly wins a great salmon.

One day the surgeon was leaning over the rail near Vian who was travelling as a passenger to Gibraltar aboard *Nelson* from the Eastern Mediterranean. 'He seemed to be keeping to himself and always wore his naval jacket buttoned tight with the collar up and his cap pulled low – in the "flat aback" style.'

Vian's name was everywhere. In May 1941 he led five small destroyers to encircle by night and help sink the feared German battleship *Bismarck*. He had also fought a 'fantastic battle, in a heavy sea' using little ships (including *Zulu*) against an Italian battleship, the *Littorio*. This ended in complete victory due to the 'tactical brilliance of Admiral Vian's brain . . . and brilliant handling of their ships', which saved the convoy.[202]

At the rail Paul 'saw, out of the corner of my eye, that he looked pinched and morose. I said, "Hello", and for a few days we engaged in casual conversation like this until he revealed he was coming home on sick leave from Port Said where he had been relieved of command of Force A,' the brilliance having inexplicably vanished. 'And he wouldn't say what the illness was. Getting closer I could see that there was a large swelling on the back of his neck; and gradually winning his confidence I persuaded him to let me examine him in the sick bay.

'I found a man who was desperately thin as if he had not long to go. The swelling on his neck was a large and infected cyst, tangled in hair, oozing unpleasant tissue and slowly killing him.

'He let me clean it up and do some surgery to remove the cyst. At the same time I fed him tinned milk and all the goodies we could find on the ship.

'Well – he began to improve straightaway, put on weight and took an interest in all that was going on. I put together a parcel for the admiral with three things in it: a Gideon New Testament, a poem and an oil painting of the crucifixion. I asked the carpenter, the chippy, to make a wooden case. The chippy said, "Did it really happen – this crucifixion?"

'"Oh yes it did," I said.

'To the admiral I said, "Don't open it till you have an hour to think it over." The PMO was Vian's friend, and I heard from him how the admiral later opened the Bible and the poem I had written out:

---

202. Lieut. Cmdr. P.K. Kemp, HM *Destroyers* (London: Herbert Jenkins Ltd., 1956).

> This day and that which hovers oer' my end,
> Into thy heart and hand Lord I commend.
> Take both to thine account that I, and mine
> On that day and on this may be all thine.
> Oh my dear Saviour make me see
> How dearly thou has paid for me.[203]

Vian read the letter twice and said to the PMO, 'That's the first step towards the cross for the admiral.' And eventually he made a complete recovery. Vian went on to command part of the invasion fleet on D-Day, and promotion with a knighthood to be Admiral of the Fleet.[204]

In the navy, a 'fighting admiral' is a leader with exceptional successes and Paul found himself up against not one but two of these at sea and a third behind a desk in London with tentacles reaching far across the waves.

Affable older brother Jack observed risks in his brother's sandpaper abrasiveness and wrote to their parents (while Paul observed that 'John's nerves rested in comfort, with no daily risk of being blown out of the water'.)

> This morning I had an epistle from Master Paul . . . I think his ship was in that Malta convoy [Pedestal]. It appears that he is at loggerheads with a Senior Medical Officer; trust Paul to smell out trouble. His sea friend said to me, 'Just give Paul my love when you write, and tell him to keep a civil tongue in his head!'

The 'trouble' confronting Paul:

---

203. Author unknown.
204. PWH to the author 1990. Vian's treatment was in the *Daily Telegraph* obituary of PWH by Captain Peter Hore. Vian's daughter spotted it and contacted us saying it had explained the mystery illness that brought their famous father home.

. . . is this shocking 'Superior' I am blessed with. In his ignorance and apathy nothing is done, no conferences are held to improve care in the light of experience and his chief concern is to get back to his family of five children. The other day he told me he 'would do his damnedest to get himself out of the vessel, but, if he failed, I must go'.

I agreed with him heartily and convicted him for his errors and omissions. It is my early Lowestoft experience all over again. And it is a general state of affairs. I met Maurice [Carpenter] and he is just mad about the whole organisation.

Thus Paul plunged in with a letter, 17 September 1942, from HMS *Nelson* to their lordships of the Admiralty, with *Nelson's* Principal Medical Officer adding a letter of support also. He begins with polite irony, which is almost unbelievable to be necessary after three years of terrible sea warfare and Pedestal:

Many surgeons are acutely conscious of the inadequacy of the surgical apparatus applied to capital ships . . . The likelihood of major surgical casualties is greatly increased in wartime . . .

Five sheets follow, listing bombshells like, '1) A review of the surgical gear supplied afloat has made it apparent that a number of instruments are obsolete, somewhat dangerous . . .' And so it goes on, even pleading for basics like, 'surgical scissors, needles, small artery forceps . . .'

With the missile launched, he sat back and took stock to his family:

We are enjoying a fairly busy time but in less exciting conditions than the Mediterranean narrows [between

Malta and Africa]. I believe there is nothing to raise enthusiasm [among the sailors] like violent action and it is very necessary.

How the war drags on through the year! 'The autumn sheaves stand dewless dry'[205] in the fields today I suppose.

Paul's heart was far too tender to take up weapons against another human being, yet he would not think it wrong to do all he could to support the final destruction of an evil empire while nursing longings, '. . . and the summer is nearly finished. What a pleasure it would be to come home for a day or two after the desperate voyaging across the seas, but I do not know if this is likely, though the Admiralty makes it their policy to release crews when it is wise.'

The needle on the tank of courage was nearing Empty again. 'I was so tired . . .' And there was the daily anxiety to fight for the highest professional standards for his patients.

He watched gifted men going to the bottom time and again. The Cruiser class of warships seem substantial now when one visits *HMS Belfast* moored up in London – but Paul saw them sinking one after the other and their men struggling amidst the debris and oil and fire. 'Maurice [Carpenter] is very fit and we have had two days in company . . . he is clever and should not be in a very small Cruiser, and how I wish we were together.'

Spiritually, he got a lift on Gibraltar because 'the Archbishop of Canterbury [William Temple] paid the squadron a visit and preached on Galatians 5 . . . "the unlimited resources of the Spirit compared with the restricted quantities of temporal goods."'

---

205. Vesperal, 1899, from *Complete Poems of S. Weir Mitchell*, American Verse Project, https://quod.lib.umich.edu/a/amverse/BAP5347.0001.001/1:8?rgn=div1;view=fulltext (accessed 15.6.23).

For five minutes, in a torrent of eloquence, he guided our thoughts to access God [through the cross of Christ], the need for redemption [from our faults] and the use of grace [the free gift of God's mercy to rescue us from sin, Satan and sickness]. He spent the day in the flagship and created a strong impression.

There is a strong consciousness of the need for military action in Europe amongst the men here. The sooner the Hun is hammered to annihilation the better, but I should like to include a few of our wasters, too.

I have enclosed a photo of our prisoners of war coming to England. Try to get a paper showing the Malta convoy.

Your loving son
Paul[206]

By now the missile had arrived on the Surgeon Rear-Admiral's desk at the Admiralty and he took umbrage, hauling Paul back for a roasting in London from which he emerged wounded. Dick heard the news and counselled afterwards:

It was interesting to hear of your adventures at Queen's House. You have three big advantages over them, viz. – a higher qualification FRCS, force of character, and the fact that they cannot send you to sea, you are there already! I'm glad that you have taken to rendering reports to the medical 'high-ups'.

As I read Dick's letter back in 2022, I am astonished at a lieutenant taking on the 'high-ups' – whistleblowers are vulnerable to invading doubts and terrors about dire consequences; and all so soon after the shell shock of Pedestal and its 'nightmare cargo'.

---

206. Letter PWH to parents, HMS *Nelson*, 13 September 1942.

Dick was enduring similar in the naval gaol: 'You see, we too are in the aftermath of the Trafalgar era – our regulations were drawn up in 1912 and have hardly altered since. We too have to battle for equipment – on a smaller scale: here a microscope, there a mercury sphygmomanometer.'

The great invasion of western North Africa was brewing and on 29 October 1942, *Nelson* departed Scapa Flow having embarked 407 commandos. The aircraft carriers *Victorious* and *Formidable* combined with destroyers formed Force H, sailing for Gibraltar.

One evening, far out in the Atlantic, the navigator invited Paul to, 'Come up on the Bridge at dawn tomorrow and you will see a sight that has never been seen in history.

'So I got up early and was amazed when the navigator checked the clock and said, "In fifteen minutes you will see the top masts around Gibraltar."'

Such skill fascinated Paul, how, using only a sextant on the sun and stars, and countless calculations of their zigzag course a man could pinpoint their place on the boundless ocean. 'And bang on time we began to see – first the top masts, Bridge structures and radar equipment and then, as we sailed around the bend of the earth and getting nearer and clustered around the Rock such a fleet like I had never seen before.'[207]

The greatest invasion – so far in history – was about to begin.

---

207. PWH to the author.

CHAPTER TWENTY-EIGHT

Another Fighting Admiral

November 1942 to Spring 1943

Saturday, 7 November 1942 – and the eve of battle: George Blundell told his diary, 'I felt very excited during the night thinking of the events due to start at midnight – our landings at, or near, Algiers, Oran and Casablanca. The secret of where they are going to take place seems to have been wonderfully kept.' *Operation Torch* was underway with *Nelson* giving cover, based in French Algeria. Four days later Blundell had counted 500 merchantmen and 350 warships engaged and was amazed it had gone so well.

And Paul was in for a surprise too. 'One lovely morning,' he recounted, 'we were in Mers Al Khabia when the PMO said, "I don't like the look of the admiral."

'So I said, "I never had done."

'"Oh! We mustn't talk like that Houghton," and, "I would like you to see him."

'So I went up onto the bridge, and Syfret was in his sea cabin looking ashen. He had in fact burst his appendix, and he should have reported it about two days earlier, but he hadn't – he had been in pain for four days. And he really was ill, in clinical shock. There was no hospital ship in miles and we couldn't get in anywhere, and Gibraltar was hopeless – too far away, so I decided to operate on board *Nelson*.'

Syfret was hoisted on stout shoulders and taken along the main deck passage, through the sick bay to the operating room. 'Much like a funeral cortege,' decided Blundell and the crew with the outriders being the Master-At-Arms and the sick birth Chief Petty Officer, followed by the Royal Marines carrying the 'bier'.

Blundell listening outside the doors to the Sick Bay heard, 'Snip, snip, forceps, gurgle, gurgle,' and "Pass the gut please".'

'I operated on him,' said Paul, 'and I was very pleased to have my instruments!'

'I was relaxing with another chap [Dr Joe Morrison] in the cabin with George, as Syfret was recovering from the anaesthetic. My feet were up on the admiral's table and I stuck his hat on my head. Taking his telescope I put it to my eye, the wrong way round. "Oh Joe do look at this," I said, "it looks like the death of Lord Nelson all over again."

'"Not yet, my boy, not yet," came a whisper from the patient. Opening one gimlet eye, Syfret's mouth gaped in a spluttering roar, "What's that b----y hat doing on your head? Take it off!"

'And,' said Paul, 'seeing me with his telescope he commanded, "Put it down."

'"It's all right, sir," I said, "it's just a hallucination from the anaesthetic."

'"No it's not."'

Blundell noted in his diary:

It was an unfortunate remark to make by the doctor, but the young RNVR doctors, who were both highly qualified professionals, took life very light-heartedly. Houghton put the Admiral's appendix in a bottle of methylated spirit and if one happened to be passing his cabin, he used to say, 'Like to see the Admiral's appendix?' and would produce it from a shelf near his bunk.[208]

Paul said:

> We nursed him [Admiral Syfret] afterwards in his Day Cabin and he was pretty bad tempered. I'm sure if it hadn't been for that I might have got the VC at least!
>
> He was making a good recovery during the next few days and the question arose: who was in charge of Force H and the fleet? The war was finely balanced with the Allies on the front foot at last. None of the senior officers wanted to face such a strong personality to discuss his fitness to command.
>
> Matters came to a head when signals began arriving from Winston Churchill asking – soon *demanding* – to know whether Syfret was in charge or not. The captain and the Principal Medical Officer did not want to tell Syfret so they came to me, a lowly lieutenant. It was clear my patient was not fit for command but Syfret thought he was. So, with Blundell and the seniors listening outside the door, I went in and told him, which he took badly. And the Admiralty in London signalled his flag must come down.
>
> We transferred him across to the hospital ship HMS *Oxfordshire*. This meant slinging him over the water on a stretcher by a wire from our ship's crane; everyone watched with gleeful anticipation of something going wrong. To the amusement of all, he insisted on his hat being transferred at the same time, resting on his stomach.

---

208. You'd be shot at dawn by the GMC (General Medical Council) for doing that now. MH.

Syfret himself was pretty annoyed with me at the time, but I did get a nice letter afterwards saying he was making a good recovery.[209]

At the start of February Paul wrote to his parents:

My eminent patient makes good progress, and I am profoundly grateful that the event went off so well.

I'm doing my utmost to get a monkey onto the Nelson's books, for my simian friend – in a ship sailing in company – is a continuous spring of amusement, apart from one or two habits. His experiences at [the battles of] Malta, Narvik and Crete have weakened his morale and I hesitate to tell you that he has found refuge for happiness on a daily tot of Rum, but Port is as nectar to his palate. He is a native of Casablanca and a very gallant monkey, useful because he has an unerring ear for enemy aircraft of which he is terrified. But he feels quite safe if he can hide inside your reefer jacket – he is only a little chap.

In cold weather, the monkey loved the plates above the stove in the cook's galley. One day he tumbled down on the hot stove top, sustaining a terrible burn on his bottom. Paul and the medical orderlies bent all their skill to dress and care for the patient and were happy to report a full recovery.

'Animals are queer things,' he noted:

I heard of a boat load of torpedoed seamen who were horrified to see a great whale approaching them. The whale, however, was concerned for them – and kept

---

209. PWH, interview with Naval History Museum, November 2000.

his small eyes three or four feet away, not so much as disturbing a ripple on the ocean. He escorted them for miles, a Chinaman was so distressed that he just laid back and died.

Changes in the mess are disturbing, especially when good men leave like our gunnery officer [Sims-Bill] who, by force of example, set a standard of reasonable living.

I wish as much could be said for the Padre. Can you understand how a paid minister of the gospel, can entertain gun room youngsters to gin five minutes after celebrating Holy Communion at sea? In the first place he is disobeying orders as junior officers are not entitled to spirits. I shall speak to him shortly but he has ruined any good he attempts.

The practical matter of Christian conduct is a difficult one and it is easy to be fanatical. But using one's common sense, a reasonable course is obvious in everyday matters. I don't think mess life is easy for anybody who sets any standards for himself, or who realises that 'no man liveth for himself'.

Operation Torch landed 100,000 American and British soldiers through hostile waters onto contested shores. From now on, new bases in north-west Africa had seized the offensive after three years of German and Italian forces dictating events.

Spirits on the ship rose and Paul noted, 'The Russians seem to be streaming west as hard as they can go. I feel a bit jealous that our armies should be in the [European] field soon, and the crisis should be forced on the German will by the sandwich effect.

'I long for England – we all do. It's impossible [for civilian sailors] to acclimatise to the sea life, but there are many worse spots than the old "Nellie". Good food, a good cabin, fine mess mates are inestimable blessings.'

Other helps were at hand:

> George and I and another officer badly needed some exercise and went ashore but ran into some Vichy French soldiers. They were none too happy with anyone looking British, having had their fleet blown to the bottom of Mers El Khabir harbour [in 1940] by our ships. They began shooting at us so we dived into a roadside ditch unharmed, and lay there for much of the day, hardly daring to look above the parapet. We expected to be shot as spies, being enemy combatants in civilian clothes.[210]

While Blundell, the professional sailor, overflowed with events: 'So much happens at Mers El Khabia. The French Admiral called, charming, but looks frightened and aged . . .' Paul struggled to see a future within the revolutionary proposal of a National Health Service:

> I really cannot describe the weary oppression which descends on one from time to time. The return to a way of living, long planned and awaited, is blurred by all the talk of state control and unlimited bureaucracy. If the brave new world is the bondage of state service, like my present existence, I shall certainly leave my profession or the country.
>
> We dwell from time to time in a land overflowing with oranges, grapes and grapefruit enough to make our table look like a Sunday school treat at home. Altogether these parts are just those I would send a duchess to

---

210. PWH to MH as a boy.

recuperate herself in after a London season of cocktails and nightclubs.
Matters [of the war] stand much more agreeably than last year. In fact I think a good shove and down will topple the Third Reich and all its evil works with it.

Something amazing happened now in that the medical powers created a post for Paul which at the time was unique for the navy – they made him Fleet Surgeon, as he laconically noted:

> I have been busy lately. We have had to depend on our own resources for surgical and medical treatment and I have filled the office of Fleet Surgeon – a responsibility recognised by high and low who fall ill, or whose nerves require sustaining, but unrequited by any increments in rank or pay – blast the Service.
> How I shall think of you at Christmas time, though there seems as much hope of homecoming as of you coming this way.
>
> Your loving son
> Paul

Preparations for Christmas went ahead and the captain christened the Christmas pudding mixture with navy rum reminding Paul of 'the story you told, Dad, of my grandfather making a sacred albatross into a Christmas dinner, and I told it to a Chief Petty Officer. I am afraid he was rather upset at this break with sailor's tradition.

'I should like to give you a Christmas present but there is little to buy and no chance of sending it and so you must wait till I come home.

'Give my love to Lucy, and to the Mission room elders. Expect me home as I have always come – when it seemed the least likely.'[211]

Albert managed to get a telegram off: 'LOVE AND BEST WISHES FOR CHRISTMAS AND THE NEW YEAR FROM ALL AT HOME. ALL WELL.'

Just before Christmas Paul confessed:

> Everybody is a bit homesick just now and I am upset at the loss of a great friend of mine. He was killed at sea in a small ship the other day a few hours after we had operated together and met on the hills during a walk. At Lowestoft he had been my assistant. How very sad it all is, especially away at sea far far from home.
>
> Tony [Houghton] must distress his parents but he is doing a first-rate job in the Parachute Regiment? And what a test! The Houghtons are doing their bit, anyway.
>
> Thank you so much for the photos. They each recall so familiar ways we all want to come back to and maybe the war will be over before we could dare to hope.

Every port in French North Africa teemed with Allied troops especially American army who Blundell found helpful and pleasant to meet. French soldiers in blue hats jostled with British khaki hats and Arab red fezzes and headdresses – 'swathed in sheets'.

Christmas Day 1943:

> We spent . . . on very high seas but the sun shone and the winds blew freshly and we managed to enjoy a very good dinner. The ship's company decorated the mess

---

211. PWH, letter to his parents from HMS *Nelson*, 10 December 1942.

decks and our wardroom was transformed to look like a Sunday school treat.

I found myself a trifle melancholy at the loss of that friend of other days. The sea looks so innocent until a ship gives a puff of smoke and crumples up before your eyes. He was a cheery helpful fellow and his captain, whom I saw recently, thought highly of him and misses him overmuch.

How splendidly the offensive is building up in strength. It cannot come too quickly if the captive nations are to survive. The atrocities seem unspeakable. It seems that the Anglo-Saxons have lost their consciousness of evil long before 1939, for these atrocities were general in Germany for years before the war and no voice of warning or threat of punishment was heard in England or America.

The redemption of Europe will be difficult beyond words, but it will be a privilege to feed and reclaim these broken folk.

Europe looks ahead to the day when we shall begin the old life again in quietness and peace. 'We seek a country . . .'[212]

Paul felt his surgical skills atrophying in the wasteland of war where he was more a general practitioner. As they roamed the heaving seas, his moods mirrored them, 'I try to tell others and myself, "we are designed for such things in a world containing hope of little else."' And, he added, 'as my C.S. Lewis says, 'Settled happiness and security which we all desire, God withholds from us . . .

---

[212]. 'These all died in faith, not having received the promises, but having seen them afar off, and were persuaded of them, and embraced them, and confessed that they were strangers and pilgrims on the earth. For they that say such things declared plainly that they seek a country' (Hebrews 11:13-14, AKJV).

> but joy and pleasure he has scattered broadcast . . . Our Father refreshes us on the journey with some pleasant inns but . . . My true good is in another world and my only real treasure is Christ.'[213]
>
> Take care of yourselves in the New Year.
> With much love from your son Paul.[214]

Five days later Paul dropped hints to his mum and dad:

> I think this letter should come home quite quickly and I should like to accompany it. Today I saw a Brimstone butterfly, a terrifying monkey, rosemary and lavender in bloom, tangerines ripening on their trees, acres of narcissi with the most delicately perfumed flowers and all of it in sunshiny weather like an English June day.
>
> Still the day is brightening in the East and the dark night of Europe's soul is nearly over. It does not do to contemplate the German tortures of Jew and Gentile, 'How shall I abandon thee, Israel?'[215]

Based on that, the war 'cannot continue in the light of such scripture and, if all nations of the earth are blessed through Israel,[216] for all Eternity, then we owe the Jews the biggest effort we can make. Whatever the curse on Germany will be – it will beggar description.' ('Whoever curses you I will curse'.)[217]

He found the ship's company 'ready for a little trouble again and the mere thought of British capital ships paralyses the enemy'.

---

213. *The Problem of Pain* by CS Lewis © copyright 1940 CS Lewis Pte Ltd. Extract used with permission.
214. Letter, PWH to parents, HMS *Nelson*, 5 January 1943.
215. See Hosea 11:8.
216. '. . . through your offspring all nations on earth will be blessed' (Genesis 22:18).
217. Genesis 12:3.

Another medical victory arrived: 'All my surgical instruments have come, brand-new and duplicated, and we could share them with other ship, so the effort [with the Admiralty] was worthwhile, and we are equipped, after three years of war, as a Battle Squadron should be.'

Then suddenly, February brought news condemning Paul to a new agony of impotence.

CHAPTER TWENTY-NINE

The Courageous Captain

As the ship passed to and from Gibraltar across to North Africa ferrying soldiers, barbed wire, milk, flour, bacon, timber, explosives and vehicles to the front line, news reached Paul provoking an urgent letter home:

> I do hope mother is getting fatter [because she is losing weight fast]. I wish to goodness you might share some of our fruits of the earth, and a bottle of wine and some of our sunshine.

And he adds, 'But you must let me know that all is well. Bad news here in this desolation would be overwhelming.'[218] The next letter lands privately at his father's office in London:

> My dear old Dad,
>
> All my heart and thoughts are with you day and night, during these awful years of war and desolation. Always, I think of you and Mummie at home in Lingfield and the country we all love so well.
> There has been so much death by sea and land that often I have tried to acquaint myself with it and prepare for the intimate blows it is bound to deal one.

---

218. PWH letter to Albert Houghton, February 1943.

Now I find the cup too bitter to swallow and the helpless isolation and confinement in a ship is awful beyond words.

I am doing my best to get home. But Dad, after more than 18 months at sea my time ought to be up. But advancement and soft jobs don't come when you seek to reform or correct. The steady gin drinkers get these. The high-ups only send for you when a calamity happens – like the admiral recently.

I can't see light at all – only this, that this world is 'enemy country' and even Christ had to come in disguise, and we have to try and 'stick our toes in' when bitterness and sorrow, come our way.

Dad, do all you can for Mummy and of course, anything I have is yours. Keep in touch with John – he's far more use than I could be and is not subject to such utter desolation of mind. Frankie will stick by you and Mummie most loyally.

I would give anything to come home. However, perhaps there is a communion of hearts and minds which transcend space.

Well, dear Dad, everyone in the old *Nelson* is very fit and there's no end of kindness. Give Mummie all my love.[219]

To Paul – feeling he should be on the launch ramp of the arc of his life's work – the reality was a valley. Disruption, destruction, danger and death amid the wasted surgical years – and now impending grief – goaded an outpouring to the other mother-figure in his life:

---

219. PWH letter to Albert Houghton, 17 February 1943, at his business office (in their first home, 438 Fulham Rd, London SW6).

My dear Lucy,

You know how all my heart and mind are with you and Mummie just now. The truth is shattering, though one must accept that it is inevitable in this world. Now it is upon us it's bitterness is overwhelming.

I would give anything to be home for only five minutes, but the captain, who is most sympathetic, says, 'The country must come first and anyone coming out to relieve me might get killed on the way.'

Oh Lucy, for years of war and before, Lingfield held everything I loved and now it seems to be dissolving. Oh, try to tell Mummie how I love her. There is no real separation, you see.

I depend on you entirely. We all do and I'm sure our Lord will stand by us, though it's hard not to be rebellious in this desolate life.

Anyway, I'm sure you are cheerful.

I sent John some money to get anything that he can. And I've enclosed a cheque in case you want some spare cash. [We found the £4 cheque to 'Miss Lucy Vine' still in the envelope uncashed by Lucy. Paul's monthly pay was £18 in 1942 – about £190 in 2021.]

With much love
Paul[220]

My dear old Mum and Dad,

We are still sailing the seas and seem desperately unwilling to set a course for home. Sometimes the days pass quickly, sometimes very slowly and we feel cheerful or bored accordingly. I wonder if you have any idea of what

---

220. PWH letter to Lucy Vine in the same envelope as to Albert Houghton, 17 February 1943.

it is to spend month after month on a warship, beating round the seven seas in fair and foul weather, or lying up in some foreign harbour at short steaming notice in case an emergency happens.

Most harbours stink. I am sure all Africa is desert; though here and there it will blossom like Eden with sweet herbs, orchids, irises and nostalgic buttercups.

A few of us have organised a squadron medical Society which meets weekly for the discussion of cases and problems, held in a different ship on rotation. Usually the captain allows us to use his cabin.

Our chaplain, enjoying quite a renaissance of godliness, is staging a course of Lent sermons. I note an improvement in his life. I should like to say the same for myself, but the temptation to fret at this life and to be intolerant is always upon me. You know me well enough, Mum and Dad, to understand this and not to condone it.

I like to think I am learning the lesson, 'Seekest thou great things for thyself? seek them not.'[221] It's far more profitable to cultivate an acceptance of tribulation and hardship in this present world, than to expect pleasure for ever more.

I cannot think of you at the Mission Room now because it doesn't exist [since the bomb] but your years of testimony are not in the least jeopardised. Living away, I know the value of the years of home life and Christian wisdom and these things are quite imperishable.

I have enclosed some dry flowers; we do see something more than blue water.

All my love, your loving son,
Paul[222]

---

221. Jeremiah 45:5, AKJV.
222. PWH to Albert and Edith from *Nelson*, 17 March 1943.

Letter, from Paul to his parents, 24 February 1943:

My dear old Mum and Dad,

I am sending another box of dates; in case the first one came to grief. You must eat them carefully, chew them well and mind the stones, as you would tell us small boys. Some of us have been together in the Wardroom for a year and a half and you can realise, Mum and Dad, how united such a number of young men can feel and we often talk of England and our homes, and these thoughts and feelings make for sympathy and cheerfulness.

At least he had a grateful patient:

A very charming letter has come from my admiral [Syfret] patient expressing his gratitude . . . and telling that he is keeping fit. You know, I'm afraid he will try and do too much, he's not a young man.

Even I am getting old and I often feel that the war of wasted years and opportunity has finished me for the future [career], but that's merely egocentric stupidity, I suppose; one must keep one's head up, remembering that our treasure, our citizenship, our lives are hid safely in Heavenly places, and things we meet day by day are to be enjoyed but not counted upon. I'm afraid my conduct and speech often belies this truth, but it *is* so all the same. Ginger Jim is ever before me because our Lady Ginger Cat – who ought to be a Wren, I suppose – is about to have kittens and she is choosing either the squadron gunnery officer's cabin or the ship's gunner's cabin. The officers in question are too soft hearted to object. You see what shocking decisions the war brings to us! A neighbouring destroyer has a hammock for their cat!

Your loving son,
Paulie

In March Paul decided, 'the news from home might really be worse [about his Mother's health] and I really cannot tell you how thankful I am for your courage and cheerfulness, just now.'

Paul was now well aware that Mother had a 'nasty' in her stomach causing the pain and weight loss, but they keep up a pretence, with Paul writing on 12 March 1943:

This indigestion is an awful nuisance, Mummie, but it's common in later life you know, and very common in wartime with the messed-up food and worry. In these parts [North Africa] the children have been in a shocking state from undernutrition and food they can't assimilate. Things are better when Allied food ships have brought flour and sugar and meat and medical delicacies, but the deficiency diseases cause awful distress. And do you know – many are still antagonistic to the British who have saved them from certain starvation.

I shall be home soon I hope – my time is coming to an end and I have done my duty on this battle wagon.

All my love, your loving son,
Paul

Dick Prewer, hearing of Edith's illness, wrote to Paul:

I can comprehend your feelings, now that you are needed most at Lingfield, and yet held far away. Would you like me to go down to your parents? You know that I would do anything for you. What more can I say of your own words, 'cheerfulness and philosophy' to give you help under present circumstances?[223]

Letter Paul to parents, HMS *Nelson*, 27 March 1943:

My dear old Mum and Dad,

I am so glad you have received at least one box of fruit, Mum, and I know the juice especially is the very thing for your disorder. Indigestion is bad enough at any time but when you can't get the right sort of fresh food it is just beastly.

The orange and lemon trees are perfectly lovely; leaves and bloom and fruit are on the tree together and the exotic smell of the flowers at evening time is astonishing.

I came back to the ship one day recently with five different orchids, a Bee, a Spider, a Fly and a Common purple orchid and one I could not identify. I have seen a Brimstone butterfly and many Large Whites. Red Campion, Bugloss and Ox slips decorate the mountain sides.

I have been a year with only a week's leave, and it seems that my life is destined to this ineffectual existence after all the years of sweated work. Sometimes I am inclined to cynicism, but one must not look beyond the present moment, for which we are told [in the Bible], there is sufficient bread for our needs and sufficient grace to cope with the present cross committed to our charge: 'Take up your cross and follow me.'[224]

---

223. Dr Richard Prewer letter to PWH, 7 March 1943.
224. See Matthew 16:24.

You may have heard on the wireless that Admiral Sir Neville Syfret is now Vice Chief of the Naval Staff and a Lord Commissioner of Admiralty. It is some consolation to know that one's scalpel has contributed to the success of the war in saving his life. The circumstances were romantic enough for any surgeon.

I have served under seven admirals, doctored three, and invalided one – apart from those ashore. So a rare experience of sea officers comes our way in this ship, and their personal habits and customs make a study as interesting as any form of natural history, and each has his fads in the matter of etiquette as to when and where he will be piped, bugled and so forth.

Lord Nelson, the sailor, remains the standard and it is to him that every sentiment of the sea is dedicated. It is amazing that one man should invigorate a Service with its own ideals [a century and a half later].

I long to be home again, to forget wars and leave the wandering years behind me, but the time is not yet.

Your loving son,
Paulie

Paul's next letter home is a folding aerogramme with a thruppenny stamp.

My dear old Mum and Dad,

I do hope my almonds, raisins and sweets have arrived safely, not forgetting the lemons and bananas and a leather water bottle.

Eighty years later, I hear his firm advisory voice that he used with us children:

I hope Mummie that the lemon juice relieves the objectionable indigestion. Anyway, do try and make use of the foodstuffs you find you can take because you must maintain your strength ... knowing of course how wartime food and worry distress one subconsciously.

By the way, try to see the film *The First of the Few*, dealing with the invention of the Spitfire aeroplane.

All my love, your loving son.
Paul

Blundell's diary locates them in Mers El Kabir; but Paul's final prediction was wide of the mark:

My dear old Dad, I am glad to know ... Mum keeps much the same, though I am not unduly optimistic; one may not be in this world. She writes saying how good you are to her and how you scour London for food palatable. See that John assists in the matter of vitamins, iron and meat extracts.

Things are going well with the army now and the War may end precipitately.

Your loving Son,
Paul[225]

Then Paul told both parents:

My dear old Mum and Dad,

Today is Palm Sunday and I attended the church ashore [in Oran, North Africa]. Perhaps a church where my grandfather may have worshipped from his square-rigged

---

225. PWH to Albert Houghton, 438 Fulham Rd, London SW6, 12 April 1943.

ship so many years ago. The service was conducted very beautifully, in the company of two or three shipmates. We all felt glad to be free of the routine and discipline for a short time.

Your loving Son,
Paul[226]

Paul to his parents, HMS *Nelson*, 25 March 1943:

My dear old Mum and Dad,

A recent storm was quite terrific and I think my grandfather would remark on the severity of the weather in latitudes where it might be least expected.

Today is Easter Sunday, and morning service was held on deck with glorious weather to remind us of the Resurrection.

You know I think every sailor looks wistfully away to that compass bearing where his home lies. Well, we shall steer a course along it one day and perhaps it may be soon, who knows.

All my love, your loving son,
Paulie

By May he reports 'my promotion to Surgeon Lieutenant Commander, which means a little more gold lace ("scrambled egg" on the cuffs, as the Wrens say) and some more pay'.[227] That pay added a few shillings a month:

All of us away here wonder what civilisation is like just now. To ease our minds from sea and sky we have weekly

---

226. PWH, aerogram letter to both parents, 18 April 1943. 'PASSED BY CENSOR'.
227. Paul to parents, HMS *Nelson*, 2 May 1943.

cinema shows . . . magnificent films one may see; *The Young Mr Pitt* or *The Great Mr Handel* are pure delight.

The war has reached a bit of a deadlock again but judging by the vast quantities of equipment in every Allied zone, the mighty and – I hope – the final clash of arms cannot be delayed longer.

Dick writes and dispatches a book or two. Old Maurice Carpenter writes from the East distressed by the climate, but what a fine job of work he has done all the war!

Now you must all keep smiling and cheer up.

All my love, your loving son,
Paulie

In Algiers, the ships company met two of the great wartime leaders General Eisenhower and Admiral A.B. Cunningham, 'ABC', whose brother had written a guide on human dissection used by Paul and later myself (a moderately helpful book). A few days later the enemy penetrated the harbour in Gibraltar setting off limpet charges under two ships but the routine possibility of being blown to bits was ignored for other matters:

Mummie, I know what distress you endure, and how very troublesome your complaints are. You know my duty is here just now, and that one must just stick one's toes in and do one's duty.

I often feel like grumbling at the life and, I'm afraid I often do in the wardroom, but I know what you would tell me to do, and so I count my blessings as well as my woes and on the whole they turn the scale.[228]

---

228. PWH to parents, HMS *Nelson* 9 May 1943

Then Paul got the confirmation he dreaded and responded, 9 May 1943:

> My dear old Dad,
>
> Jack has written recently confirming the state of affairs with Mother. I wish my prayers might achieve what our wishes would attain. For myself, I have long ceased to pray for personal deliverance from danger or disaster, for there is no evidence to show that Providence exercises supernatural power to give immunity from the general misery. It is unchristian to expect it. We, too, since we are found in the fashion of mankind, must humble ourselves and be obedient unto death.[229]
>
> This is a hard doctrine as God demonstrated on Good Friday at the crucifixion of His Son, but that demonstration was the answer to it all, too. We shall rise to life immortal. As a great Catholic puts it, 'Whatever lies ahead beyond the limits of our senses, I know that God holds us *alive*.'[230] This seems almost enough to me, and far away at sea, even before the depths of sorrow and pain called to me in the voice of loneliness, when the isolation seemed very great, the great doctrine of the Church, the Communion of Saints, became vitally important: 'I believe in the Communion of Saints.'[231]
>
> I speak as a fool, and can scarcely comfort myself, and sometimes the Christian creed seems as insensitive as this armoured ship. And as ridiculous in a world of sin and death. But it is not of course, our eyes are covered, lest we should be dazzled at the triumph of the Redemption, 'glorious as an army with banners'.[232]

---

229. Philippians 2:8, AKJV.
230. The original source cannot be found, but it's based on Philippians 3:13.
231. The Apostles' Creed, https://apostles-creed.org/interpretation/the-communion-of-saints/ (accessed 22.11.24).
232. See Song of Solomon 6:4,10, ESV.

You know how all my heart is with you and Mummie and Lucy. There is so much I have left undone that I should have done. Don't forget to share your doubts and troubles, old Dad, and John has broader shoulders than myself – always a broken reed.

Your loving son,
Paulie

What happened next amazed Paul and everyone else:

As if to emphasise my helplessness at home their Lordships at the Admiralty have been good enough to appoint me 'Surgical Specialist' to this Battle Squadron and ship, post-dating it for pay. I know you at least will be proud, especially as the appointment is a unique one made specially for my humble self!

Everybody out here is very kind. In fact one is amazed at the amount of sincere kindness in this poor old world. And senior officers who happen to know that you are laid up at home Mum, often ask about you.

Then our new flag lieutenant called Aisher comes from near Blakeley Heath. We pace the quarterdeck and travel together in mind to all the old familiar paths and lanes and roads we both know and love so well.

This sunny land of oranges and lemons and remote mountains is particularly lovely and I often read *Pilgrim's Progress* and, knowing that our way through life is at best a journey, I pass through Bye Path Meadow and the Delectable Mountains to the land of Beulah. I think I have seen too much violence and destruction to get a very firm grip on things of home again. We must enjoy them while they are at hand, happy in the present joys, humble under the present cross, confident of persevering to the final victory.

Now I must not write more. There is no distance, really in the kingdom of our God, or separation, unless sin or folly hinder our vision. And I can send you all my love and kisses. This letter is travelling by famous vessel across the desperate sea.

All my love, your loving son,
Paulie[233]

Paul to parents, HMS *Nelson*, 15 May 1943:

My dear old Dad and Mum,

I have enclosed a photo taken on board a hospital ship to tell you how I look these days. A lot older, I fear.

I know you are not at all well these days, Mummie, but Dad and John and Frankie write and tell me how jolly good you are and how you do your best to take all the nourishment you can, and it is very important to try you know.

Since I can't take old 'Nellie' home, you must try to realise how very often I think about you and pray for you. Then I realise, again, that distance does not really separate – as the psalmist said, when he thought how remote the sea could be . . . 'If I take the wings of the morning and dwell in the uttermost parts of the sea; even there thy hand shall lead me'.[234] Not of course that he ever went there. However, he was quite correct, as it happens.

Maurice Carpenter wrote the other day and wished specially to be remembered to you. He is in a very hot spot and if any man has deserved well of his country

---

233. Paul to his parents, HMS *Nelson*, 18 May 1943
234. Psalm 139:9-10, AKJV. Note: 'even there shall thy hand lead me' in AKJV.

he has done so after nearly 4 years at sea in very ill protected cruisers.

Dick is very sorry to hear how upset you have been Mummie – no one is softer hearted than Dick, and he holds you both in high respect and with great affection.

We are expecting a flareup some time out this way, but things are going so well that victory seems quite near. I believe the Hun is as brittle as he is cruel and will crack up very suddenly and quite soon.

Paul witnessed the enormous flow of men and supplies building up for an invasion *somewhere* in the Mediterranean – so he had reasons for hope. But that brittle quality did not materialise, and ahead lay two years of bitter fighting that would scar the Houghton, Swift and White families.

So that was it. His mother was dying. He languished on a battle wagon, circling the seas from stinking port to port with his surgical skills fading like a bright star behind clouds.

Yet a little later the Senior Service reached out:

In May 1943, the signal arrived, unknown to me – that my mother had been ill some time and was dying. Captain Jacomb sent for me. He was tall, slim, silver-haired, a fine countenance and a cultured voice. Such was his manner, his transparent personality, that it seemed to me that any man would instinctively respect, admire and trust him. He would never be rough or discourteous. He would have no sentry outside his cabin but was accessible to all.

I climbed up to the bridge, wondering if my domestic problems had betrayed me. But the captain greeted me seriously and gently and took me into his sea cabin alone. He had just received a signal from the Admiralty intimating a lapse in my mother's condition and as he read the signal he seemed deeply distressed., 'Houghton,' he said, 'what I'm about to say is secret – you mustn't tell anyone – but the ship is returning to England in a week for urgent reasons and I shall see that you have leave to visit your mother. Let us hope she will be alive.' He said words of comfort. And do you know? his eyes filled with tears, and mine were overflowing. He was terribly nice. I thanked him and left the bridge.[235]

We sailed into Plymouth Sound on a glorious June day, and I got immediate permission to go home. I went up to London with my friend Lieutenant Geoffrey Bullock and I went home. Mother knew me and I spent the night with her. Then I got permission from the Admiralty to stay another night. I stayed by her bedside and said some prayers with her and next morning she died. Died of stomach cancer which was very common in war – the poor wartime diet I expect.[236]

That day, when Edith died, a jubilant British Jew in MI5 – Ewen Montagu (co-working with Charles Cholmondeley) – popped into *The Times* Deaths column the announcement of a Major William Martin's death, Friday, 4 June 1943. Martin never existed. He would become *The Man Who Never Was*[237] in Montagu's book after the war. It was another false titbit to a long string of Spanish and German spies who had already fallen for Montagu's bait.

In one of the most astonishing deceptions of war, a British submarine had dropped a body into the sea off Spain carrying

---

235. *'Reminiscence,'* handwritten account, by PWH, June 2000. Also in interview with Naval History Museum.
236. Secretly recorded round the fireside at our home in Sheffield 1998. Also interview with Royal Naval Museum, November 2000.
237. Ewen Montagu, *The Man Who Never Was* (Philadelphia and New York: J.B. Lippincott Company, 1954).

a briefcase of (false) information about where the allies would assault Europe. Paul would have been delighted to know that, not only was it a Jewish genius pulling the strings at the London end but, the distal spy on the string, was following his Christian conscience. Baron Von Roenne had the absolute trust of the Führer himself. Determined to set the Nazi terror up for destruction, Roenne duped Hitler into defending the wrong Mediterranean coastlines from the coming Allied onslaught – which greatly helped *Nelson*'s adventures ahead. *Operation Mincemeat* was being 'digested', as Ben Macintyre put it, in his gripping 2016 book.[238]

As for Albert, 'My poor father had to stay behind, and I went back to the distraction of sea life', back to the roving gypsy life. *Nelson* sailed north for the Orkneys, on 7 June. The ceaseless round of naval routine and community was a comfort: dawn action stations, watch on watch off and the hundreds of men from every corner of the British Isles' slinging hammocks to sleep anywhere they could find.

Edith had lived just long enough to see Paul promoted – and she died knowing that thirty-one years of steering her precious son had contributed to the fight – and always confident of ultimate victory. Two days later Paul was trying to support his father:[239]

My dear old Dad,

My thoughts and prayers are with you and for you very often these days and I am sure your hope and confidence will illuminate the way we have had to tread just now. I cannot believe we are really separated and I do not feel it although one or other of us – whether you, Mummie,

---

238. Ben Macintyre, *Operation Mincemeat: The True Spy Story That Changed the Course of World War II* (London: Bloomsbury Publishing, 2016).
239. Letter PWH to his father, 9 June 1943, HMS *Nelson*.

me or Jack – may be called to serve on a different station in the kingdom of God.

I should like you to read the life of Cowper the hymn writer and seek a change in direction in 'Dover Harbour' which will be a great tonic. [*Dover Harbour*, a novel of the Napoleonic wars by Thomas Armstrong.[240]] I was lucky to get you a copy because with its great popularity it has sold out.

We had just left the evening service in our little chapel and the knowledge of the communion which has not been broken could not have been greater away here on the wide and desolate ocean. The familiar sentences of the evening service were infinitely soothing, 'The souls of the righteous are in the hand of God, there shall no evil come near to them'[241] by land or sea, in heaven or earth. It is enough and we need not ask for more.

The old ship is rolling heavily tonight and we all wonder where our star is leading us and to what great adventure the sea will bear us. The atmosphere seems laden and importunate with crisis on crisis. These days might be lonely but there is so much kindness in the world that half the sting of life is removed at once, and when you meet it, you can't but feel ashamed and unworthy of it.

How strange my return home last week was, becomes more and more apparent to me, timed to a day, so that I could see you and Mummie before she repaired to a better commission and at least be together for a few days. The mercies of God are very amazing and we should cultivate the grace of hopefulness.

Paul was desperate to do something for his grieving father and made a recommendation – at least on tobacco – that he

---

240. Thomas Armstrong, *Dover Harbour* (London: HarperCollins, 1942).
241. Based on Wisdom 3:1, RSV.

would never have done in later years. He would become one of Sir Richard Doll's fifty-year follow-ups comparing the fates of 'non-smokers v. smokers'. He lived to see this study clinch the facts of 'the killing' the tobacco companies made selling their weed. Also, Albert was a nervous man, as his son knew:

> I hope the cigarettes came safely, and finally I want to say this. Do not let your conscience take charge of your wisdom in the matter of seeking the benefit of cigarettes and a tot of whisky offers you. It is foolish to doubt their benefit and to deny yourself when times of strain and age require them. Do not imagine it will make me smoke or drink more or less, Dad!
>
> Your loving son
> Paulie

He wrote a second letter, the same day, 9 June 1943, overflowing with grief and concern:

> My dear old Dad,
>
> I have been thinking of you a great deal and wishing that you could share the distractions of life aboard ship. But the sea is never quite the same and above all there are one's mess mates whose courtesies and kindnesses are so many that the world becomes less lonely and the heartache of life more tolerable.
>
> I could not have stood the experiences you and Lucy have shared so manfully these latest months and now I feel a great coward and a fortunate one. All our life we have been wanting something that cannot be had in this world, and even when we seemed nearly

to have attained it in this life, when some ambition or wish is achieved, it somehow evades us and we can only continue the search. We must not despise such earthly blessings, though we come to find they were never meant to satisfy; but we must not mistake them for the reality or cease to pass on to that other country. We are, then, linked to heaven by our very ambitions, united with those who have our affections and precede us. And how much more must they be with us in their perfect humanity no longer dependent on faith or even the means of grace. This is the community of the church.

I cannot express the bitter heartache and the sorrow at my past meanness, and the longing for the truant years which have fled so rapidly from our experience, and the bitter sweetness of every remembrance in village and garden and household, and the tender care of my childhood and wise guidance of the later years, repaid with so little care. They form only a memorial to the impermanence of this very temporal life. But it is surely gathered up into all of that redeemed world which we have made our own, never to be lost when we stand together at the great Easter day [of general resurrection of those who died in faith in Christ].

We shall all re-employ ourselves in some great service together in that serene sphere. We must cultivate the sense of continuity of life and experience and knowledge [for all who have new life in Christ]. This very frail and mortal body, always perishing and scarcely repairable, is the poorest shadow of the superb new creation Mummie now enjoys and we shall inhabit – 'in my Father's house are many mansions'.[242] While the stumbling service we

---

242. John 14:2, AKJV.

render here is absurd beside the great missions we shall be expected to occupy later.

Paul strove to describe how Christians will, in the age to come, be responsible for cities and kingdoms:

> These are odd views perhaps but as Sir Walter Raleigh said, 'Of death and judgement, heaven and hell, who oft doth think must needs die well.' And though we may scarcely see a step ahead in one sense in these decimating experiences, these objective facts remain and we ought to reckon on them.
> I ought not to write in this strain, I am not a good man, and I am one to whom much has been given and from whom much will be expected, and I know I ought to be consumed with the urgency of every hour instead of idling away the years.
> Have no qualms from your intolerant tyrant of a conscience about a cigarette and a glass of wine. It is intemperate for you to abstain from these very proper pleasures when they correct a strained temperament.
> At the moment my company is feathered, every sort of seagull and Fulmar petrels.
>
> With much love from your son
> Paul

These thoughts do not speak of trying to contact the dead; 'Nonsense!' he would have snorted, at the thought.

Paul writes again, trying in their mutual grief to turn the language of war to their benefit:

My dear old Dad,

I have just got your letter of the 11th of June in record time.

I'm so glad you find chinks in the blackout, Dad, and I do too. As dear old Dr Johnson said, 'Cheerfulness breaks through,' and with the support of friends and mess mates and the courage of conviction one ought to be up to face the 'enemy's [Satan's] heavy artillery with some confidence.

Sailing away from his father, towards more deaths at sea, Paul reflected:

Whatever one feels subjectively, we know objectively that all is well, absolutely right and shipshape with Mummie. That's what I tell myself and it is true. And 'the sufferings of this present time are not worthy to be compared with the glory that shall be revealed in us'.[243] In fact, the whole emphasis of St Paul's writing and every truly Christian writing is the continuity of the redeemed life beyond physical death.[244]

Then the guilt and loss surge back:

I have been looking at old letters from home, books and little things Mummie gave me – so indifferently accepted at the time, I fear, and (with little but sea to look at) recalling a hundred incidents across the years and feeling with utter dejection that these are trophies of life past, and written off, though we might offer all we have for one more day [together].

---
243. Romans 8:18, AKJV.
244. Paul to his father, 12 June 1943.

But are these feelings and emotions Christian? They are very human, but 'blackness, and darkness, and tempest'[245] are far removed from the comforts of the Spirit of God. All is redeemed that is of God, and the very details of the past are not lost to us but persist to be eternally enjoyed if they are worthy of it.

And he pauses to consider questions confronting every doctor:

> I write in this strain to release my own mind and express something of a doctor's outlook to pain and the circle of suffering which encompasses a man from birth to death. And, when all is said, we cannot escape pain and, by definition, it hurts. Our very conceit will not allow us to humble ourselves and become obedient unto death – in ourselves or our best loved hearts. Only the very Deity might attempt this, and so the Cross throws its shadow across our valley of the Shadow and answers all our problems. We are not separated, 'Death hath no more dominion over us.'[246]
>
> Once more I say, do get *The Problem of Pain* [by C.S. Lewis] at the Catholic bookshop opposite Westminster Cathedral.

Then he ponders the future:

> I do not know our next move, old Dad, somewhere on the seven seas we shall try to do our best and then I hope I'm for home. John writes and speaks of a move to Shrewsbury for you. Well, the way will open up. Lingfield has the softest memories for me – from the

---

245. Hebrews 12:18, AKJV.
246. Romans 6:9, AKJV. 'Death has no more dominion over him' in text.

age of twelve, but I shall have to leave at some time and, anyway, distances in England are not great.

Read my 'Dr Johnson' and he will echo round your mind, 'Deep calleth unto deep'[247] from the eighteenth century. Books are priceless in their store of wisdom and to read of other men in similar circumstances and how they dealt with the situation gives you a great sense of companionship. It's good to take a bird's eye view of time and watch [in *The Pilgrim's Progress*] Mr Valiant-for-Truth, and Mr Great-heart and Mr Fearing and Mr Ready-to-Halt and Hopeful and Faithful struggling, fighting, wrestling their way to the city 'which hath foundations'[248] We shall never be lonely in their company.[249]

Perhaps Paul had hints that the 'high-ups' have noticed his long sea-time and needs the refreshment of a posting on land.

I shall be very glad to be ashore again. It felt quite odd just to see ordinary folk behaving like ordinary people and I could have watched for hours the other day ashore in the South. The 'lines have fallen in extraordinary places'.[250]

Your loving son
Paul

The crew's beloved Captain Jacomb was replaced and, Paul reflected:

We all thought it was time he must be awarded his flag as an admiral in place of Syfret. But he was passed over.

---

247. Psalm 42:7, AKJV.
248. Hebrews 11:10, AKJV.
249. All these are characters in John Bunyan's *The Pilgrim's Progress*.
250. Based in Psalm 16:6, AKJV: 'The lines are fallen unto me in pleasant places'.

He was an excellent man. But he couldn't get on with the senior officers of the Navy – or so the story went – along with the rumour that the high-ups scoffed because he had 'married a Portsmouth blond'. They were deeply attached.

Jacomb went home poor man without any medal. He became a rear-admiral or something in a shore establishment at Portsmouth. He had commanded big ships all the war and that was his reward for all his services.

Captain the Honourable Guy Russell took over – 'no end of dog'. He was a tall, handsome youngish man; coming aboard with a bicycle. As I had a bicycle as well, he would order George Blundell and me ashore to cycle with him. He told us no end of stories about the Admiralty, terribly funny. George and I felt that while he was cycling with us the ship could not sail, so we cycled over Malta and over North Africa, where, in the latter, lay lonely forts of whitewashed mud walls from the French Foreign Legion – as if straight out of *Beau Geste*.

On 9 June, as *Nelson* and Force H exercised their great guns off Cape Wrath, Scotland, no one on board could know that one of warfare's supreme deceptions – *Operation Mincemeat* – was about to make all the difference.

CHAPTER THIRTY

Malta and Sicily Saved

June to September 1943

Secrecy, and surprise were essential if a stepping stone to Berlin was to be won.

'Our warlike activities are obscure but we all try to prophesy and those with the gift of fortitude hope to do great things', noted Paul:

> We listen to stupendous news and try to imagine what 700 bombers, could do in half an hour to a German city. And then we picture the Hun when he knows that he is reaping the whirlwind he has been sowing for ten years. He cannot appreciate the might of sea power. Well, these specs on the ocean have laid a net about him and we are drawing it tighter and tighter.[251]

The great docks at Gibraltar were alive with ships and troops when the *Nelson* arrived. Paul shot off a letter to his father:

> I'm glad that you are keeping your chin up and looking ahead rather than astern . . . I seek to do the same and

---

251. Letter, PWH to his father, June 1943.

find the prospect good. I daily thank God for tempering the storm of Mummie's departure to my capacity. I enclose a little cutting from *The Times* expressing a Christian view of life and death, titled Love and Memory.

'Those who died in Christ are at peace; they rest from their labours. This rest does not rule out a continued activity of love and blessing in prayer for those still on earth, but it is an activity unmarred by mistake or weariness or sin.'

And, Paul continues, 'What is the good of the Christian creed of belief if you do not objectively use it?'

On the reverse of the cutting, British film producers were preparing for post-war markets – optimism was growing.

And then he counsels his father:

You need not allow yourself to be beleaguered by remorse, Dad. Remorse is the devil's repentance – his ruin is final; but our loss and failure are not final. For in that city which has foundations, sorrow and sighing, bitterness and regret are done away in the atmosphere of perfect knowledge and love and right mindedness.[252]

The past forty years of your married life – on a human basis – why, they have been happy, profitable and successful. And you must remember that they have had a purpose for us boys in shaping character, developing perseverance, tolerance and humanity.

We must endure as seeing Him who is invisible and be confident that there is grace enough for the present cross we bear.[253]

---
252. See Hebrews 11:10, Isaiah 51:11.
253. Letter, PWH to his father, 27 June 1943.

It would be character tested very shortly in great events.

An old flame – a nurse Paul loved in Brighton[254] – sent a letter full of longing. Elizabeth Blackwood wonders why they have drifted apart? But Paul had told his brother he would not commit to marriage because he did not want to leave a war widow.

On Gibraltar, Paul was in the naval bar and overheard two men talking. They were navy divers and one of them was saying, 'I found a gold ring today 80ft down and here it is.' Paul looked over his shoulder. Sure enough it had a Scotch thistle engraved on it – the Houghton family crest – and the lost ring came home. He lost it again later!

The long-anticipated recapture of Europe was about to begin. Malta would be the headquarters and from her airfields roamed deep-ranging war planes. So in early July, *Nelson*, flying the flag of Admiral 'ABC' – led Force H and an armada of warships and troop ships towards Sicily, for the long-awaited invasion of British troops on European soil. Codenamed *Operation Husky*, the aim was to take the large Italian island lying between Malta and the toe of Italy.

On 4 July, 'ABC' announced to the fleet the invasion was 'on'. The array of more than 4,000 ships, the largest ever known, assembled south of Malta, with the big ships there to keep the Italian fleet from threatening the invasion troops. *Nelson* had diverted towards Greece, 'sailing,' said Paul, 'blue seas in brilliant sunshine,' to reinforce the *Mincemeat* decoy of the Germans that the landing would be on Greece.

This was high summer and 'you can have no idea how extremely uncomfortable the ship can become when she has been battened down for days on end. Scuttles are closed

---

254. The letter was found in one of his books in 2010.

and watertight doors locked. No amount of air conditioning refreshes the stuffiness and stale air, spaces between decks. However we keep fit and the fresh air on the upper decks compensates for it'.

On July 16, the *Nelson* was in Malta to refuel and Paul could get a letter off:

The Sicilian operation proceeds in fine form and I suspect the Italian peninsula will welcome the Anglo-Saxons if it means the eviction of the Hun. They know now how they will be treated – better food rations, plenty of cigarettes and other animal pleasures their folly has denied them for years.

Meanwhile his cousin, Tony Houghton was in the Paratroop Regiment prompting Paul to ask:

Is he safe and sound? I have offered a few prayers for his welfare. I should be very distressed if he came to grief.

Let's hope that after the war we can travel ourselves to see some of the places I have explored. Our commander [George Blundell] and two of us are making plans for holidays in the Shetlands and Orkneys.

My mind longs for civilian life again with its regular life and ways and the practice of my profession properly. I sometimes feel that all the knowledge I struggle to attain has been for nothing.

But self-pity is useless – wicked – and we must soldier on! Expect me home by autumn with any luck.[255]

---

255. Letter, PWH to his father, 16 July 1943.

No sooner had his letter gone than they were fighting off a heavy air attack. Just after midnight their old friend *HMS Indomitable* was hit once again by a torpedo so *Nelson* escorted her back into Malta where, three days later they were attacked by thirty bombers, but came through unscathed. Terror had become commonplace.

'Sicily', Paul wrote, 'has the dignity of a British Governor ruling with mercy and judgement. Our casualties for the invasion seem to be few', because, of course, *Mincemeat's* outstanding success in keeping German forces far away in the wrong parts of the Mediterranean.

> But I have been saddened by news of the loss of a close friend in these parts; we had planned all sorts of events... and now he has perished, leaving a wife and lots of old mess mates to mourn him. We need to sit very loosely to life and health, surprised to retain either in ourselves or our acquaintances.
> On Sicily the fascists seem to be hated, and now Rome has been bombed. I hope the old city is unscathed – a small price to pay for the extraction of the fascists. The Sicilians are close to starvation rations.
> I often think of you, old Dad, and always pray for you. I'm sure you are taking a rational view of the inevitable mutations of this changing life. The very fact that we dislike the fatigues of the passing days surely hints that we are destined for a more beloved country.[256]

With the capture of Sicily, Paul is at liberty to reveal where they are:

---

256. Airmail, PWH to A.J. Houghton, 20 July 1943.

My dear old Dad.

The Sicilians received the Allied forces most willingly and even the Italian forces showed very little fight. The locals assisted with the invaders *impedimenta* and welcomed the food and cigarettes and the liberty the Anglo-Saxons brought to their island. The Germans were completely double bluffed, and, unable to prevent the landing being in the wrong place.

Our journey has taken us back to Malta. An island – the very keystone of Allied victory – lay a thousand miles from an English base and proved a persistent source of ruination to his convoys supplying his North African forces. Yet a [German or Italian] naval expedition could not be arranged to deal with the dwindled resources of Malta's Grand Harbour.

The great ship moored up, amid shattered half sunken wrecks, and Paul, idling at the rail was stunned by a sight he never forgot. Field Marshall Lord Gort the governor was greeted by the admiral and a guard of honour and waved aboard at the foot of the gangway. Gort, the three times decorated soldier – attempted the climb – had to halt. Slowly it dawned on the onlookers – he was too weak to move. Gort had put himself on the same rations as the islanders.

Among the crew the hopes of an Axis collapse were dominant: 'I feel, as many in authority believe, that the days of warfare are very nearly accomplished and that we may lift up our heads.'

But the agonies ahead could not be foreseen.

'I have enclosed £10, and I'm delighted to do so Dad. Use it as you feel best, perhaps to a *really* efficient missionary for his *personal* use.' Paul had no time for Christians living off the church when they could be working. 'But *I am* satisfied that many working overseas endure great distress from climate and lack of minor luxuries. Living in this very hot climate my sympathies are with them!'

Then he turns to the pain besetting countless families:

> I know how very bitter the cup of bereavement is, Dad. Sometimes I wish I were at home; in a fit of loneliness or recollection I would give anything to see the countryside again. Or again the prospect of the future seems too bleak to contemplate now that the familiar landscape, the background of all my life, is far away. The temptation is to cease to struggle or plan in a life bereft of any permanency.

Just across a few miles of water 7,000 British and American soldiers were dying; along with 10,000 Germans and 132,000 Italians taken prisoner. When Cholmondeley died in June 1982, Ewen Montagu wrote to *The Times* of his 'invaluable work and . . . Many who landed in Sicily owe their lives to Charles Cholmondeley'.[257]

Amid all this Paul penned a philosophy to help father and son push on:

> But you know, this [longing to go back to life with Mother] *is* a temptation and it is *not* reality. The truth is that nothing is lost to us. In the matter of 'separation' we do well to repeat St Paul's views, 'that I am persuaded, that neither death, nor life, nor angels, nor principalities, nor powers, nor things present, nor things to come . . . shall be able to separate us from the love of God, which is in Christ Jesus our Lord.'[258]

---

257. Macintyre, *Operation Mincemeat*, p. 334.
258. Romans 8:38-39, AKJV.

And so the grievous loss in the bittersweet memories, stirred by the sights of familiar things – well, one day all these will be gathered up into that Divine present where past and future are not known.

For the present we pray that God's will be done on earth – as it certainly is being fulfilled by the church in heaven; and also for grace for the present Cross and bread for the present day, knowing that not long ahead, grace will be no longer needed and the sacrament of bread an anachronism.

Now he gets brutally honest:

It is very easy to talk, and I cannot express to you the feelings which overwhelm one away at sea as week succeeds week, but feelings do not make facts any less objective, and faith is to be put to use or else discarded.

Then comes a confession which to me as his son, awakens an 'Aha! me too' reaction:

Biological death has ever been a terror to me. It came so strongly to me as a student that I very nearly jettisoned the idea of qualifying and only persisted because to retreat would have been the end of me.

I wonder now where I found the courage or the philosophy to persist in a lifelong study of morbidity [disease]. But I came to know that death is a universal phenomenon of nature, upon me so close at hand as I write, and not to be avoided by blinkering my intellect. Indeed, death is the sacrament of life, the gateway to newness of life ahead and therefore, not to be feared.

Nailing his colours to the mast, in order to overcome death's fears, he bangs the nail home with, 'except a grain of wheat fall into the ground and die . . . It brings forth much fruit. He that loves his life shall lose it; and he that hates his life in this world shall keep it unto life eternal'.[259]

'I write, Dad, to emphasise the heartaches and the thousand natural shocks of life as I find they are not fortuitous [random], but part of the process of moulding our spirits for the city which has foundations.' He rounds off with poetry his young family would hear decades later:

I like Tennyson's lines from *In Memoriam* –

That life is not an idle ore,
But iron dug from central gloom,
And heated hot with burning fears,
And dipped in bath of hissing tears,
And battered with the shocks of doom
To shape and use.[260]

And I suppose it is by such tribulations that we become prepared for the splendours of our next commission [work in heaven].

But we are human beings – and incidentally we shall be even more so when creation has been redeemed – so do not neglect the comforts which are at hand. Especially do not neglect the companionship of friends and their letters, a glass of wine and books.

---

259. See John 12:23-25.
260. Alfred, Lord Tennyson (1809-92), 'In Memoriam A.H.H.', www.azquotes.com/quote/ 526360 (accessed 22.11.24). The original poem uses the words 'dipt' and 'batter'd').

Malta was now the base for Force H, which had mastery of all the supply routes through the Mediterranean. As *Nellie* entered Grand Harbour, she wiggled her skirts in attempting a pretty turn in the bay to impress the crowds ashore and got in a terrible tangle with tugboat *Restive* to the amusement of Paul and friends leaning on Nelson's rail.

Paul went ashore on 23 August to help after a big explosion in Valletta, probably from a timebomb dropped from the air. *Nelson* sent parties to help dig people out of the wreckage.

Once Sicily was secured, the two sister ships *Nelson* and *Rodney* began using their terrible guns to soften the way for Allied troops to land on Italy in *Operation Hammer*: the bombardment of Italy's coast defences north-east of Reggio.

Paul and his friends revelled in the smoking volcano, Mount Etna but once inside the Messina Straits the whole ship closed up to Action Stations ready for the bombardment which began from seventeen miles (30,000 yards) out. Allied pilots were spotting and directing where the shots fell and broke into jubilation over their radios when *Rodney* hit an ammunition dump with a mighty explosion.

A film crew was there as the triple 16-inch guns thundered, stabbing flame and belching smoke and rolling the ship from end to end. Watching that movie you can see men drinking from an earthen ware jug, while a Chief Petty Officer, wearing anti-flash and steel helmet, scans the horizon with a telescope. Other crew are wheeling 16-inch shells along the deck and lowering one into the magazine.[261]

As the Allied invasion of Italy took shape, the German infantry was about to prove their mettle. They were dug into the Italian cliffs in concrete fortresses, on their own

---

261. Imperial War Museum, https://www.iwm.org.uk/collections/item/object/1060020189 (accessed 22.11.24).

continental turf, with their backs to the wall of Berlin far to the north; they were in no mood to give way.

Preparing to face these troops was a pipe-smoking vet, turned doctor, who Paul would come to know. Peter Swift, Jean's brother, would shortly meet the enemy in the closest quarters possible.

Paul was relieved to write:

> You write more cheerfully, Dad, and I'm glad you find comfort and consolation. They do abound though I am lucky living a roving life. In fits of vile self-pity I sometimes wonder how the future can be faced or the present endured. Then I remember that well-being has been my lot so far and I commit an act of faith and accept the future confidently. 'I do not ask to see the distant path, one-step enough for me.'[262]

Then, at the start of September, Albert got a military update:

> I'm sure you heard our ship's name broadcast yesterday. We have had a good crack at the Hun on the Calabrian peninsula and they will need to spend a few days licking their wounds before they can recover any military ability.
>
> The morning of our bombardment was a perfect Mediterranean day as we approached the Messina Straits. Mount Etna looked very fine, rising 10,000 feet above us and he had the goodness to smoke a little to oblige us.
>
> We all wanted to go ashore and climb the hillsides and lay in stores of lemons and grapes and figs which abound

---

262. Letter, PWH to his father, 28 August 1943. Poem, John Henry Newman, 1801-90, 'Lead, Kindly Light', https://newmanu.edu/about-newman/history-of-newman/lead-kindly-light (accessed 22.11.24); the actual words are: 'I do not ask to see the distant scene; one step enough for me.'

in Sicily just now. Our 11-inch and 6-inch guns were soon showing Etna what they could do and the destruction onshore must have made her quite jealous.

How all the world waits for the next round and wonders where the attack will fall. It almost seems as if the Western war will have burnt itself out in Germany by November as the last one did.[263]

Alas, the recent victories were firing hopes too far and too fast.

---

263. PWH letter to his father, HMS *Nelson*, 2 September 1943.

CHAPTER THIRTY-ONE

Hope for Italy
1943-44

The British Eighth Army began to cross the Messina Straits onto Italy on 3 September. On the 7th, the day before more mighty events, Paul was sparkling:

> The food has improved to make me very portly! A run ashore and a chance of a 10-mile walk came along the other day and four of us enjoyed the most wonderful time and finally descended a long, fertile, terraced valley to the sea. We had seven sorts of fruit to eat, melons, grapes, mulberries, figs, pears, apples and prickly pears – all in such abundance that we seem to be in an earthly paradise after enduring the heat of this great ship.
>
> A wonderful bath in the bluest of deep-sea water completed the outward trip and then we needed to hurry back. I think we all breathed deep sighs of relief when we saw our top masts over the hill and knew Nelson had not sailed.
>
> My thoughts are with you in the problems which beset your 'interior life' as the Catholics say. We do not do well to worry unduly about our future in this

world – though I am the chief offender in this respect. Nor about the supposed loss of those our hearts hold dearest. Sometimes I think we worry because the future existence will be so different that we shall not recognise ourselves or our friends in it but 'what if this earth be but the shadow of Heaven?' That is the answer, I do believe.

I am in a hurry to catch the mail.

Your loving son,
Paul[264]

Then on 8 September the BBC confirmed the wonderful news of the Italian government's surrender. The imposing Force H lay off the coast of Salerno and there was the feeling that it would be a walkover – a feeling quickly blown apart, as Paul vividly recalled over fifty years later:

> The landings up the Italian coast at Salerno south of Naples were terrible for the troops. The army landed and the RAF thought they had destroyed the German batteries in the hills behind – but in fact they hadn't. Our army was pushed right back into the water, while we were lying some distance offshore. We had a spotter ashore who directed us to aim our 16-inch canon straight at the batteries in the cliffs. The great guns roared with everyone battened down below decks to escape the shockwaves – that silenced those guns all right. And the army got back on the offensive.[265]

During that first night '20 to 30 Heinkel 111s came at the flagship and one of them came close down the port side in

---
264. PWH to his father, 7 September 1943.
265. PWH, *Naval History Museum Interview*, 2000.

a mass of flame. Noise, smoke and gun flash enveloped the ship as *Nelson* fired everything she had with such intensity it shocked their sight and hearing. One able Seaman name Studley passing 6-inch cordite passes collapsed from heat and exhaustion. For the rest of his time everyone called him "Cordite"'.

The Germans turned in fury upon the Italian ships steaming to surrender and sank the brand-new battleship, *Roma*. What a sight greeted them when *Nelson* arrived off Malta on Sunday 12 September:

My dear old Dad,

The Italian fleet will no longer annoy us. Their ships, great and small, are lined up at in neat rows and never having had any spirit or pride or tradition they lack any now and surrendered most willingly, being nauseated at supping with the Devil for so long. They came to us for protection as much as anything and the arrival lacked the suicidal pomp of the Teutonic naval debacle in 1918 [when the Germans sank their own ships at Scapa Flow].

We all feel our duty is done in this sphere of service and look for England and home pitying the wretched soldiery who must proceed up Italy under his own steam.[266]

A fortnight later, Paul watched the first great national surrender to happen on *Nelson's* deck. Admiral Badoglio, commanding the Italian Navy came aboard.

The Italians seem to be as pro-Anglo-Saxon now as they were Axis-minded a year ago. The vigour they display in

---

266. Paul to Albert from HMS *Nelson*, 13 September 1943

racing their ships behind the security of the British naval division is remarkable!

They are received aboard without any humiliation or imposition of the stigmata of defeat and wear their ensigns [flags] with all the conceit of hard-won victory. There may not be much to laugh at nowadays, but we find the Italian fleet a great figure of fun.

These snaps show the Italian admiral boarding our ship as pleased and proud as he can be. They are all so absurd, lacking any military ardour, and longing for a quiet life from whoever will offer it. Keep these photos, as they are historic events.

In this photo, the legendary General 'Alex' Alexander, the British army commander in Italy is on the Marshall's left. He had been the last soldier to leave the beach at the Dunkirk disaster. Always looking as if 'he had just come from a steam bath and had a letter from home' Alex had the priceless gift of giving calm and confidence to soldiers in desperate places. He visited the front line almost daily, and was another general who knelt by his bed and prayed. British troops were not always polite about their American brothers in arms but Alex praised the US soldiers, saying, 'Sometimes a soldier must obey and die.'

Paul found 'Marshall Badoglio... an old man to look at and performing a rather gallant service to his wretched country in this office [of Prime Minister] he now holds. By the time the Anglo-Saxon tidal wave has reached the Alps the Italian peninsula will be pared to the bone of all essentials'.

Paul had a particular disgust for the yellow tapeworms many feet long that he met during bowel surgery or rectal examinations – easily spread by hand to mouth while eating local delicacies:

The countryfolk loaded us with the most delicious grapes and the ripest of melons and figs so that we could scarcely bathe for distension! No sea in the world can possibly offer such aquatic delights, and, looking up when diving deep, your companions seem fossilised in a lake of lapis lazuli. But we look forward to the smell of English soil and woods in autumn rain.

The heat is trying on our tempers which become irritated by trivialities and querulous at inactivity – until we settle down to the truth that the ways of the Admiralty are inscrutable past comprehension.

An arrival of edible bread and supplies has heartened us, and, best of all, the day when I say goodbye to the ship. But, if only our company could keep together! So many of us have served together for so long that it will be a grievous thing to part.

Paul begins to hope, but the years of war have added realism to his thirty-two-year-old outlook:

I do hope things look up for you, Dad. Life is mostly uphill; I think we expect it to be otherwise and are surprised at the truth. We expect permanency in a world where everything is temporary – until we learn our folly.

I am terribly sorry to learn of Albert Chandler's violent death by enemy action. How his sister and brother must be distressed. It is idle to try to explain these events. No explanation satisfies the honest mind; all we know is that most people who survive birth die before their 10th year. In fact, this is a cosmos of violent catastrophes and chronic miseries. It is obvious, as John in the Bible observes, 'the world lieth in the evil one'.[267] Only our

---

267. 1 John 5:19, ASV.

absurdity surprises us when evil crosses our path and stalks our destiny – rather, we should be surprised that we continue to enjoy any measure of security at all.

Yet Paul did not linger on the melancholy:

I gain confidence in a better future from the fact that surprise and dismay at disaster remains in every human mind despite its inevitability at some point in time in personal experience. Surely, this means that we have fallen from a state where calamity had no part, where no agent could behave maliciously. That is Paradise Lost. The story of Paradise Regained[268] is the summation of all faith and knowledge, 'the redemption of the world by our Lord Jesus Christ', as the Prayer Book for Soldiers and Sailors 1941, has it.

And he had another reason for hope:

My dear old Dad,

My duty to the sea has been completed and I long to pick up the threads of my own work again. The chance of my being drafted home are bright now.

I have had Sandfly Fever and mild dysentery for nearly a month, very irritating in this hot, old ship. The 'big ship' war is over in the Mediterranean. It will be strange to live ashore again after 2 years of this incarceration and sea life. I have little to bring back. Frankie begged me to buy a Maltese lace christening shawl and I sought high and low and finally bought one in the old

---

268. A reference to the poems by John Milton (1608-74), 'Paradise Lost' and 'Paradise Regained', www.goodreads.com/book/show/336518.Paradise_Lost_and_Paradise_Regained (accessed 22.11.24).

capital – a delightful walled city. The lace is still made in the convents. The priests and churches are devoted to the name of Saint Paul.[269]

Paul was based on Malta into late 1943, carrying on twice daily GP clinics where crew could come with anything. As the surgical specialist to Force H, he went around the fleet, operating on anyone who needed it and bringing back some to the *Nelson* for her operating theatre.

After the fiery years, it was a time to reflect on human greatness while the army fought their way up Italy. As a boy, my dad would say to me:

The heights by great men reached and kept
Were not attained by sudden flight,
But they, while their companions slept,
Were toiling upward in the night.[270]

For sure, Paul never thought of himself as 'great' – heading some autobiographical notes, '*An Unimportant Life.*' And if he was tempted to think of himself too highly, 'Anyone in the Navy knows what an unlucky thing it is to boast.'[271]

Paul made no pretence to physical courage and told me plainly, 'When I was afraid at sea I tried to distract myself with sucking a boiled sweet or sharpening a pencil.' For years I could not understand how that could help. Then one day in my twenties, I was stretched out face down on freshly ploughed soil on the Mount of Olives. I had just dived into a roadside

---
269. PWH letter to his father, 21 October 1943.
270. Henry Wadsworth Longfellow (1807-82), *The Ladder of St Augustine*, by Poetry Foundation, www.poetryfoundation.org/poems/44636/the-ladder-of-st-augustine (accessed 21.11.24).
271. Admiral of the Fleet, Sir Hedworth Meux, to Parliament, excoriating Winston Churchill for boasting about the navy from the time when he was First Lord of the Admiralty. Quoted in Roy Jenkins, *Churchill, a biography*, (NY: Plume – Penguin Group), p. 305.

orchard evading crossfire between Israeli army and the PLO. Heart pounding I found myself examining crumbly grains of soil beneath my nose – a helpful diversion.

As a teenager I had stood beside my father staring at portraits in the Imperial War Museum, London. They all belonged to an exclusive club – they had all won the Victoria Cross, the highest award for courage. Dad remarked, 'They seem to possess a calm outlook; it's as if they had faced the worst and were not overcome.'

Yet Paul had something else. Military historian Sir Max Hastings observes, 'Heroes are tremendously useful when there is a battle to be won but most of the time they are thankfully redundant.' Hastings, a soldier himself, finds 'moral courage is far more valuable.'[272]

Confronting the naval medical authorities for vital medical equipment, possibly cost Paul a good deal more than bombers and U-boats. And he had another courage, noted by a colleague: He always sat down with his patients and told them with kindness and compassion the truth about their medical prognosis. He had the rare ability, to look at the facts and yet maintain hope. It was a hope that arose from knowing his prognosis could be wrong; and that higher hands might intervene for healing and that, even if the gates of death opened, death was not the end.

Then at last, in the autumn of 1943, his ship was heading home from the Mediterranean and the famous Force H – formed when Britain fought alone – passed into history. They carried senior Nazi prisoners of war who Paul cared for and found 'rather pleased with themselves.' He amused the mess about General so-and-so taking Calais in 1940 and taking Calomel [a purgative] in 1943.

---

272. *The Times*, 2 January 2021.

By 1944, far away in Portsmouth, Wren officer Jean Swift was gently re-training some of the battered survivors of HMS *Manchester* after Pedestal. She watched how her warm personality began to restore their faith in humanity. And, through the window she was watching the unmistakable buildup for a massive invasion by more than 4,000 ships – coming on some French beach *somewhere*. 'It was,' she said, 'all enjoyable *except* when the Doodlebugs came over.' [rocket powered flying bombs -- Hitler's terror weapon.] Her twin brother John was a junior infantry officer training for France, while older brother Dr Peter was reaching the front line in Italy. Everyone in the Swift and White families wondered if the gates of death would shake them.

CHAPTER THIRTY-TWO

Home Is the Sailor

Winter 1943-44

Here he lies where he longed to be;
Home is the sailor, home from sea
Robert Louis Stevenson (1850-94), Requiem[273]

Back in England, Paul was drafted to a hospital for naval officers, Durham Down, Bristol for a few months with the illustrious Christian surgeon Professor Rendell Short. Paul facetiously saw Short, in the Brethren circles, 'as about as near to sainthood as any mortal could come. But one day, I was beside the great man in the operating theatre peering into a patient's bladder from below, when he dropped his cystoscope on the floor – and out slipped a mild expletive! What a delight to my ears – what a relief to discover he was fallible like the rest of us.'[274]

As a Christian, Paul often felt short of some arbitrary mark – not 'witnessing' enough and not enough in control of his temper. But what he could not bear were 'humbugs', people

---

273. https://poets.org/poem/requiem (accessed 13.10.22).
274. PWH to the author.

talking religion but not living it. Rendell Short was no hypocrite and both agreed: everyone is equal at the foot of the cross. Furthermore, they knew Christ did not come to doctor the 'well' but the 'sick'.[275]

At last Paul could pick up the threads of home life, telling them:

> If Frankie is fit enough, maybe we can all meet at Lingfield. I have a bottle of sherry stored away that will keep us merry.
>
> It is disappointing that Frankie should lose her third child and I sympathise with them. Maurice Carpenter writes from Portsmouth and I hope he will come to stay.
>
> I am enjoying much of the work here and it is very varied. I have had two half days at the University and that is great. The soft weather has brought masses of crocuses and a few early primroses into bloom, promise of good things to come.
>
> We enjoy undisturbed nights from enemy action and wonder when the war in the West will open. The hospital bulldog is growing fast. I have seen no dog with such spirit and ferocity.[276]

By April, he tells his father:

> Tonight the church was packed and pretty with spring flowers. Our scholarly vicar preached quite wonderfully on the Easter theme of resurrection from death. Sometimes heaven and earth seem to meet. It's strange this world of spiritual forces and beings and values. It's within us too, *He hath made every thing beautiful in his*

---
275. See Mark 2:17.
276. Letter to Albert, 7 February 1944, from Royal Naval Hospital Durham Down, Bristol.

time: *also he hath set the eternity in their hearts*, says the Preacher.[277]

Another matter was bringing some healing from fighting:

> The sequence of the seasons is most glorious to watch – I have missed the English spring for two years and more, you see. One cannot cease to wonder that a Creator should offer his creatures such Divine variety as morning and evening, sunrise and sunset, light and darkness, spring and autumn and so on to his own infinity.[278]

Leaving Bristol, he moved to be a surgical specialist at the Royal Naval Hospital, Liverpool, 'an awful hideous old building down at the docks – and intensely busy', where cutting-edge clinical trials were progressing:

> They were beginning to use *muscle paralysing agents* like curare from the poisoned arrows of South American Indians.
>
> Curare was revolutionary because now the abdominal muscles were soft and unresisting, enabling us to work inside the abdomen with freedom. It was fortunate at sea that, when I had to put Admiral Syfret and others to sleep for surgery – without the new muscle relaxants – I was already used to giving anaesthetic agents myself. We had no anaesthetist on board.
>
> I didn't like being ashore again as I had got to like the life at sea, and you make friends aboard ship.[279]

---

277. Based on Ecclesiastes 3:11, AKJV.
278. Letter PWH to his father, 10 April 1944, RN Hospital Durham Down, Bristol.
279. PWH, interview with Naval History Museum, 2000.

Through Fire and Water

D-Day arrived, 6 June 1944, and Second Officer Jean Swift, twenty-three, glued herself to the window watching the armada of ships, great and small, sailing out of Portsmouth Harbour. The skies were dark with bombers towing gliders, Spitfires and Hurricanes passing over in a continuous throbbing roar towards France. Her heart swelled for her dear Twinny John in the infantry and Brian White, her brother-in-law, with 45 Commando, who had been training in secret for such a day. Were they up there?

One morning some weeks later, in her lodgings, her landlady asked, 'What's up, Jean? You don't seem your normal cheerful self.'

'I just feel so miserable,' and she burst into tears. 'It's John. I'm sure something's happened to him.' A few days later Alice and Harry Swift at Leighton Home Farm, Shropshire, got the telegram that their son Captain Swift had been severely wounded near Caen, by shrapnel in his leg on that very morning his sister felt miserable. And he would probably lose the leg.

Then they heard grave news from Normandy. Brian had landed on Sword Beach, before two months of non-stop fighting near Caen. Infiltrating into enemy lines, Brian led his troops over a bridge on the River Orne and met a panzer in hiding which they engaged with hand-held weapons. Death came quickly on 20 August 1944.

Brian and his new wife, Muff, had been living in a farm cottage on the Home Farm. He must have returned on leave, because Jennifer appeared in September 1943, and there is a tiny black and white photograph of Brian 'holding me, with Muff and Morny and Pod [Alice and Harry Swift]. Legend has it that he prodded me and said *Oh! And it all works!* I didn't know the photograph existed, until a year or two before Mum died in 2006. Brian's father, well I'm afraid that the shock needed tranquilizing, and alcohol I gather he found soothing, or perhaps hoped it would be'.[280]

Jean, reeling from this double catastrophe, knew that her other brother, Peter, in Italy, had been in the forefront of the terrible fighting at Monte Cassino and continued to face ferocious German resistance as they edged forward. He 'participated in the Indian frontal attacks during the second battle up the infamous Monastery Hill – making pencil sketches while waiting in the forward dressing stations and supporting the Ghurkhas and Poles in the third battle. Peter's upbringing with horses became invaluable in managing very frightened mules on the steep slopes. After a bloody four-month battle, Peter was reportedly the first doctor into the Monastery for some hours when it finally fell to the Allies in May 1944'.[281]

Then, during the 'bad fortnight' of the Swifts', Harry and Alice got a casualty telegram saying Peter had been badly wounded in a minefield north of Casino, but was off the critical list. Later they gathered he had crawled forward in a minefield 'to rescue a casualty, been blown up himself – and had to apply his own tourniquet and get both of them out – with an audience "cheering them on" from the edge of the minefield. Later Peter said it felt a 'bit like getting kicked on the shin playing football'.[282] He lost the leg below the knee.

As yet Paul knew nothing of these events. From ashore he followed the news about the D-Day landings on the BBC and President Roosevelt's D-Day broadcast from the White House, which struck a powerful chord with the nation:

In this poignant hour, I ask you to join me in prayer:

---

280. Mrs Jennifer Evans, daughter of Brian and Muff White.
281. John Swift, the son of Peter Swift, Jean's older brother.
282. Ibid.

'Almighty God: Our sons, pride of our Nation, this day have set upon a mighty endeavor...
 Their road will be long and hard. For the enemy is strong...
 They will be sore tried, by night and by day...
 The darkness will be rent by noise and flame... Some will never return.
 Embrace these, Father, and receive them, Thy heroic servants, into Thy kingdom...[283]

Nelson, arriving off the French beaches, astonished Field Marshall Rommel, who told Hitler that operations were impossible for miles inland due to the naval gunnery – a 16-inch shell blast could flip a 45-ton German Panther tank, even with a near miss.

What were Paul's lasting reflections on the war years?

When I look back on it all, I think my most useful time was ashore in Lowestoft in the air raids. There were a lot of cases and we were rather understaffed, and a lot of action going on overhead. There were only two of us – even in England at a naval base – silly really, isn't it! However, once you got to sea and had all the tremendous defences of the ship itself – and you got better food too I think, much better – life seemed less precarious.

In the last fifteen months at Liverpool, we were immensely busy in bad circumstances. I was back into surgery and working with the senior surgical consultant. He was a great expert in general surgery; so it was wonderful revision training.

---

283. www.presidency.ucsb.edu/documents/prayer-d-day (accessed 22.11.24). See also, https://fdr.blogs.archives.gov/2019/06/05/fdrs-d-day-prayer/#:~:text=FDR's%20address%20took%20the%20form,powerful%20chord%20with%20the%20nation (accessed 15.4.24).

That was surgeon Mr J.B. Oldham FRCS, who gave Paul this reference during a personal crisis ahead:

> I have known and worked with Lt. Cmdr. Houghton for fifteen months during which time he has been surgical specialist to the Royal Naval Hospital, Seaforth. He did an immense amount of work. He is a first-class surgeon, meticulous in his technique . . . steeped in the literature and science of surgery.
>
> His personal qualities are of the highest order, he has exceptionally high principles, untiring application to his work and an extremely good presence. He has, too, a keen sense of humour and is an excellent colleague and messmate. I am sure he would make an excellent surgeon to a teaching hospital.

And Paul continued decades later:

> In the meantime, new discoveries were coming on – antibiotics being the greatest. But these were not being integrated into routine treatment. The only time in the war that I remember when we used antibiotics – apart from the sulphonamide I mentioned earlier – was at Bristol. I was there for a few months, and I got to know the orthopaedic surgeon and he said, 'I have got a nun, from the local convent, and she is desperately ill with staphylococcal septicaemia infecting her blood and bones.' He said, 'Do you think you could get me any penicillin?'
> 'No,' I said, but our pathologist here is quite advanced, and he is brewing his own.' He was just brewing it – and it looked like beer too – fermenting.
> 'Shall we filter it off, sterilise it and drip it into her?'

I said. Well, he did – a terribly risky thing to do with this awful looking stuff – and, do you know, it cured her! In two days she was a different woman. The difficulty was to get enough of the drug; you might have enough for four days, but that wasn't enough, so patients relapsed and died. All this took time to discover, and it was the Americans, who were able to produce it in bulk.[284]

In the dying weeks of the war an SAS jeep full of British soldiers drove past the guards into Bergen-Belsen extermination camp. Almost retching from the stench, they struggled to believe what they saw: tens of thousands of skeletons – some still stumbling about. Richard Dimbleby broke it to the world on the BBC.[285]

Paul was horrified but not over surprised. The Germans had recruited the doctors to their infamous T4 assisted dying plan years before. 'By having a doctor make every decision that sent an innocent person to death, murder became a medical procedure. Actions that were unacceptable for the state to undertake became acceptable if a physician did them . . . In this way murder was sanitised.'[286]

With victory won, Paul 'got talking to a group of Wrens at Portsmouth who were miserable. They couldn't imagine a country not at war; the loss of the comradeship in the mess – so strange, isn't it – after six long years'.

So, Paul reflected, though the long years seemed like the death of the good seed of surgery, perhaps a green shoot showed in Liverpool – except the peace now heralded a new crisis.

---

284. Interview with Royal Naval History, November 2000
285. Ben MacIntyre, *SAS: Rogue Heroes*, 2016, Penguin Books.
286 Friedlander H. *The Origins of Nazi Genocide: from euthanasia to the final solution*. The University of North Carolina press, 1995:219. Google Scholar.

Part Three

Senior and Son, 1945-2009

A grain of wheat...if it dies,
it bears much fruit.

John 12:24, ESV

CHAPTER THIRTY-THREE

Crisis in England

Sometimes a weariness ... comes over me, and I feel that I would give almost anything to be on the high seas again ... I get it crossing one of London's bridges when the tide is in, and the salt tang strikes one's nostrils.

Dr J.J. Abraham, The Surgeons Log[287]

Paul 'was waking up sweating after nightmares about not getting a job'. At least he had one thing in common with Sir Winston Churchill, they had almost no money – after five years' naval pay for Paul. Doctors were pouring out of the Armed Services and flooding towards the few jobs in the hospitals. As for the proposed National Health Service – it was no more than an idea bitterly opposed by the doctors' union, the BMA. Doctors had little career structure to chart a path ahead.

He visited his father in Lingfield, pleased to find Lucy keeping house, as in the days when Mother was alive. Thence to London looking for surgical work, and reading a classic, *The*

---

[287]. Dr J.J. Abraham, 1876-1963. *The Surgeon's Log*, Epilogue, 1911 and 1932 versions, by www.shipsnostalgia.com/threads/the-surgeons-log.15759/ (accessed 22.12.21). See also, J. Johnston Abraham, *The Surgeon's Log* (London: Chapman & Hall, 1947).

Surgeon's Log, reflecting his longing for the sea again and to be heading for the warm South. General Practice seemed like second best, and anyway, the GPs were fleeing to Canada.

Furthermore, his heart nursed dreams for the 'far off' Welsh Marches and – of course – a woman to share those with. Brother Jack and Frankie had gained a foothold up there in Shrewsbury; maybe in them lay a door of hope.

As for a woman – a persisting inner whisper muttered, 'How is a man as shy as me with girls, ever going to reach, "Will you . . .?"' And where was nurse Sister Blackwood now? An enquiry on this fifty years later elicited the vague, 'Oh she went away in the war,' in a tone trailing off and uninviting to further questions. Pippa once found a letter hidden in a book – was it Elizabeth's last? – wondering wistfully why he acted so distant? Was she the victim of his dark moody days when close friends felt as if they had said something wrong?

And week after week, in Lingfield, Albert's 'old biddies' kept praying for their star.

By 1946 the war had been over for more than a year and Paul was thirty-five. Food and fuel shortages were worse than during wartime. Most major cities had bombed-out centres. A ferocious winter killed more than a million much-needed sheep in monumental snowdrifts. Stranded people were recovered as frozen corpses in isolated houses. From 1946-47, 'perhaps half a million Germans starved or froze to death in their ruined cities. The British sent food, fuel and clothing they could ill afford to spare themselves'.[288]

Paul's nightmares make little sense at face value. He was a surgical specialist, with an excellent Confidential Naval Record, though he had not seen it. But he did know that confronting the senior naval doctors to get surgical tools for the fleet had

---

288. Daniel Johnson, *Daily Telegraph*, 28 August 2022.

made enemies. They didn't care that he kept a letter from a grateful Admiral Syfret. They could have concocted a court martial for insubordination and drummed him out of the Service like his grandfather.

The years of prolonged professional and physical threats had left Paul with a jumpiness to loud noises and a dread of poverty. Jack found him temporary surgical work in the Shrewsbury Hospital. One of Jack's obstetric cases, in 1943, had been Mrs Theo ('Muff') Granville White at the birth of Jennifer. So, 'Dr Houghton' was a household name on the Home Farm at Leighton where 'Muff' lived, a war widow, in a cottage with little Jennifer.

To bolster his prospects, Paul even wrote to his original surgical mentor in Brighton and received back a letter, though they had not met for nine years:

November 6th, 1945

Mr. Paul Houghton took meticulous notes on cases. He had excellent judgement . . . A man of character, painstaking and reliable who always does his best for his patients . . . a loyal and good colleague.

Similarly, with Sir Cecil Wakely, by then the senior surgeon at King's College Hospital London, who sent back:

I have known Houghton for many years . . . I have seen some of his work, which is beyond all praise. He is a competent surgeon . . . Has a happy knack of getting on with his colleagues . . . A cheerful optimism, which goes a long way to endear him to his patients . . .

It gives me pleasure . . . to recommend my friend, Paul Houghton, and support his candidature at the Shrewsbury Royal Infirmary.

Perhaps his tendency to mood swings and melancholy were accentuated in the years following these testimonies. It's hard to say now whether this was from post-traumatic stress disorder or the dislocation of everyone's lives following the war.

Paul pined in a letter to his father: 'Today [25 January 1947] is cold and snowy, wretched weather that recalls by contrast the southern Mediterranean shores. There the mimosa bushes are in bud and the almond trees about to blossom. How I should like to take you to the warmer climes and search out the ancient monuments together...'[289]

A difficult senior in Shrewsbury added workplace bullying, casting ever longer shadows over employment. Paul confessed privately to his father, 'These five years of war were endless in retrospect, "leeway" I shall never make up.' His hope of a surgical career was now a drifting ship nearing angry rocks, and he told Albert: 'As the months pass, I wonder where I can best use my one talent... Life is short and zeal fades and finishes and too soon it is too late.'[290]

Also he longed to share the wartime 'fellowship of suffering' with his cousin Tony Houghton, who had survived the terrors of parachuting into Holland trying to capture the 'bridge too far' at Arnhem. Brother John could never bridge the gulf to those who had seen action. 'When I have a weekend, Dad,' wrote Paul, 'we must have Tony down to Lingfield.'

Life had become like fighting to find his key to escape the dungeon of Doubting Castle. Maybe Giant Despair could be clobbered again somehow – if only one knew how. So, Paul concluded: 'One may commit one's way to the Lord and in patience possess one's mind in peace; in the meantime learning to labour and to wait.'[291]

He was out of the navy and out of proper work – more 'at sea' than ever. Suddenly a magical missile hit him amidships.

---

289. PWH, letter, 25 January 1947, to Albert Houghton from 1 Council House Court, Shrewsbury.
290. Ibid.
291. Ibid.

CHAPTER THIRTY-FOUR

Moored Alongside

1946-47

> Shall I compare thee to a summer's day?
> Thou art more lovely and more temperate:
> Rough winds do shake the darling buds of May...
>
> *William Shakespeare (1564-1616), 'Sonnet 18'*[292]

After the war's end, Wren officer Jean Swift, twenty-four, was enjoying herself with the navy. She jumped at the chance when some naval friends asked her to help sail two captured German yachts along the coast from Portsmouth.

Out in the English Channel, a stiff onshore wind sprang up, bringing the sailor's dread – the threat of being blown onto a lee shore. Furthermore, the rigging of these pre-war beauties was rotten. Hoisting more sail – to try to claw off the beach – was met with the snapping of ropes and shredded sails. By now, with the breakers roaring on the beach, an officer ordered Jean to let go the anchor. Up forward in the bows she watched the chain rushing out and remembered no one had

---

292. William Shakespeare (1564-1616), 'Sonnet 18', www.poetryfoundation.org/poems/45087/sonnet-18-shall-i-compare-thee-to-a-summers-day (accessed 22.11.24).

checked whether it was tied on at its other end. Instinctively she dived at the racing snake with her hands. One hand got yanked into the steel hawse pipe and, pulling back, she saw the bloody mess of her finger.

The anchor held, giving companions time to hustle Jean below for a temporary dressing. Once back ashore, a naval doctor sent her north by train to the Home Farm.

Her parents, Harry and Alice ('Pod and Morny' in the family) were delighted to have more children at home. Jean was pleased to be with her beloved 'Twinny' John, convalescing from his leg wound and leading his little niece, Jennifer, on important 'work', like checking which rabbit holes were inhabited. Pod drove Jean to Shrewsbury Hospital where the Casualty doctor was called.

Jean's heart fluttered as she saw this 6ft2in dark-haired man approaching in a white coat. Taking her injured hand, she noticed his blue eyes, and then 'Mr P.W. Houghton' on his lapel. 'Better put my feelings aside,' she told herself, 'because this must be the obstetrician who attended Muff – and he is married.'

As an opening gambit Mr P.W. Houghton remarked, 'I see you have naval buttons – where were you stationed?'

A few days later Alice and Harry invited 'Dr Houghton' for tea, to thank him for caring for their two daughters. But when Muff arrived, she deduced that this was not Dr John Houghton who had attended her, but his brother, Paul. More invitations for tea arrived to check the patient's finger and unwind from duties in the peerless countryside – why not?

One warm afternoon, Paul and Jean took their tea down the grassy lane from the old redbrick farm and sat on the bank gazing down the rows of mown grass and away towards the Welsh hills. He was, he realised, sitting in the very Welsh Marches of his dreams. The smell of sun-baked hay hung sweet, and the bumblebees droned among the hedgerow flowers.

Suddenly Jean heard, 'Shall we get moored alongside?'

'Moored . . . ? To what and why?' she wondered. 'Or who?' Suddenly the penny dropped!

With the engagement fixed, the fridge door well and truly fell off the cold storage room, and Paul's long frozen feelings tumbled out in a torrent of love letters which were repaid. They enjoyed silly rhymes and nicknames which would last for more than sixty years in the form of 'Beakle' or 'Beaky' which came forth in everyday life.

Paul's heart for spiritual matters was widening. He began to distance himself from the Brethren, though they would forever retain a tender place inside. He got to know the Bishop of Shrewsbury, who privately confirmed him into the Anglican Church; so now he could take Holy Communion with his fiancée.

They were to be married by the Bishop himself on 27 September 1947 in her local church at Leighton. A sunny day dawned and the three surviving parents of the bride and groom, her three siblings and guests gathered in church as Paul waited at the front with his best man . . . and they waited and waited. Forty-five minutes later the flustered prelate dashed up the aisle with the organ beginning – just ahead of the bride on the arm of her father. The Bishop had gone to the other village in Shropshire with the same name.

As the happy couple walked out of the church door into sunshine, Paul – no doubt still fuming – brushed past the verger who whispered, 'Cheer up, sir, it's only for life.'

Neither of them had money so, for a honeymoon, Peter leant them his wagonette with a pony in the shafts, and they set off west into that 'never-never land' of Paul's dreams. It began to dawn on the 'towny' that his new wife really did know a lot about 'four-legged beasts'. This knowledge had emerged rather late – in fact, at the wedding reception – where yeoman farmers extolled the bride's escapades in the saddle – including a foxhunt that had carried her for forty miles.

Stopping the wagonette in sleepy Clun, Jean instructed Paul to stay at the pony's head while she bought groceries. On return she found her husband had wandered off to examine the local church and the pony and all their belongings had wandered off towards home.

In Shrewsbury, before they were married, Paul's unhappy relationship with his senior – along with a disturbing clinical investigation and his nightmares about unemployment – continued. Jean's first courtship letter is revealing:

The Home Farm,
Leighton,
Shrewsbury,
Tel. Cresage 50

May 1947

Paul Darling,

This is just a note to try to cheer you up on Saturday after you will have heard the great decision. Whatever it is, I pray that you will be happy whether you stay here or go somewhere else – please God, make it here. But one thing is certain, Paul, and that is that whatever you do, you will make a great deal of good out of it; other people know that too and therefore they are jealous. Don't, please don't let them hurt you; it is hard, though, isn't it, not to be hurt, especially when you are convinced that it is not just.

There is another thing that is certain too, darling, and that is that wherever you go and whatever you do, my heart will be there with you, if nothing else of me can be; it is going to be very hard to try to keep any interests in Shropshire if you are not here. Something good seems to come from most things, and I'm sure that there is so much good to come for you – you were not put on this earth to be long unsettled or sad, and soon these troubles must pass darling, they *will* pass.

It is a heavenly evening and the birds are singing; how lovely it would be if we were together now – it is such fun to share the things one loves and enjoys with somebody who has the same feelings. It makes them doubly good and the bad things half as bad – all the little things become such fun – climbing mountains, walking, playing with boats; pouring out our troubles and just doing nothing by the fire, watching the coloured counties and having the larks in the sky on Sundays; do you remember Bredon in 'The Shropshire Lad'? If not, look it up!

> In summertime on Bredon
> The bells they sound so clear;
> Round both the shires they ring them
> In steeples far and near,
> A happy noise to hear.
> Here of a Sunday morning
> My love and I would lie,
> And see the coloured counties,
> And hear the larks so high
> About us in the sky.[293]

---

293. AE Housman, Bredon Hill, www.britainexpress.com/counties/worcestershire/az/bredon-hill.htm (accessed 1 February 2022).

No doubt Paul did not look it up because he knew it already and Jean continues in words that were prophetic:

> There are so many good things in the world, and yet the bad things sometimes manage to shadow them, but the shadows cannot last forever, and for you they certainly will not – you have far too much of all that is good for that to happen.
> Good night, Darling; God bless you and make you happy always.
>
> With very much love,
> Your
> Jean XX
>
> PS. Please let me know their Lordships' decision quickly, and please, we must see each other soon, and then we can laugh! And one more thing, please forgive this horrid green ink.

All that sunny personality in Jean, her love and faith, devotion and adventure would be tested but, time and again, it would balance out the mercurial mood swings of her husband.

Little did they know as Jean wrote the letter, that the 'Bredon Hill country' beckoned.

CHAPTER THIRTY-FIVE

Work

1947 and after

Judging by my early memories at home, I am now sure that my dad was suffering from PTSD into the late 1960s. Mood swings and feelings of deep darkness, flashbacks to horrific events and outbursts of temper characterise this condition.

Yet, the new NHS brought hope bursting in when suddenly the possibility presented of working in Worcester. So, with Jean in the car, they travelled south down the River Severn, the age-old border where England blends into Wales.

To Paul's delight, he was appointed as a new consultant at Worcester Royal Infirmary in the fledgling NHS of 1948. There were two main hospitals that could not be more different. The grand old eighteenth-century infirmary stood half a mile from the cathedral with its own charming chapel. There the doctors' trade union, the British Medical Association, the BMA, had been founded in 1832 in the midst of a cholera epidemic.

The BMA had opposed the formation of the NHS, fearing it would eat into their wallets. Before the arrival of the NHS, surgeons were appointed to Worcester Royal Infirmary in a purely honorary, unpaid capacity. Places were keenly contested, and it was a great honour to be chosen. Paul joined eminent surgeon Mr George Marshall, who said later:

I suppose doctors today would think we were absolutely mad to take on all this extremely demanding surgical work and be paid nothing at all for it. There was no salary, so it was essential to be in general practice as well to make money to live.[294]

The advent of the NHS was like day after night. Everyone got treated without cost to them, which relieved the worry for the doctor treating the poor. Even better, the medical staff got paid! Paul set to work on a starting salary of £1,500 a year (about £69,000 in 2023).

A couple of miles away, and up the hill on the edge of the city, was a prefab hospital constructed from American kindness during the war. It was rows of ground floor wards laid out on the 'Nightingale' pattern, with beds down each side the ward. All the wards were connected by a central corridor. Paul loved it. As kids, that corridor seemed to reach to infinity; our wonder doubled when Dad and another consultant, Mr Hamish Chalmers, challenged each other to a race one Christmas day. Soon they were off – white coats flying and sending alarmed dinner ladies pressing themselves flat against the wall. Designed to last ten years, the hospital served thousands till the late twentieth century.

Paul found a friendly, well-run establishment and – with one, perhaps two, exceptions – was to enjoy his consultant colleagues for the next thirty years. Gone was the snobbery he encountered in Shrewsbury and – most important – work could flourish along with great fun night and day.

Now firmly in the land of 'fairy tale thatched cottages and fairy haunted woods', Jean and Paul took a bank loan for a

---

294. Miriam Harvey, SRN, *Tales from Worcester Royal Infirmary* (Malvern: Aspect Design, 2012).

tiny, thatched cottage at Severn Stoke, a few miles south down the river. The loan was repaid within a year.

On the wards, Paul took time and trouble to coach his junior assistants and lectured the nurses in training. Dr Bruce Roscoe was one of his house surgeons, fresh out of medical school: 'I have to say he was extremely kind to me and furthered my career considerably. We got on extremely well – but in a slightly wicked sort of way. He was a lovely warm man – but he used to lose his temper quite quickly. Of course, if he didn't like you – you were doomed. To the horror of the operating theatre, he sacked a surgical registrar right there in theatre – the chap deserved it but, yes, he was fired, and Paul said, "I don't want to ever see your face in here again." He wouldn't survive today, would he! That was the worst instance of him losing his temper – and he always had a good reason for it. People were extremely fond of him.' [295]

Paul read medicine avidly, often coming home and falling asleep feet up on the sofa with the *BMJ* (*British Medical Journal*) over his eyes. Roscoe recounts how:

> He had read somewhere about a description of piles [haemorrhoids] called 'jumping piles'. So he got his team to ask any patient with piles if they jumped. And then they were given a score for 'research' according to their answer. A junior doctor said it wasn't really research but great fun. Paul would come into the consulting room from next door saying, 'I found another case of jumping piles – most enlightening.'
>
> Concerning research, he once quipped: 'My only contribution to furthering medical science is discovering that men swim faster when the sea is on fire.'

---

295. Interview with Dr Bruce Roscoe, Paul's anaesthetist in Worcester, by the author, 24 August 2020.

His pastoral care approach was unique. A colleague remembers being called into his office to be asked, 'Are you going to marry Dr -------?'

'Well... well, yes, sir. We are engaged and the wedding is in about a month's time.'

'I don't think you should. That's all. You can go.' It was that blunt. And of course, he was right. The marriage lasted a few years. How did he know? He based it on incompatibility. He had the guts to say these things.

The recent war was never far away, and Paul used to get very emotional about it. He delighted in an outstanding anaesthetist called Freddy Park. Freddy had been a prisoner of the Japanese on the infamous Burma-Siam railway, highlighted in the film *Bridge on the River Kwai*. He hardly spoke about his experiences of starvation and slave labour, but he and Paul were very close. Paul could even pull his leg gently with a suggestion to buy a Japanese car because his British Triumph was going wrong. While Jean declared firmly that we British should reach out to the Germans in friendship and peace, Paul brooded and felt less willing until the latter years of his life.

Paul was unusual in his readiness to talk openly about the Second World War. And I think that, along with his skills as a raconteur, detoxified much of its horror. In Sinton Green, the village where they later came to, lived a godly man who had been with the Chindits under Orde Wingate in the jungle against the Japanese. He and my father would discuss the ethics of flushing the enemy out of their dugouts with flamethrowers and whether to shoot them, or not, as they emerged. But if a man came out holding up hands full of grenades, one had little option. Yet sensitive men could be tormented by these memories. Paul would move the conversation to the cross of Christ where mercy and justice deal with all past deeds.

The marvellous Sister Pullen was running Paul's surgical ward at Ronkswood Hospital. They were swapping stories one day on the ward, and she told him how she had been torpedoed twice in the Atlantic. To their mutual astonishment, Sister revealed she was rescued – not once but twice – by Paul's own ship, when he was aboard. (Probably his destroyer, HMS *Zulu*.)

In the 1960s, George Blundell, living nearby in Warwickshire, phoned Paul to say one of their old shipmates, Commander Archdale, had found the Italian pilot who dropped the torpedo that struck the *Nelson*! What ensued was incredible:

CHAPTER THIRTY-SIX

A Reunion of Enemies

In Paul's Words

As a boy, I remember my father coming home from a social night in London, fizzing with a story that astounded us:

HMS *Nelson* was struck by an aerial torpedo delivered by a squadron of Italian planes off Sicily in November 1941. The planes flew low through an intense barrage. The torpedo struck the ship on the port side forward of A Turret blowing a hole 40 feet x 20 feet and weakening the ship's hull on the starboard side.

Archdale was a cultured man and knew everybody in high places while he was working in Italy in the 1950s. There he had traced the Italian airman through their Ministry of Marine to discover that the airman had continued fighting with German forces after the Italian capitulation and that he fled to the Argentine after the Allied victory, lest he be imprisoned. Archdale persevered and got him a free pardon, with a job back in Bologna airport. Then, Archdale suggested that Blundell and I should invite him to London and hear his story.

We entertained him at Brown's hotel and had dinner, together with his Austrian wife. We were soon on easy terms despite a language problem. We guessed he was not less than forty years of age, and a little care-worn but very much at ease with us.

He explained that he led a flight of three torpedo planes and decided that, attacking at sea level made it hard for our guns – to depress their barrels low enough. He got through but two planes and their crew were lost. At this point he became quite distressed.

My place in the ship was in the forward dressing station. The ship had just altered course to the North through an intense barrage when the torpedo hit. There was a tremendous crash. She lifted in the water, shook like a dog, rang like a deep bell, and settled low in the water.

After dinner, George Blundell produced a hefty fragment of the torpedo. The Italian glanced at it and wrote down the number on the fragment, and they matched his records. The torpedo was made in England! Britain had sold such weapons to Italy before the war.

Then Archdale brought us to his flat and George showed a 'movie' of the aerial attack that he had taken himself at the time. The Italian squadron of three planes came down through a ferocious defence, the sea was boiling with falling explosive. He recognised his own plane, stood up in horror, saluted and burst into tears as he watched his wingman go to his death.

And he added a final touch, round the supper table to us family:

Then – to our amazement – the Italian said he had used his on-board movie camera, fitted to all warplanes to confirm claims of successful kills. He showed this film at the meeting. We watched the *Nelson* getting larger and larger.

The episode of this dinner party was quite extraordinary. We reflected later how mortal enemies could be such good companions.[296]

---

296. PWH, *A Reunion of Enemies*, handwritten in March 2001.

CHAPTER THIRTY-SEVEN

More Work

What made Paul a good surgeon? I asked Dr Bruce Roscoe, who watched him operate over many years:

> He made decisions very rapidly, and he was usually right. He had good clinical acumen. Like a good businessman, he could decide and carry it out even if he suspected it might be wrong.
> And he wouldn't fiddle around like some surgeons I watched. He took a scalpel and made his incision, and it would always be just in the right place. He worked hard and if the surgical list was going on until midnight – you went on until midnight.[297]

His theatre sister in Worcester told me, 'You'd better look out when the patient was haemorrhaging as Mr Houghton elbowed his way through the huddle of nurses and doctors, scattering trays of instruments, to get to work. And he could throw an instrument on the floor saying he would not need that – only to find a little later it was essential for his operation. In spite of this his sense of humour always shone through and he was popular.'[298]

---

297. Interview with Dr Bruce Roscoe, Paul's anaesthetist by the author, 24 August 2020.
298. Harvey, SRN, *Tales from Worcester Royal Infirmary*.

Another nurse watched when, 'He noticed the operating theatre clock was running slow. "Get it put right, please, Sister," came the order. A week later and dog tired, it was still running slow, so he strode up to it, took it off the wall and threw it out of the open window.'

As his son, I joined my dad in theatre twice and it was the sense of fun in the team that stood out. Failing to find the femoral pulse before a planned amputation – the patient was already asleep – he burst out in a mock panic, 'Sister, do you know I can't find a pulse? What are we going to do?'

In the early days, he did most of the emergency and night work because he had no registrar. GPs knew that he would go out at midnight on a 'domiciliary' to quite distant parts of Worcestershire. Then came the wait while the ambulance got the patient to hospital. He would follow it in, perhaps operating until breakfast, before doing the routine day's work.

The 1960s were an exciting time for technical advances. One day, Paul and his team were experimenting with the miracle of a flexible tube that could see round corners – the fibre optic endoscope. Paul poked it into a woman's colostomy opening from her abdomen. 'What can you see, sir?' asked the registrar, breathless with anticipation.

'I can see a magpie!' The instrument had gone right through, and out of her back passage so the bird was visible beyond the window.

'Bruce,' he said to Roscoe one day. 'I will give you a tip about domiciliaries. When you are in a patient's house, and you see something you like, you always want to admire it – pick it up and look at it. The chances are when they die, they'll give it to you.' One lady had an old carriage clock with a button on top. Paul would press the button for the joy of hearing it chime. The grateful patient gave it to him – no wonder our mum would wring her hands at the clutter collecting round the house – much of it picked up through nosing around in antique shops. But, she added, 'I think these distractions help lighten his load.'

Consultant colleague Dr Nick Dyer, who Paul greatly liked and respected, commented, 'Paul was unusual because I noticed that most surgeons lost their edge in their mid-to-late fifties. But Paul didn't; his decision-making, hard work and surgical dexterity remained sharp until he left the health service at sixty-six.'[299]

As a Christian in the workplace, Paul was reticent to talk about his faith with colleagues. He had a horror of being like one local doctor, notorious as a 'good Christian but a bad doctor'. Yet, Roscoe noticed, 'You were left in no doubt that he was a committed Christian. He would pray briefly and unobtrusively before each operation. But you wouldn't make a joke about religion in front of him or tell risqué stories in the operating theatre.

'He could be quite rude about the higher clergy in the Church of England who appeared to renege on their beliefs. He formed opinions about people very quickly – not always correct ones – yet these weaknesses were very endearing.'[300] Privately he waged theological war by letter, challenging more than one Bishop of Worcester to live up to his calling; while his good name with patients rose and rose.

But it was the chest physician Dr Edgar Moyes whose 'quarter of a century of unclouded friendship' meant most to Paul among those he admired in Worcester. 'If only I had Edgar's energy,' Paul would groan to Jean after a 'working day' as long as two for most people. And it was Paul they called on

---

299. Dr Nick Dyer, conversation with the author about 1979.
300. Interview with Dr Bruce Roscoe, Paul Houghton's anaesthetist in Worcester, by the author, 24 August 2020.

to speak at Moyes' memorial service when he tragically died of lung cancer in 1974:

> He came to Worcester in 1952 and in the next five years... tuberculosis was conquered and Moyes brought in the new compounds defeating that Captain of the Men of Death.
> The fountain of his buoyancy flowed from his nature, but another tributary sprung from his home. The matchless affinity between Hester and Edgar is almost legendary, there is no scale to measure the loss.
> Perhaps this was the wellhead of his great compassion for all who were distressed . . . And his unlimited time for others. With this went his wisdom and good sense. His clear mind and high principles dispelled the mists of perplexity for peoples' personal problems.
> As his life ebbed away, he came to me deeply troubled about the future of his profession, as he had to contemplate the desecration of the service he had done so much to develop, by that venomous and bitter woman in the Ministry of Health.
> Sleep – to wake! Few men have done more for their fellow men ... few done more for the City of God, denying not one instant's toil ... So instinctively last Monday his family brought Edgar back to the security of the Church and found awaiting him all the love of the Redeemer of the World.[301]

Everyone seems to have a story to tell of Paul. Dr Rick Thomas, another of his junior house surgeons, remembers tearing up

---

301. 'In memoriam, A service of remembrance and thanksgiving Edgar Napier Moyes, the cathedral church of Christ and the Blessed Virgin Mary, Worcester, 2nd May 1975 with address by PW Houghton FRCS'. The Lancet and BMJ published Moyes' obituary by PWH, May 1975.

the long corridor at midnight with a patient on the trolley who was entering into the fun. One doctor sat on the front, whooping it up as the stagecoach driver, with the patient and the other doctor shouting encouragement from the rear. Suddenly the fearsome Night Sister stepped into the passage from one of the wards, screeched at the 'coach' to halt and gave the drivers a verbal blast they would never forget.

The next day they slunk about wounded until Paul put his head close to Rick's ear and whispered, 'Good job in the corridor last night.'

'Yet,' adds Rick, 'you knew, though he was a maverick and a legend, that he was a Christian without him saying it: because of his care and compassion for patients and his commitment to maintain hope.'

Concerning hope, he was ahead of his time in being honest with patients when the outlook was bleak. On occasions, as with the Sisters at Stanbrook Abbey south of Worcester, he could discuss openly the guarantee of eternal life in Paradise that Christ keeps for anyone who puts their faith in him. The Mother Abbess became a friend, shared devotional books with Paul, and became a well of spiritual water he could visit during domiciliary rounds. Well-thumbed classics like *Palgrave's Golden Treasury*[302] of Christian readings lay in his car's glove pocket for quiet laybys when out on the road.

I noticed my father was apt to admire colleagues as better people than himself whether they shared his faith or not. 'Surely he does the work of our Saviour too, with such tender care,' he murmured, as we drove away from the Worcester Royal Infirmary one day.

---

302. Francis Turner Palgrave, *The Golden Treasury of English Songs and Lyrics*, first published in 1861, see also www.goodreads.com/book/show/1237210.Golden_Treasury (accessed 22.11.24).

He would not pass judgement on a colleague he knew was gay. Not that he saw gay activity as good, since he saw from the Bible that God did not design his masterpiece to function that way. Yet he strove to maintain Christ's unconditional love and interest in those who differed from him.

Paul had a succession of Indian and Pakistani registrars who, once trained, could relieve him of some night work and delighted him by their company. Roscoe says:

> He was a bit like Napoleon with his generals who said, 'I don't want good generals I want lucky ones.' He would say that he was not a good surgeon but a lucky one – which of course he wasn't – he was extremely skillful, very good indeed. What Paul meant was that he wanted to hone the surgeons with the gift of 'knowing what to do,' and acting on it.

Several Asian doctors brought their families to our home and cooked fiery curries, an alarming experience for us children. Mr Ahmad FRCS fascinated my father because he had gone on to become professor of surgery in a remote part of the North West Frontier region of Pakistan. In 2022, I had an unexpected letter from Dr Sajad Ahmad a GP in South Wales:

> My father never tired, all his life, of talking about his time in Ronkswood Hospital. He absolutely adored your father; I grew up with stories of how highly he regarded him and I have often tried to Google and find out more.
>
> My father, Mr Riaz Ahmad, was Mr Houghton's surgical registrar in Ronkswood Hospital. I was born in Ronkswood. Sadly, my dad passed away in 2006 quite suddenly in Pakistan.

About the curry! Yes, I remember this . . . and being a religious person myself I am eagerly waiting to meet my father one day and hear all about what it was like.

There was the story of my dad attempting my own religious circumcision and then doing an incomplete job, probably because he was scared, only to have help from your father who then took over and completed the procedure – and being told 'never operate on one whom you love'.

Yes, my father trained thousands of surgeons, and many would have heard of his stories from Worcester as the Head of Surgery at Khyber Medical College.

In retirement, Professor Ahmad had rung my father from the Hindu Kush, pressing him to come out with my mother for a visit. Paul and Jean were very much tempted by this kindness, but just didn't quite have the strength, he being well into his eighties.

In his heyday, Paul's juniors chided him to slow down or he would have a heart attack. Sure enough, chest pain set in when, as was his habit, he was walking two miles uphill from the Royal Infirmary to Ronkswood Hospital. Realising he was having a heart attack, he walked straight into Casualty, lay down on a couch and told a nervous junior doctor the diagnosis.

'Well, sir,' she responded, 'I will just examine your heart,' and began to undo Paul's waistcoat buttons. Immediately, the chest pain disappeared, and Paul exclaimed, 'You know! I think it's that tight button causing the pain.' And it was – so, roaring with laughter, he strode off to work. Apart from some atrial fibrillation, that heart kept ticking for another half-century.

With a love for practical jokes, Paul presented Miss Hulme (Matron) with a birthday cake covered in white icing, lovingly prepared. She received the gift with expressions of warm gratitude which turned into a different sort of warmth when she discovered Paul had got the X-ray girls to make it out of plaster of Paris.

Committee work was unavoidable, and Paul did his bit. When one interminable meeting dragged on, he began to study the faces round the table and liken them to his butterflies. Pieces of paper began circulating to friends present asking, 'Have you noticed the lovely Painted Lady over there?' Or, for a florid gentleman, 'We have a Red Admiral in the chair', and 'an Orange Tip' for some pointy spectacle frames.

Recognising the huge expense ahead from the new breed of hospital administrators in the 1960s, he took to the local newspapers to warn the public. As a schoolboy he told me one day that he had found an administrator in the corridor with a clipboard and asked, 'What are you doing?'

'A time and motion study to see how hard people work.'

'Not here you are not,' came the retort.

Another had parked in Paul's own place. 'So I pulled on the car door handle, which came off in my hand.'

'What did you do with it, Dad?'

'Oh, I threw it into the garden.'

It's not to excuse such behaviour, though we loved these stories as kids, but he would not have done this a few years later. 'Triggers of PTSD dysfunctional behaviour can fire off chaotic responses in the fight-or-flight sympathetic nervous system.' [303]

There was always the humour to fall back on. When The Beatles and long hair came along, an administrator parking in Paul's hospital space found his face at the window saying, 'Excuse me, *miss*, would you mind moving your car?'

---

303. Dr Rhona Knight, *The Ripple Effect: Vicarious Trauma and Vicarious Resilience*, CMF National Conference lecture, April 2024.

Far-seeing as ever, he would be unsurprised to hear, as I write, that his old medical school Barts has had doctors in a fury because senior managers get 'sleeping pods and wellbeing rooms' while doctors get plastic chairs to recover in.[304]

---

304. Lizzie Roberts, 'Doctors furious at NHS bosses' TikTok video showing off gleaming offices Clip by Barts Health, which boasts of having a £1,000 coffee maker, sparks anger from front-line staff working in poor conditions', *The Daily Telegraph*, 11 October 2022.

CHAPTER THIRTY-EIGHT

Worcestershire

Had I been Norman William possessing for my goods,
Fairy tale thatched cottages, and fairy haunted woods,
I would have spent my days, far from battle frays,
Drinking sweet apple cider, at the inn of The Four
Cross Ways.

Quoted by Paul, source unknown

Clifton, where their first home lay, was a hamlet with two farms and two or three houses. Cleve Cottage survived from medieval times – a frame of oak timbers slung between two curved 'crucks' or tree trunks at each end of the house, curved in to join at the top. Between the timber frames was 'wattle and daub', good red mud and straw to keep out wind and rain. Paul taught Sunday school at St Denys Church, Severn Stoke with his old school friend Rev Wilfred Miller.

No one told them – until after they moved in – about the sagging hollow in the thatched roof. To their alarm they heard that this showed where a very large occupant had been removed by boat that was floating at roof level during one of the Severn's floods. 'Neverr moind,' growled a neighbour, 'that medieval flood baa-nk 'olds most of them waaters back – but ya' never knows.' On winter nights, when the river had spread like an inland sea, Jean and Paul could hear it lapping on the brim of the bank *above* their bedroom.

The cottage had a well and no electricity, but to their delight it came furnished with plentiful oil lamps and the basics. A wartime sofa was purchased and served them well for the next sixty years – so long as you had enough cushions in the right places.

Worcester Eye Hospital employed Jean part-time with her orthoptist skills. But to her surprise she discovered her husband had the idea that wives shouldn't work. So, 'I was determined not to be an unhappy housewife, and I began to keep the hens for meat and eggs and make the best of the damson trees.' Mr Gittins, local horse dealer (affectionately known as Old Git), valued her riding skills to exercise his sparky horses – one of which 'bolted' like an arrow across the Severn's river meadows, and was closing in fast on the roar of the weir. A plunge was only avoided by hauling on one rein with both hands to circle until horse and rider were exhausted.

And they had room for two pigs, on a government initiative. Jean, looking out of the bedroom window early one morning was diverted by two pink bodies running round the orchard. It was her husband, stark naked from his cold bath, in pursuit of an escaped pig.

A bumper crop of damsons granted Jean the chance to sell a ton of them in 1951; money she spent on a proper honeymoon to Ibiza by train to London Airport.

The cottage was tiny and always needing renovation somewhere. 'Never again a thatched roof,' Jean concluded, 'a bedroom for the mice.' Paul had watched Sir Winston Churchill bricklaying one day at Chartwell. So he bought himself a bricklaying pamphlet and set to work building a small bathroom to avoid going outside to the privy in all weathers. His particular joy was creating some stairs on a bend. In later years, we would look at his slapdash bricklaying and carpentry and wonder, 'How on earth can any patient survive?'

My sister, Pippa, was born 15 October 1952, at the cottage. She was christened Philippa but always known as Pippa – or Pippy. Their neighbours, Adam and Mary Letham, living on the next-door farm, had their firstborn, Margo, at about the same time, followed by Bruce, who was about my age. In later years that farm with its huge bulls, tennis court and grain silos was a place of endless adventures for us.

It was time to find a larger place for the family, and Paul's shipmate, Lt Commander Geoffrey Bullock, a local auctioneer, found a broken-down smallholding called Yardway just off Sinton Green. The village was a scattering of cottages, a pub and some council houses around the green. Going West was a lane, sunk 10ft deep by centuries of cart wheels leading to the brow of a little hill where Yardway sat back from the road. Geoffrey and his (rather commanding) wife, Joan – also ex-Royal Navy – were living nearby.

Paul and Jean went looking and found a redbrick house, of the early nineteenth century, with a magnificent view to the Malvern Hills from a small rise. Their hearts leapt, especially when they saw an old, tarred barn, boarded with waney elm, and a redbrick double stable with a hay loft. There was no running water or electricity, an overgrown garden and much to be done. Fields both sides of the lane made up eleven acres, ample for a few ponies and hens.

Geoffrey Bullock did the bidding and went to £2,500, because as he knew, 'You just can't beat this position.' Again the bank loan was paid off within a couple of years. Yet Paul continued to feel financially insecure which, combined with his devotion to the patients, helped drive his work ethic to dangerous levels. Jean got used to him returning from work almost too tired to eat. She prepared a flask of hot milky coffee and sandwiches round the fireside.

When I was a little boy, he would come to read to me in bed, sat on the floor with his back to the bed until both of us were sleepy. Before that he usually knelt down with us to say the Lord's Prayer or read a few verses of a psalm in the King James Version – oddly comforting and confusing at the same time. In a frosty winter, the iron bedroom windows helped fern patterns of ice crystals grow on the glass.

A favourite story was Admiral Nelson in the Ladybird book.[305] Could we ever do what he did in this picture, Dad and I wondered? Sword in hand, Nelson is on the rails of a Spanish ship, about to leap into a forest of enemy cutlasses and spears. Probably not, I decided.

Dad's Saturdays and Sundays 'off duty' involved popping in for a quick ward round to check his sicker patients. 'Surgery is like war,' he said. 'Eternal vigilance is essential.' Pippy and I came on Sunday mornings for proper strong orange squash from doting nurses – not like the weak stuff from Mummy made with wartime economy. Then he took us to Shrubhill station to watch the steam engines. Years later, I had an interview to do medicine at Birmingham Medical School. A professor sneered, 'I see you like fly fishing. No doubt, being the son of a consultant, you can afford not to tie your own flies.'

'Well, sir, my parents never made that obvious to me.' They offered me a place.

I was born three years after Pippa in September 1955, when Dad was already forty-four. But he aged well and I comforted myself through school that he never looked much older than Mum, ten years younger, but greying younger. When the

---

305. *The Story of Nelson (An Adventure from History)* (Loughborough: Wills & Hepworth; Early Edition, 1957).

midwife had delivered me, she rang round to tell my father that he had a son. He dashed down to have a look but was barred entry by the senior midwife. Mummy, lying exhausted on the couch, overheard a terrific row behind the door, which could only have one outcome – and he soon came striding in.

Disaster struck when I was only thirteen months old and beginning to crawl. Unseen by either Geoffrey Bullock's wife, Joan, nor Mummy, I crawled out of the kitchen onto the drive as Joan backed the car – right over me. In the ensuing panic, the teenage home help, Susie, soon to be married to David Moule, a farmer from Sinton Green, took charge and somehow got me into Worcester Royal Infirmary, where they examined a squashed left leg in Casualty. The paediatrician called my father, and I joined the Children's Ward. Long years later, as a junior doctor there, I dug out my file (not recommended) with the laconic entry: 'Fracture of the femur and tibia. Six weeks traction.'

Once again, as with the war memories, it was a trauma that both parents talked over openly – which I think helped detoxify their pain. 'You were so small, I can't think how the wheel did not roll over all of you,' he told me in my twenties.

Give sorrow words. The grief that does not speak
Whispers the o'erfraught heart and bids it break.[306]

However, both parents were troubled when I developed disabling back pain in my thirties that persisted over the rest of their lives. My father did the orthopaedics in his early days at Worcester and treasured anonymous letters that came from two patients every Christmas:

---

306. William Shakespeare (1564-1616), *Macbeth*, Act IV, Scene III, when Malcolm speaks to MacDuff, who has just been informed that his wife and all his children have been slaughtered and evidently stands speechless trying to take it in, www.folger.edu/explore/shakespeares-works/macbeth/read/4/3/ (accessed 25.11.24).

27.5.80,

Dear Mr Houghton,

Approximately twenty-one years ago you did a laminectomy for me. Just in case you have the misfortune to be like me and only remember your failures, spare a thought if you feel depressed, for the thousands of people who have benefited from your skill.

My back has not given me the slightest problem since you operated. I don't want you to waste your valuable time in an acknowledgement so will remain.

Anon

Watching me struggle in pain as a GP with a growing family, he applied his skills in spinal manipulation – no doubt praying under his breath. Improvements didn't last and it challenged his faith. He died a year before he could witness a remarkable miracle in 2010. It happened to me by the simple laying on of hands and praying in the name of Jesus at a church in Sheffield. Anyway – he's witnessing it now from Paradise!

Yardway proved a brilliant buy. Like homing pigeons Pippa and I, and later my wife, Esther, and our children Celia, Dan and Fiona, flocked back, never failing to find delights in the funny old house, its timeless buildings and the patchwork of meadows and woods. Inside, pastoral prints and watercolours hung on the walls, and the old dining room with its huge fireplace – never lit because it smoked – was watched over by the dark oil painting of Dad in naval uniform. We kids pitied other children who didn't have a stable and an old barn of reclaimed ship's timbers, with rats and a terrier and cobwebs and hay bales to make houses and the lurking dread of Injuns' arrows in Monkwood that could transfix one's cowboy hat.

First they got a water pump installed in the well and mains electricity laid on. The hens and geese didn't last long because it was too painful to slaughter them. There was a rough division of labour: 'Jean, you will make the tennis court.'
'Really?' she queried. 'That ground is covered in old plum trees.'
'Yes, and I have bought you a wheelbarrow.' Mummy managed it with seventeen wheelbarrow loads a day while Pippa watched from her pram. Curved rose beds appeared and a fine grass court (with mossy patches to catch out your opponent). How I loved – all my life – to lie on that lawn, watching the clouds sailing above the apple branches and wonder why the chimney did not tumble, while the clouds stayed still.

Dad installed himself in the 'study' lined by growing cabinets of books, from the Saxon Charters to the great twentieth-century wars, with literature, love, Christianity and adventure in-between.

Among my earliest memories are watching, from my bedroom window, my dad striding across the gravel drive waving a small cricket bat, which I still have, his present from a visit to his old father and Lucy in Lingfield. Beyond him I can see the red stable roof, painted in yellow ochre streaks by lichen. Climbing roses frame my bedroom window and white clouds sail over the caerulean sky.

At weekends he got into his old naval jumper and laid into hedges with a billhook until the sweat poured off. The same approach prevailed in whitewashing the house, making Mum throw up her hands: 'Oh, Paul! It will take me hours to get that paint off the windows.'

The farm pond for the working animals was in our kitchen garden – a bog of rushes, moorhens and stagnant water. I can just remember Pippa and me riding in the hay cart behind Kitty, the carthorse from George Knight's farm next door. She had a docked tail. We were at the very tail-end of a way of farming husbandry that stretched back unchanged for centuries.

There in the pond, our father got to work, digging out a sizeable pool. He shored up the walls with a homemade concrete and there we swam in green water with frogs and newts, watched by amazed ponies. In the fierce winter of 1963, Mummy, an elegant skater, fixed some skates on a pair of old policeman's boots and tried to get Dad onto the ice . . . hopeless.

Beside the pond was a pollarded willow tree with three vertical trunks – ideal as my three-masted ship on which I sailed the oceans when the breeze blew, creaking most realistically. With a stay-at-home mum and the home-help, Glenys, to tease, life was very heaven before school at four. Mummy would summon us for meals from far and wide, on her boson's pipe, kept from the navy.

Children's parties went well with the pond, though I was always embarrassed our water was green and other swimming pools were clear. On the rare occasions when Dad did get home in time for my party, there was wild outdoor chasing and water fights with ear syringes he handed out. One of my girlfriends laughed till she had an asthma attack, upon which Dad commanded calm as we all goggled at her.

After work Paul's relaxation was a brisk walk in the lanes, often taking a child or two in hand. As we approached Monkwood, verses would bubble out:

There was once a road through the woods . . .
Of a summer evening late,
When the night-air cools on the trout-ringed pools
Where the otter whistles his mate . . . [307]

---

307. Rudyard Kipling (1865-1936), 'The Way Through the Woods', in *Rewards and Fairies* (New York: Doubleday, Page & Company, 1910). This poem is in the public domain, https://poets.org/poem/way-through-woods (accessed 31.10.24).

'Who wrote that, Dad?'

'Oh, Rudyard Kipling. He was a bit of a mystic.'

As a boy under twelve on a 'summer evening late', Dad escaped work and took me up the River Severn in our little boat, rowing through the warm air trapped under the willows – times I look back on with fondness.

Later, that boat was nearly the end of us when we were blown out to sea in South Wales.

Holidays with him had a habit of the unexpected. Sitting on Croyde Beach with our cousins the whole beach was diverted to see Uncle Pat White (Brian's brother) and Daddy swimming just beyond the breakers and waving their shorts in the air, laughing wildly. Dad loved all our cousins and did what he could for fatherless Jenny and her mum, Muff.

In the 1960s we visited Grandpa in Lingfield. Dad showed me the apple tree which his father had climbed to prune it. He had slipped and fallen but, shooting out a massive hand to a branch, was left dangling by one arm – reminding son Paul of an ape in the zoo. This provoked helpless laughter in Paul until inevitably Albert dropped.

History repeated itself. At Yardway we had a fair-sized elm tree in the kitchen garden leaning over the pond. My toy plane got stuck up the elm tree, so Dad fetched his long ladders, home to countless woodworm.

The first rung gave way – one of the higher ones. A chain reaction began where the descent accelerated as one rotten rung led to the next. 'Help Mark, ow! Help!'

I was unclear how to help, because his long body had got wedged between the two uprights like steel wedges in the shaft of an axe. I began to laugh and lay helpless on the ground with tears streaming down my face ... which repeat as I write.

Then the ladder began to rotate on one of its feet, threatening to pirouette father and ladder into the green water so I flung my body round the lower ladder and the fatal gyration was arrested.

Our parents taught us to garden and lay hedges, build fences, and outdoor carpentry. We learned when the hay was sweet and ready, and the delight of turning it on a summer's evening. Mummy and Uncle John made catapults for us from nut branches and showed us how to pull supper from tiny trout streams in Wales. And stern advice came from Mum to never ever leave wounded prey suffering – and never ever ever point your gun at someone.

My father began sex education round a bonfire in the old apple orchard. 'Mark, have you ever seen two animals mating?'

'No,' I lied.

'It's very interesting . . .' – my eyes widened at this worrying direction of travel.

'Is it?' And to my huge relief, there the matter rested.

But Yardway had a feature for my father which became a conflict area with Mum – the ponies. Having plenty of time, she decided to start breeding Welsh Mountain ponies 'so as not to be an unhappy wife'. These progressed to the larger Welsh cobs which we rode locally, and on which Pippa and Jean competed successfully.

Dad was in a double bind: emotionally he loved seeing his wife and children enjoying the dream he had won by the sweat of his brow. Yet if one walked into the house asking, 'Where is Mum?' then he might sigh in resignation, 'She is *doing* the ponies.' The hours of time and energy they consumed could infuriate him. I got wind of incidents where dinner was not even ready for invited guests, to his embarrassment. However, he got some relief from viewing it as a cross to bear and received – in later years – forgiving and humorous coping strategies, whispering sardonically in any sympathetic ear, 'Put no trust in the legs of a horse – it says so in the Bible.' In time, Mum realised the peril to their relationship and reined in her horsey hours.

Mum and Dad were popular in the neighbourhood and often invited to parties to which Dad usually felt too tired or shy to go. Once there, however, the problem was to get him away at the end – riveted in conversation, so long as it wasn't small talk.

Mysterious parcels began arriving when I was about ten, and they were opened with Dad announcing, 'We are going to do chemistry experiments,' hoping to grow a thirst for science which would lead to medicine later. He lined up glass jars of sulphuric acid and set fire to sodium which, as he said, was 'burning like a flare hanging over the Atlantic at night'. Bunsen burners, petri dishes, glass flasks and tubing were prepared, and he said, 'Now we have made hydrogen. Mark, light the end of the glass tubing with this match – it's quite safe because no air has got in.'

The explosion blew us backwards and brought Mum rushing in to pick glass fragments from around our eyes – miraculously undamaged.

Despite his horror of burns from the sea years, Dad's homemade gunpowder grew more exciting and sowed in us a thirst for higher technologies. My friend Rob and I began packing this mixture into metal containers when my parents were out. A faultless prototype rocket launch rose with aeronautical control that would have had the SpaceX team speechless with envy. We were ready for a demonstration before a parent.

'Uncle' Max was dragged out of his study. Max and Marjorie Holdsworth were great friends of my parents. The paint tin packed with gunpowder had the flaming match applied as before. The ensuing flash sent us boys reeling backwards. I peered anxiously through the smoke in case we had killed

Rob's father – revered by us as the Commander of the British Signals for the D-Day landings. He emerged nodding approval at this 'success'. Afterwards, at our secret debrief, Rob decided his father's sangfroid came from his First World War trench warfare – when ten out of twelve in his school class had died. (Max once told me his first experience of being shelled drove him to take off his helmet and try to get in it.)

To Mum's sorrow, Paul could never be persuaded to dance until a strange thing happened in Jerusalem in the 1980s. I got engaged to a lovely Swiss girl, Esther, when we were both working in the Nazareth Hospital. My parents came out to meet Esther, and we stayed at the Scottish Hospice just outside the walls of old Jerusalem. It was Burns Night, the one night of the year when the staid and steady Scottish expats became wildly transformed. Suddenly, in the middle of a careering Gay Gordon's dance, I saw my mother's eyes wide with surprise – it was her husband, flying up and down the hall in the arms of Esther.

1965 was the year my father splashed out on our first foreign holiday – to Corsica, which was amazing; except that my poor school report arrived on holiday. After that he began hanging over me and 'helping' when I was trying to do my homework, and it was a relief to get into Malvern College as a boarder in 1968 where I was free to find my own path.

Our relationship was helped by the discovery that I could score 'bull's eyes' with a rifle better than most. At last, I had something to excel at. Dad was delighted and, by fourteen, I had persuaded him to get me a sporting .22 rifle and six boxes of ammunition. With quiet excitement we read the warning, 'Dangerous within one mile'. I progressed to firing army .303 rifles at 500 yards in the school team. 'Dad,' I exclaimed. 'Through the telescope we can see the bullets in flight.'

'Can you really! We could see our 16-inch shells heading over the horizon as well.'

When Frank Harris, our shooting master, mooted sending me to Canada with the England schools rifle team I became alarmed at the cost to my parents and backed away. But on one glorious occasion at Yardway my .22 downed a pheasant on the wing. 'Mum, I paced it out – 30 yards away – imagine that!'

'I saw you in Sid's field,' she retorted, ever the farmer's daughter set against the poacher.

'Well only just in his field.'

'Pah!' Nevertheless some years later, the photo of the pheasant and I appeared on the sideboard.

At school I discovered that my father's handiwork was walking nearby; more than one master sidled up with a shy smile and shared their gratitude for my father's care. Others kept their distance concerning delicate anatomy – indeed, Dad himself had had his piles 'done', which he referred to obscurely as 'a sore bottom'.

And in that region of anatomy, Trevor Pargeter, a farming neighbour, roared with laughter as he repeated Paul's reply to, 'Do you think Sid will be well enough after the operation to come to the church fête?'

'Yes – but *not* on his bicycle.'

Nearby lived a family with their tiny baby, Sally. She had an 'acute abdomen', so Paul operated and found an 'intussusception' – where a section of bowel swallows itself in a lethal tangle. The miniature damaged bowel was excised and then reconnected end to end. Sally grew up to become our much-loved neighbour next door with her family.

Walking through the village with me, Dad would meet patients like the man who bared his belly in the road, complete with the scar, exclaiming, 'Oh, Mr Houghton, just look at your handiwork – isn't it wonderful!'

Such a lively mind brain 'did not suffer fools gladly' and, while the succession of vicars were not fools, it's hard to remember one that came 'up to standard'. Nevertheless, Paul cycled down to take the vicar a bottle of wine one Christmas Eve, without lights. Hitting the kerb he somersaulted to land seated on the grass, still grasping the bottle intact.

He was churchwarden at times over the years.

Seeing some rising damp on the inside mediaeval masonry, he hacked off the Victorian plasterwork down to the original stones. Hearing of this happening I brought him a flask of tea at the church one afternoon. Pushing open the door I was horrified to see a sight like an infantry dugout after a direct hit. Pews and church lay covered in rubble and dust.

'Dad, did you ask the vicar if you could do this?'

'No.'

As an adult, I noticed my father thirsty for fresh 'spiritual water'. Hearing my stories of remarkable spiritual renewal in my church at Worthing he too longed for more, and asked me, 'Did I grow up too bound by tradition and rules?'

'Perhaps,' I replied, 'but now the good Lord is again opening blind eyes to the great news of life and hope through the cross – liberating us to walk and talk with the same Man who thrilled Israel 2,000 years ago.'

As a father, he was sparing with instructional Bible verses. But on one occasion he rang up and quoted Isaiah 5:8, saying quietly, 'I think this could be for you: "Woe to you who add house to house." It steered me off my foolish idea of joining two semi-detached houses into one.

Once he dropped me at Worcester station on my first foray to the Nazareth Hospital Israel. I was twenty-eight and excited but nervous of the unknown ahead. As he said goodbye he added, 'Well, you are an experienced traveller now.' I swelled about 6 inches at this unexpected encouragement for a new venture.

The ancient St Bartholomew's Church, Grimley, across the Green and down Dark Lane was our usual Sunday worship site. The pews were hard and the services from the Book of Common Prayer seemed tedious. When he spotted a glazed look on my face as I sat down, I might find myself sitting on his great fist and leaping to my feet. Soon the whole pew was rocking with suppressed laughter.

The church lay on primaeval gravel beds in the meadows near the River Severn – a goldmine for the Church Commissioners. As our parents observed, the commissioners, having lost faith in the riches of the Lord, mined the worldly wealth the good Lord had left them – and this led to an incident.

Deciding to 'get out of the house' one wet afternoon, Dad and I rode down on bikes to look at the flooded gravel pits near the church. The real attraction wasn't the wildfowl but several gigantic diggers lined up along the top of sandy cliffs some 20 to 40ft high.

Climbing up onto the caterpillar tracks of one of these, I hoisted myself in and sat there pulling levers. Dad poked his head in and saw a knob, 'Pull to Start Engine'.

'Pull it,' he said, with the foolish grin of a ten-year-old.

I pulled and the behemoth burst into life, roaring and swaying. 'Jump!' I thought. But my exit was blocked by my gibbering father.

'Mark, Markey, Mark!' he shrieked, leaning in and pulling feverishly at every knob in the cab.

'I must keep my head,' I thought, 'or this nutter will jam it into gear and we'll all be in that water.'

Mummy's calm tuition kicked in. The year before, sitting on Sid Knight's Ford Dexter tractor in our top field she had drilled me in the essential knob on a diesel: 'Pull to Stop Engine'. Glancing here and there I spotted those happy words – and hauled – the engine shuddered and died. We leapt on our bikes and fled.

Later, back home, my mother and I agreed Dad had a gift for turning a problem into a crisis. Like the time we were returning from Uncle George Blundell and Auntie Marcelle in high spirits. Mum was at the wheel and the old Rover 12 sailed crabwise down the main road with Dad shouting, 'Jean, Jean,' and lunging across to wrestle her and the steering wheel.

The sea was never far away. Once, when we had a rope tight to pull down an apple tree, he remarked, 'I saw an officer's legs cut off on a ship, when a steel cable snapped and whipped back. I could not save him and he died where he fell. Another man had a buttock sliced off by the ship's propeller when he fell in the water.'

One summer afternoon, walking into the house from the tennis court, Pippa and I were alarmed to hear Dad do something we had never seen before – in loud floods of tears. We glanced at each other and said, 'Uncle Geoffrey Bullock must've died from that lung cancer' – a window into the shared pain of two shipmates.

CHAPTER THIRTY-NINE

Africa

1975-85

Retirement from the NHS at sixty-five brought him a leaving dinner and a solid silver tray inscribed, 'From his many friends in general practice'. Dr Bernard Dawes, a Worcestershire GP, wrote saying, 'I feel I have never met anyone in my life who has exercised his vocational calling with such zeal and sympathy.'

But he went straight back to work, effortlessly moving from General Surgery to fill in for a Urology colleague off sick. Out walking in the woods with my father-in-law, Jules had to go behind a tree; after a long wait, Paul's voice floated over, 'Plumbing trouble?' Taken to the cathedral, Jules was astonished to have various patients pointed out in the crowd covertly. 'There's another "survivor" – gallbladder, then his waterworks.'

At last Paul felt free to pursue his youthful hopes of being a missionary surgeon and – as in 1937 – wrote to a mission society offering his services. Again they never replied. Instead, he was led to All Saints Hospital in Transkei, a 'self-governing homeland' of South Africa, just one year into so-called nationhood.

So off he went alone. Jean stayed at home for the first months caring for Yardway and the animals. Pippa was settled in Barts Hospital as Sister in charge of Theatre G, the Surgical Professorial Unit where the photo of our father's surgical 'firm' with Prof Geoffrey Keynes still hung on the wall. Naturally our father was delighted Pippa was there and later she was doing the same in Nazareth, Israel and Worcester.

Paul arrived at the remote All Saints Hospital at sixty-seven. Looking around, he took in the far-off smudge of the Drakensberg mountains. Near at hand were wide-open hills, immediately inviting for walks and dotted with mud rondavels. Hard-working 'blanket women' festooned with broad headgear and blankets greeted him with smiles in their extraordinary clicking language. Their men trotted past on scrawny ponies to Engcobo, the local township, looking like the film set of a western. Goolandodo, the sacred mountain, reared up nearby, capped with its rocks and a colony of baboons.

Altogether this was a recipe for delights, and he soon struck up a friendship with one of the few white residents, Ashley Hessel. 'Hessel' and Melba ran the town store and impressed Paul by ploughing their profits into their ceaseless outreach with the great news of Christ to bolster Christians near and far in their tin and wood churches.

The other white doctors included socialists – as different from him politically as night and day. Debate raged around the dinner table over the white versus black struggle, but relations remained good-humoured. They became a tight-knit working group where TB, malnutrition and tetanus raged in ways not seen in the West. He became adept at plastic surgery to restore penises virtually skinned by witchdoctor circumcisions.

Pippa and I visited, and I, as a medical student, studied my dad at work: his caring and gentle hands, and his habit of getting down on his knees to examine a child's abdomen, and the praise he ladled out to the African nurses whose bedside fluid charts were 'the best ever'.

Some miles away, St Lucy's Hospital became Paul's refuge for laughter and enjoyable conversation with thirty-five-year-old Dr Richard Devonshire and his wife, Felicity, living in their *rondavel*. Richard remembers, 'The Cowley Fathers had founded St Lucy's in the late nineteenth Century, leaving behind a fine library. Paul was thrilled to see this as he was very knowledgeable about Church history. We found Paul as an Anglican who had been unsettled by *Honest to God* published in 1963.'[308] This notorious piece had scoffed at classic Christianity, such as the resurrection of Christ. Paul blamed the bishop's apostasy for helping to undermine the foundations of society from the 'swinging 60s' onwards.

'St Lucy's,' Devonshire recalls, 'was surrounded by fine landscape, with flat-topped hills a thousand feet above us. I marvelled how a man of his age had so easily managed the steep climb.

'For weekends we would occasionally go to the Wild Coast, on the Indian Ocean. I remember his delight on seeing on the hotel bookshelves a *History of the RNVR* – an extraordinary title to find in such a faraway place. He was pleased to find in it events and people he knew.'

One day, down at their favourite beach, Umghazi River Mouth, they joined in with some little children dancing on the beach – at which point Paul's Achilles tendon snapped and put him in plaster. Devonshire said:

---

308. John Robinson, *Honest to God* (London: SCM Press, 1963).

How amazing it was to meet a retired senior surgeon who could find fun in the ridiculous. Earnestness, particularly, he found very funny. One of his stays at St Lucy's coincided with the visit by a team of educators who had come to look at how we taught our nurses. They happened to meet Paul and one of them asked him what role he liked. He wished he had replied, 'Do you mean sausage roll or Swiss roll?'

On his visits to St Lucy's, Paul would help with the clinical work. It was a great experience to assist him and to watch the fine handed technique of a senior surgeon, and always the master raconteur with his stories of old cases.

Lunch in the hospital was a shared meal with the other doctors. His accounts of the dreadful things he had witnessed at sea, were heard with disbelief by some colleagues. His stories were so personal and immediate.

Some locals brought Paul a lamb born with an imperforate anus. Gently taking the woolly bundle, scalpel and scissors, he soon had things functioning to everyone's delight, including the patient.

And Africa gave Paul something he rarely knew in Worcestershire. He wrote back to us:

Last night the Minister of the Church of Scotland mission came to supper. They are just splendid, rock-like people of God, and a pleasure to meet. I asked him to read the evening Psalm and heaven seemed to open for a while. The black African vicar is also a good chap, young and right on course. All this is a great experience in this friendly community.

CHAPTER FORTY

Caribbean and Israel
1985 and after

Back in England after the year in Africa, Jean and Paul made three short-term visits to St Jude's hospital in St Lucia on the Caribbean as a volunteer surgeon. The almost bare room they were given, the balmy air, cricket with the local kids, sea swimming and good conversation with devout Roman Catholics felt almost ideal.

No surgeon is perfect and I was present at a major problem. He and I, with few obstetric skills between us, found ourselves on a remote island helping a woman whose child had got stuck in the birth canal. No obstetric help was at hand, so together we had the grim task of destroying the infant and removing it piecemeal. This saved a family from being orphans. I wish now we had rung an obstetrician, and they could have told us the simple *symphysiotomy* procedure to widen the birth canal. While the destructive procedure was horrible, I feel no guilt at all. Contrast that with my guilt after I approved a social abortion as a GP; the shame was so deep that nothing but the blood of Jesus could wash my conscience – and that many years later.

Having lived to see medical 'miracle' cures become commonplace, Paul retained that physician's awareness of being often powerless and prone to error; he kept a framed inscription nearby, written out for him by a patient:

> Often reviled when remedies prove vain,
> But ever welcome when the shadow falls,
> Daily at grips with death, disease, and pain,
> In slums, and darkened homes, and hospitals,
> Who tend the sick, and heal the tortured limb,
> Both do Christ's work, and do it unto Him.[309]

Whenever I was back in Yardway, Dad was ever ready to discuss rural life and its classics like *The Amateur Poacher* by Richard Jefferies.[310] He would turn a Nelsonian blind eye when, with my friend Rob *et al*, we would set off to lay waste to and pillage the furred, feathered and scaled citizens going about their lives in rest and quietness. One day, lying low with thumping hearts in a patch of brambles, as an angry farmer scanned the undergrowth, the law student took the opportunity (unhelpfully) to inform the medical student that it would not do for a barrister in waiting to have a police record.

'Bah!' scoffed the medic as we vaulted a barbed wire fence; and, but for two interventions, the law might have had us.

Firstly, Trevor Pargeter and his father-in-law, Mr Burrie Wood, helped the poacher turn gamekeeper, by inviting me on winter shoots and conservation work in good company – a lifesaver from the desert of London. (Dad would slip a bottle of port into my hands for Mr Wood.)

Secondly, in my final year at Charing Cross Hospital Medical School, I wound up a heated argument with a vicar using

---

309. Source unknown.
310. www.goodreads.com/book/show/19273078-the-amateur-poacher (accessed 25.11.24).

an unassailable fact, 'Neither you nor anyone else could guarantee God will meet and speak to me today.'

'Oh yes, I can,' came the return salvo. Then, God very unfairly ambushed me with some plain truth about my lifestyle and character – defects that needed fixing. The message arrived direct from Christ hanging onto life with his arms pinned out by nails: 'Trust me with full control of your life and all your wrongdoing and unhappiness. In exchange I will pour in my love and presence, make sense of life for you, and pack my life into yours to the *full*.' Fearing I might never get this chance again, I said, 'Sorry,' handed him control of my future, and found a Friend who 'sticks closer than a brother' (Proverbs 18:24). I have lived happily ever after.

There is little doubt my father and mother must have noted – but tactfully kept quiet – that their uneasy son was changing for the better. I bet they had been praying for years!

Once qualified, I did a job in Worcester where the medical mess dinner invited Mr Paul Houghton as guest of honour. Seated with his wife at the top table, all went fine until someone threw a bread roll at the opposite table. War broke out with rolls flying like shot and shell at the Battle of Waterloo. Jean and Paul affected table conversation as if nothing was happening until, grabbing a half-empty wine bottle, Paul stood up on his chair and called everyone to order before delivering a fine speech. Who was there the next morning to clear up the mess? Mr Houghton.

But trouble was brewing between my father and me. I went south to work in Worthing and there it was clear that I had to make some career choices, and surgery was the elephant in the room. Going into medicine was entirely my choice – but in the past year or two I could tell my father was hoping I would do surgery. I came home one weekend to talk it over, hoping for his guidance. Instead, he lost patience, leading to a nasty row between us, just as I was about to depart for the long journey to Worthing. My mother, who had been out at the time, stepped in with oil on the waters, insisting such a bad leave-taking must never happen again.

An excellent pastor helped me forgive my father – not only for putting on undue pressure, but for the times he had been absent at work when I needed him as a child. It would have helped if he had said 'Sorry' at home for grumpy moods and unkind words to Mum (as I hear he did at work) – and countless tensions would have been defused in family life.

That crisis, where the pastor brought the peace-making Jesus between my dad and I, unlocked a new and happy relationship for the years ahead, as if God was restoring the years that the locust had eaten.[311] What is more, it helped me find my identity in God's view of me as his son rather than following a career to please a parent.

As he mellowed, Dad became more accepting of weakness in others. He was more comfortable to be with. He took an interest in us children as we were, rather than as he would want us to be. Of course, he was delighted in Pippa's career on the surgical unit at Barts.

He said to me one day, 'You had better read this,' and handed me Tennyson's poem 'Ulysses': I began reading:

There lies the port; the vessel puffs her sail;
There gloom the dark broad seas . . . [312]

And, he added, 'You seem to have an insatiable thirst for adventure.'

---
311. Joel 2:25.
312. Alfred, Lord Tennyson, 1809-92, 'Ulysses', www.poetryfoundation.org/poems/45392/ulysses (accessed 25.11.24).

'Well,' I thought. 'You are a fine one to speak on that!' But I smiled to have his support for another sailing voyage in the stormy Hebrides.

Seeing my career unfolding differently to his own, he got behind me, especially in praying for my abortion prevention work – remaining resolutely opposed to mass abortion as a travesty of good healthcare. We knew that rare situations demand difficult deeds – as we had done on that remote island.

Paul's far-seeing eyes, steeped in his knowledge of the kind yet awesome Creator for the people and nations he made, gave him cause for grave concern. He had seen the fate of nations who practised the systematic destruction of children – whether by ancient Israel or Nazi Germany. He knew from the Bible that no profession or nation could presume on God's patience for ever. He agreed with me that corrupt medical 'advice' to women seeking abortion was harming women,[313] and that responsibility rested with one profession – doctors. We were sowing the seeds of our own destruction.

In 1985, when Paul was in his mid-seventies, I was an anaesthetist at a Christian hospital in the Holy Land, the Nazareth Hospital, serving a mix of Israelis, both Palestinians and Jews. We suddenly needed surgical help, so he came out to help.

Standing at our door in the May sunshine, I pointed to the distant plain: 'That's the village of Nain there.'

'Nain! The village where Jesus went to an open coffin, and gave a widow her son – living!'[314]

'Yes, and just to the left, out on the plain of Jezreel, in that cluster of palm trees is where King Saul met that dreadful witch of Endor.'[315]

---

313. See Dr Mark Houghton, *Pregnancy and Abortion: A Practical Guide to Making Decisions* (Welwyn Garden City: Malcolm Down, 2020).
314. Luke 7:11-17.
315. 1 Samuel 28.

'Is it really?'

'And to the left you can just see the top of Mount Tabor.'

'Goodness gracious – that's back in the dim past of the early Old Testament!'

Later, the kindly urologist Dr Basel Fahoum enthralled Paul with his tales of growing up in Nain.

Stopping me one day in the corridor and waving a patient's notes, Dad beamed, 'Do you know, Mark, I've got a patient from Ashkelon – the last time I heard of Ashkelon it was a forgotten historical site in the Old Testament!'

I looked at the file. 'Yes and he has a Russian first name. Thousands of Jews are coming back from the north, west, south and east, just as the prophets foretold.'[316]

Work was light, so borrowing a car we spent days together, poking around the reedy, rocky shores of the Sea of Galilee, swimming on our backs to see the skylines Christ saw and walking the old dusty tracks where he walked down from Nazareth.

We went dabbling in the spring of Ein Harod, drinking with cupped hands where Gideon famously tested his men – were they lappers or cuppers?[317] I watched as seven decades of Bible knowledge sprang into 3D from within Dad's heart, making his face shine.

Pulling off the main road, we took the single track to Nain and found my acquaintance who stood erect and introduced himself in broken English, 'Saleh Omri, shepherd of Nain.' In the welcome coolness of his little house, we drank coffee and he showed us the upper and lower millstones his mother and wife had ground corn in. He got out the key to the church –

---

316. For instance, Isaiah 43:5-6, '. . . I will bring your children from the east and gather you from the west. I will say to the north, "Give them up!" and to the south, "Do not hold them back."'
317. Judges 7.

being a Muslim, the warring local Christians had entrusted it to him as a neutral.

Then we walked across the cornfields to explore a vast pile of rocks, with shame. As Dr Basel had said without bitterness, 'The Arab village of Endor was destroyed by the British as retaliation for an attack on their soldiers.' In the shimmering silence, it seemed strange that for 2,000 years the biblical site had kept its name thanks to Arabs – only to be wrecked by us. When I last visited, there was nothing to be found.

One baking noonday, we stopped at Jacob's well in the West Bank – a place from two millennia *before* Christ. Had not Christ himself sat down thirsty here and asked a Samaritan woman for a drink? This story had always thrilled Dad. We peered into the depths and remembered together his provocative:

> 'If you knew ... who ... asks you for a drink, you would have asked him and he would have given you living water ... a spring of water welling up for eternal life.'
> 'Sir ... give me this water so that I won't get thirsty ...'[318]

I took him to Armageddon (Megiddo)[319] a few miles from Nazareth, and the enormous archaeology trench down through layers of Bible history. Pointing at a table of stones I said, 'That altar is where they found children's bones, sacrificial victims.'[320] We stood in silence thinking of the terrible double Exiles that God reluctantly unleashed to end that practice.[321]

At night we revelled in hospitality from the expats and Christian Arabs, cramming into a little stone house with

---
318. John 4:4-26.
319. Revelation 16:16.
320. www.thattheworldmayknow.com/innocent-blood (accessed 24.4.24).
321. 2 Kings 17:17-21.

a domed roof and roaring out their songs such as Father Abraham having sons and we can all be his sons too.[322]

A Palestinian Arab child came in with an acute abdominal emergency – cause unknown. He decided to operate, and I gave the anaesthetic, suddenly and acutely aware that he had not operated for several years.

Having confirmed she was asleep, I looked up to see the scalpel hovering at his chest height and something in his look urged me to shout, 'Dad, stop!' I was too late – slash flashed the blade in a long cut. When I opened my eyes expecting a lacerated bowel, I saw a perfect incision from end to end, a millimetre above the organs... his gift had not deserted him.

The child went home happy and so did a Jewish boy, delighted to have his 'bat ears' put in their beautiful place by Paul's plastic surgery.

And so, forty years from the end of the war – when he had supposed surgical ambitions must die – Paul's final operation had finished, near where another Jewish lad had grown up to become the Master healer, whose ways he tried to imitate.

---

322. See https://missionbibleclass.org/teaching-ideas/songs/english-songs/old-testament-songs/father-abraham/ (accessed 17.12.24).

CHAPTER FORTY-ONE

Season of Mists and Mellow Fruitfulness[323]

1985-2008

And I have asked to be
Where no storms come,
Where the green swell is in the havens dumb,
And out of the swing of the sea.

Gerard Manley Hopkins (1844-89), Heaven-Haven[324]

Sophie, their Staffordshire bull terrier, kept in step as their pace slowed with age. 'I think we shall go out together,' Paul would say. In fact, he was still strong enough to bury her by the pond he had dug beside his tiny children. Horizons contracted but Jean and Paul's pleasure in the garden and kitchen garden, the purple hills and nearby woods never faded. They managed Switzerland at ninety-three to see Jules and Klara Lüthy, my parents-in-law, renewing an enjoyable friendship.

---
323 From John Keats (1795-1821), ode: 'To Autumn', www.poetryfoundation.org/poems/44484/to-autumn.
324 www.poetrybyheart.org.uk/poems/heaven-haven/ Out of copyright (accessed 2.11.22).

He sorted his papers, retaining snippets from our childhood, like this prayer by Pippa:

Dear God,
Please hear our prayers,
When we are at thy house,
When we are all quite still.

With the sea long gone and horizons bounded once again by the garden, Paul treasured the sight of a snail 'sailing' across the flagstones, its shell rolling side-to-side, like a ship on a great sea swell.

Both our parents grew more attached to each other and deeper into the Bible together. They offered willing ears, and nuggets of wisdom, to neighbours and family who came in. Paul gave generously near and far – while always wrestling about not giving enough. The Master Craftsman had refashioned a cynic with an uncivil tongue into sincerity and gentleness.

They kept Yardway going as a home-from-home for the grandchildren, coming down from Sheffield for weekends. Grandpa – 'Paul' to them – was always asking how they were doing. Repeatedly, as parents, we were astonished at some crisis in a child working out well – eventually deciding it was God's mysterious ways blending with the prayers of four grandparents.

He and Jean came often to Sheffield to hear the prophetic preaching of the Bible applied to today's issues by the late Philip Hacking in our own Christchurch, Fulwood. Paul watched the national and world scene with foreboding. Coupling his insight into the greed of a nation which had become morally rudderless – having kicked out God and his enormous generosity – meant the 2008 financial crash came as no surprise. 'There will be worse to come,' he foresaw, as the pillars of peaceful society were knocked away: the authority of the Bible, the integrity of politicians and priests, state bloodshed from too many unnecessary abortions. 'They sow the wind and shall reap the whirlwind,'[325] he said.

He mocked the attempts of modern thinkers and theologians to save society: 'All you must be now is nice. Then everyone else will think you are nice and niceness will spread like treacle all over the world.'

As the climate crisis deepened and the River Severn burst its banks, he noted the record high water levels on a medieval flood scale fixed to Worcester's Bishop's Palace. '"The floods have lifted up their voice",'[326] he said, adding, 'It's the voice of God, pleading with people to return to him for security and climate solutions.' And Paul held to that expectant certainty that Christ himself would return . . . any day soon, because 'the day of the Lord will come like a thief in the night'.[327]

The Church of England was wrestling with the gay clergy issue in 1998 and the courageous Nigerian Archbishop Ben Kwashi, well used to murderous persecution for his faith, wrote to Paul from the Lambeth conference, 'There is no doubt the children of God at this conference are aware of the prayers of saints . . . Thank you for your prayers.'

Paul washed dishes at Worcester's Maggs Day Centre for the homeless, so long as he could drive. And he found convivial conversation with the Worshipful Company of Clothiers, a mediaeval guild, at their ample dinners with good wines. He bored us by indulging some light-hearted vanity in applying to Garter King of Arms for a coat of arms – duly granted for surgical services at sea. On the shield is a gold cross on a

---
325. Hosea 8:7: 'They sow the wind and reap the whirlwind.'
326. Psalm 93:3, AKJV.
327. 1 Thessalonians 5:2.

blue background: picturing his marine life. For the motto in Latin he chose *pietas et amor*, 'duty and love', which sounded abominably sanctimonious to me – but, I had to admit, it was true to the times I crashed his cars or got sent home early from a school rifle match at Bisley.

He could preach, provoking Jean's great-niece Caroline to write after Muff's funeral, 'James and I both wanted to thank you, Paul, for that beautiful address you gave. We were both very moved . . . What a tremendous effect it had on everybody there. You were so beautifully frank, . . . and generally gave her a marvellous send-off.'[328]

He sorted-out his desk retaining a tiny clothes iron and a battered toy hammer – relics of a London boyhood nearly a century before.

In his final years, from about the age of ninety-five, when stirring deeds and surgical success were past shadows, he was forced to examine his personal beliefs. A bowel haemorrhage brought him to hospital where a couple of treasured younger colleagues stood at the end of the bed muttering *sotto voce*, 'I thought he was a goner – perhaps he is.'

'Not yet, not yet,' emerged from the moribund figure. Admiral Syfret and Surgeon Lt Cmdr Houghton had swapped places sixty years on. He was soon home to normal life again, but death was knocking at the door.

With his sight failing and the joy of books fading, he began to recall those first words committed to memory from Lucy's lullaby almost a century before:

My sheep know My voice and they follow,
Yes, they follow Me, they follow Me.[329]

---

328. Letter to Paul and Jean Houghton from her great-niece and nephew Caroline and James Evans, 12 November 1995.
329. Based on John 10:14. Unpublished in this form.

He kept imagining the tenth chapter of John's Gospel and how the King himself would shepherd him and his loved ones into his presence for ever.

Even so, the immense question of what happens during and beyond death gripped him. He said several times, 'I am very old now, Mark, you know.'

'I know you are, Dad; you told me already.'

'Well learn this:

"When the will has forgotten its lifelong aim
And the mind can only disgrace its fame
And a man can scarcely remember his name,
The power of the Lord will raise his frame."'[330]

Giveaway comments appeared: 'You know, death is a very big thing to face.' He really had to wrestle this through, along with swollen, ulcerated legs which kept him downstairs or isolated in Worcester Royal Hospital with MRSA. Pippa and her husband Chris were living 10 miles away in Clifton-Upon-Teme. Inevitably they bore the brunt of his care, supporting Mum's day and night devotion, 'Its my duty and I love it.'

It seemed to help to hear the great Bible anchors like, 'The LORD is my shepherd . . . though I walk through the valley of the shadow of death, I will fear no evil: for thou art with me'.[331]

In his bed downstairs, he loved one of us sitting beside him holding onto each other, which for such a man was a huge change. He came to a place where it was settled: 'Yes, Jesus did rise from the dead and if he rose, I am going to hold onto that and I will rise too.'

One summer afternoon, I was with him, with Mummy and Pippa nearby. He had another haemorrhage in his bowels.

---
330. I cannot trace the author and wonder if it was my father himself.
331. Psalm 23:1,4, AKJV.

And a fine GP helped hugely by reassuring us there was no point in going into hospital.

Dad remained conscious to the last and reasonably clear in mind. I said, 'Let's have a prayer, Dad.'

'Yes, yes.' So I read those words from Psalm 23 above.

'Amen, Amen, Amen,' he responded (in the same words as the dying Admiral Nelson though I doubt that was in his mind just then). And that was it. It was August 2009, just a month short of his ninety-eighth birthday on a summer evening at Yardway. Sally, their neighbour, who he had saved as a baby, was sat holding his hand on the bed – the roles reversed.[332]

No sooner had Dad gone than Mum's mental confusion came to the fore and she often asked, 'Has Dad really died?' When we confirmed it, adding, he was alive with Jesus in Paradise, and they would meet again – then she became peaceful.

Without him, she couldn't settle in their old home, and it dawned on us that home for Mummy was simply wherever Dad was. She had been his main carer and was exhausted, so we brought her up to a care home in Sheffield. There the grandchildren in their teens visited Jean often.

Some minor strokes intervened and on one occasion she appeared to die in the ambulance. Afterwards her face shone with joy for some days even though she was unconscious. We concluded she had an advance visit to Paradise and the Good Shepherd. My mother died about two years after Paul, in 2011.

Bruce Roscoe and I discussed all this, and he asked, 'Do you think the Church has made faith needlessly complicated?'

---

332. I was amazed to hear on *The Rest is History* podcast, Trafalgar (Part 3), 2022, that Admiral Nelson died saying, 'Amen, Amen, Amen' also. Perhaps Paul knew that story. But I doubt Nelson was on his mind as he was translated to a new world.

'Well,' I reflected. 'I never heard my parents say they ought to get to heaven because they were good people. They didn't think they were. It was a simple childlike trust in that Good Shepherd which kept them balanced through many trials.'

Paul's funeral in Grimley church was packed with folks squashed into the pews beside the mediaeval stonework which he had hacked and repointed so many years before. On his request, and feeling weak, I mounted the pulpit steps and said he would be surprised to see so many here.

As I recounted the feelings of a man locked in a sinking ship I could see people listening intently:

> Work, war, wife, worship and Worcestershire capture the man. So, I see him now, no longer shrunken with age, but as I first knew him and as he now is in his indestructible body – tall, dark-haired and forever in his prime. I can't wait to meet him again like that, for a laugh and a hug.

Jean and Paul are buried together in the graveyard they had tended for decades. On their headstone is Lucy's song, from the tenth chapter of John's Gospel:

> My sheep know my voice, I know them, and they follow me.

I think he had persevered to achieve the goal that he often mentioned: 'He that shall endure unto the end . . . shall be saved.'[333]

---

333. Matthew 24:13, AKJV.

Postscript

Captain George Blundell turned up for parties in his magnificent 8-litre Bentley with huge headlights and his beaming smile. He lived until 1997. Paul spoke at his funeral about the anchor cable rescue of HMS *Nelson* – which his son John had been unaware of.

Admiral Vian was one of the two senior naval commanders for the D-Day invasion and then led British naval forces against the Japanese in the Pacific. Retiring in 1952 he was specially promoted Admiral of the Fleet to recognise his outstanding career.[334]

Admiral Syfret, following *Pedestal*, was made a knight 'for bravery and dauntless resolution in fighting an important convoy through to Malta in the face of relentless attacks by day and night from enemy submarines, aircraft and surface forces'. After the war he became Commander-in-Chief of the Home Fleet, retiring in 1948.

The *Nellie* steamed on to host the surrender of Japanese forces Penang, 2 September 1945. Rear-Admiral Uozomi signed at the same table where Admiral Badoglio had signed the surrender for Italy. By war's end she had steamed more

---

334. Royal Museums Greenwich, www.rmg.co.uk/collections/objects/rmgc-object-63999 (5.4.24).

than 135,000 miles, fought in the bitterest actions, been torpedoed and mined, targeted by countless bombing attacks and lost not a single man in action. No wonder she was a happy ship. In the quiet church at Burnham Thorpe, where Admiral Nelson's father was rector and young Horatio learnt about the sea, one can see the White Ensign, the flag which *Nelson* flew during the Second World War. She 'sank' at the ship breakers in 1950.

Rear-Admiral Humphrey Jacomb visited Paul and Jean at Yardway once or twice. How I wish I had been old enough to remember him.

Dr Dick Prewer became a world-famous prison psychiatrist for the most disturbed and dangerous cases (despite saying as a junior doctor he would never be a prison psychiatrist).[335] He and Paul kept up their letter-writing habit. Sixty years on, Dick remembered Paul at their first student lecture 'dispensing hope and encouragement in Barts'. Dick wrote in 1995, 'I think of you every day especially your singing: "There's a call comes ringing over the restless tide – send the light, send the light."'[336]

Paul wrote, 'Dick remained a godly man and a happily united family man, eventually becoming a Roman Catholic.'

Lucy Vine was known to us as children when we visited Lingfield from Worcestershire into the late 1960s. She always made us welcome. She lies in Lingfield churchyard, not far from Paul's parents and next to the Austin family.[337]

Albert Houghton never remarried and died in 1961. As a small boy I found him bending stiffly to pick up a garden fork; how can I help? I wondered helplessly.

---

335. Paul Hooper, 'Richard Russell Prewer', *Psychiatric Bulletin*. 1996;20(1):62-63. doi:10.1192/pb.20.1.62
336. Chas. H. Gabriel (1856-1932), https://hymnary.org/person/Gabriel_Charles (accessed 6.11.24). The lyric is actually 'restless wave': https://hymnary.org/text/theres_a_call_comes_ringing_oer_the_rest (accessed 25.11.24).
337. Paul Houghton written record, 1998.

Postscript

Tony Houghton, Paul's cousin, married a delightful Chinese lady called Kitty. He was admitted to a mental hospital, so Paul went to visit. There Paul diagnosed the 'madness' was actually a brain abscess, got it treated and saved him for many more good years of life.

Dr John Houghton was a consultant physician in Shrewsbury Hospital. With his wife, Frankie, they had our two cousins, Peter and Timothy. Frankie died of cancer, and John remarried Ann, who outlives him.

Dr Peter Swift, our uncle with his pipe (oh, the smell!) became Senior Paediatric Consultant, FRCP, at Farnborough hospital. He married his physio, Barbara Minchin, who cared for him after he lost his leg in Italy. They served in a Uganda hospital during the dictatorship of Idi Amin. Their children are our cousins Jane, John and Sarah.

'Twinny' John, our beloved uncle who chased us kids and invented games, married physiotherapist Brenda after the war and they had our cousins Christopher and Rosemary. John stayed in the Royal Welch Fusiliers, serving in Palestine and the Korean War. His calm people skills were prized for peace-making during the Cyprus crises. Then at forty-nine, John died tragically in a car accident while Chris and I were at Malvern College. He had just been appointed full colonel and would have been a general, said his fellow soldier to me.

Mrs 'Muff' Theo Granville White never remarried after Brian's death. She brought up Jennifer in a cottage on the farm at Leighton. 'Twinny' John helped little Jenny love the countryside before she and Muff moved to Dorset.

HMS *Zulu* was sunk by Axis aircraft off Tobruk during the *Operation Torch* landings in late 1942.

As grandfather, Paul was delighted to know that his grandchildren follow Christ.

Acknowledgements

I am indebted to Captain George Blundell's children, John and Liz, who saved his films and diaries for the Imperial War Museum (IWM) in London. John and his mother had patiently deciphered and typed the secret handwritten diaries. Sadly, John Blundell died during my writing but not before he had been of huge help with his father's diary. Many thanks to IWM for their permission to quote the diaries free of charge.

I am indebted to Dr Chris Howard Bailey of the Royal Naval Museum who recorded invaluable interviews with my dad, and our naval mum, Jean (née Swift) of the WRNS, when he was ninety and she was eighty. Her book *The Battle of the Atlantic: The Corvettes and their Crews: An Oral History*, Royal Naval Museum (Stroud, Gloucestershire: Alan Sutton Publishing Ltd, 1994), contains invaluable eyewitness accounts. She wrote in her gift copy, 'To Paul and Jean. Thank you for being such gracious hosts and talking with me. Chris Howard Bailey 24 November 2000.'

Paul also left various handwritten accounts from about the age of eighty.

My sister Pippa, thanks for your tireless help reading our dad's spidery handwriting and laughs over, 'The ponies loved it too!' And at last, we have got to know Dad's redoubtable mother.

Captain Peter Hore, naval historian and writer of Paul's obituary in the *Daily Telegraph*, thanks for your invaluable advice at short notice on any matters naval.

Mr John Black, President of the Royal College of Surgeons, thanks for your recollections as a surgeon just after Paul in Worcester and your love of all this history and the Foreword.

Dr Bruce Roscoe, thanks for your warm encouragement. Interviewing you about Dad was unforgettable.

Dr Sajad Ahmad FRCGP in South Wales, I thank you for your initiative in getting in touch and warm anecdotes of our fathers.

Dr Richard Devonshire, thank you for reconnecting so willingly since we last met when I was a medical student in Transkei.

Dr Andrew Ferguson, I'm so grateful for that full read-through and your recognition of the revolutionary benefit the NHS brought us all. And thanks for suggesting 'Surgeon, Sailor, Senior'!

I'm indebted to these professional authors and their insights: Mark Stibbe, Ralph Turner and Stephen Poxon.

Last but not least, well done the wider family for rooting out dates and events of our parents. Cousin John Swift, I remember you saying, 'I'm often astonished how our parents coped with the Second World War.'

Above all thanks to Esther, my dear wife, along with our Celia, Dan and Fiona for tolerating boxes of letters clogging the home and your laughs and thoughts during early drafts. And Samuel, with the babies, Klara and Barnabas – you kept Grandpa smiling and diverted.

Publisher Malcolm Down, designer Sarah Grace and editors Sheila Jacobs and Micah deSilver, thanks for your unstinting patience on details.

Acknowledgements

Every effort has been made to attribute photos, quotes and facts correctly. I apologise for any errors or omissions by copyright holders and would be grateful to be notified of any corrections for future editions.

Appendix
Online Links

The Telegraph obituary of Paul Houghton, www.telegraph.co.uk/news/obituaries/medicine-obituaries/6409316/Surgeon-Lt-Cdr-Paul-Houghton.html

British Medical Journal obituary of Paul Houghton, www.bmj.com/content/bmj/341/7768/Obituaries.full.pdf

The Royal College of Surgeons, obituary of Houghton, Paul Winchester (1911 - 2009), by Mr John Black PRCS, Identifier: RCS: E001723. https://livesonline.rcseng.ac.uk/client/en_GB/lives/search/detailnonmodal?qu=%22rcs%3A+E001723%22&d=ent%3A%2F%2FSD_ASSET%2F0%2FSD_ASSET%3A373906%7E%7E0&ic=true&rt=false%7C%7C%7CIDENTIFIER%7C%7C%7CResource+Identifier

Glossary

Aft – the rear end of a ship.

Ack ack – anti-aircraft gunfire in wartime slang.

Action stations – a crewmember's place of duty on a warship when an enemy was threatening.

Amidships – the middle of a ship.

Axis – Germany and her allies in the Second World War.

Battleship – the largest and most heavily armoured type of warship in the British fleet.

Beam ends – the side of a ship, thus named from wooden ships that had cross beams ending all along the side.

Broadside – when a warship fires her largest guns.

Blue Belt – a State Registered Nurse at Barts Hospital.

Bofors gun – a large single- or double-barrelled rapid firing cannon used against attacking aircraft. Originally a Swedish product, BAE now owns the company.

Bo'sun – (boatswain) a senior rating in charge of rigging, boats, seamanship on the upper deck.

Bows – the sharp end or front of a ship.

Bulkhead – the internal steel walls designed as watertight compartments in the ship.

Chief Petty Officer – a senior non-commissioned officer.

Fo'c'sl – the forecastle or front section of a ship.

For'ard – towards the forward end of a ship.

Davits – small cranes by which to lower the lifeboats.

Destroyer – a fast, manoeuvrable warship such as HMS *Zulu* which Paul sailed on in the Battle of the Atlantic escorting and protecting larger war ships.

Dog watches – a short duty slot in the changing rota for officers and crew. Dogs ran in two shorter watches: First Dog 16:00 to 18:00 and Last Dog 18:00 to 20:00.

HMS – short for His Majesty's Ship, for instance HMS *Nelson*.

DSO – Distinguished Service Order, a military medal almost always awarded for gallantry, one level below the highest, the Victoria Cross.

Knot – one nautical mile-per-hour. One knot equals 1.15 miles/hour or 1.85 km/h.

Make my number – Naval slang for paying someone a visit. It derives from a ship's obligation to report their pennant number to the admiral on joining the fleet.

Oerlikon – a famous Swiss-made, rapid-firing gun with a single barrel, made in Oerlikon, Zurich. Highly effective against aeroplanes. A Swiss spy smuggled the design to England where they were made in substantial numbers under licence.

Ops Room – the ship's operations room, the nerve centre.

Pharmacopoeia – a large book of approved medicines and mixtures.

Glossary

Pom-Pom – a rapid firing naval gun with multiple barrels firing a 2lb shell.

Poop – the extreme rear end of a ship.

PMO – the Principal Medical Officer of a large ship or shore base.

Quarterdeck – an area on the ship, apart from the bridge, where the captain has special authority.

Scuttled – Deliberately sinking one's own ship by opening sea valves and laying explosive charges.

Stern sheets – the rear end of a ship's rowing boat.

Tin fish – naval slang for a torpedo.

Top brass – naval slang for the most senior officers.

Pips – small brass stars worn on shoulders of the uniforms for officers to denote their rank.

Port – nautical expression for the left side.

Sawbones – the ship's surgeon in naval slang.

Starboard – nautical expression for the left side.

U-boat – a German submarine.

WRNS – the Women's Royal Naval Service, affectionately known as the Wrens.

VC – the Victoria Cross, Britain's highest award for courage in battle.

VD, Venereal Disease – Sexually Transmitted Infection (STI). In the 1960s Houghton predicted that STIs would explode in a global pandemic, and he saw it happen. He foresaw the national consequences when the pillars of cohesion – family, Church, government, education and social norms – lost their moorings of respect for Christ and the Bible and drifted into the worship of 'sex without boundaries'.

Yardarm – a thick horizontal poll fixed to the mast and holding square sails out to the wind.

People and Nicknames

Aaron Houghton – Paul's paternal grandfather. Father of Albert, Paul's father; also, father of George, and Herbert Houghton killed in First World War.

Albert Houghton – the father of Paul.

Anthony (Tony) Houghton – first cousin of Paul, son of George Houghton, who was Albert's brother.

Admiral Neville Syfret – the famous fighting admiral from South Africa, who Paul sailed with on Malta convoys and the Allied invasion of North Africa.

Barts – St Bartholomew's Hospital, London where Paul trained in medicine.

Captain George Blundell – the Commander of HMS *Nelson* and Paul's greatest friend at sea. Awarded the OBE (Order of the British Empire) – 'a piffling award for what he did' in Paul's eyes – after repairing the steering gear aboard HMS *Kent* and saving her from destruction. Also called Torps, being the Torpedo Officer.

Captain Humphrey Jacomb – Paul's first commanding officer on HMS *Nelson*.

Captain the Honourable Guy Russell – took over HMS *Nelson* from Captain Jacomb as Paul's commanding officer and cycling companion ashore.

Edith Houghton, née Winchester – Paul's mother.

Dick – Dr Richard Prewer, Paul's lifelong friend from Barts Hospital medical school.

Flagship – a warship carrying the admiral and flying his flag in command of a fleet.

Frankie Houghton – Paul's sister-in-law, married to John Houghton, mother of Peter and Timothy.

Ginger Jim – the Houghtons' family cat; prone to disappear for long periods, which they decided was on business in America.

Kitty Houghton – wife of Tony Houghton.

Lt Geoffrey Bullock – Paul's shipmate on HMS *Nelson* and later neighbour in Worcestershire.

Geoffrey Keynes, Sir – the eminent London surgeon, polymath and surgical inspiration to Paul. He was the brother of the economist Maynard Keynes. He built up a collection of delightful woodcuts by Samuel Palmer, the friend of William Blake, author of the hymn 'Jerusalem'.[338]

Iver Salvesen – head of the Christian Salvesen logistics company.

Jack – Paul's brother John.

Jean Houghton (née Swift) – Paul's wife.

Mrs King – Paul's maternal grandmother. See Mrs Winchester.

Maurice Carpenter – a boyhood friend, Barts student and later medical colleague at war in the Royal Navy.

---

338. 'Sir Geoffrey Keynes, had honorary doctorates from Oxford, Cambridge, Edinburgh, Sheffield, Birmingham, and Reading.' Fussell, *The Great War and Modern Memory*.

Marion Salvesen – the wife of Iver Salvesen, living in Aberdour House near Rosyth.

Ops Room – the ship's operations room, the nerve centre.

Old Bill or Billy – the Houghton family's spaniel.

Old Brodie – Paul's medical student friend from Barts Hospital days.

Pram – the smallest motorboat of a ship with a blunt end.

Sawbones – a ship's surgeon.

Torps – nickname of George Blundell as Torpedo Officer on HMS *Nelson*

Mr Winchester – Paul's maternal grandfather

Mrs Winchester – the maternal grandmother of Paul and the mother of Edith Houghton, née Winchester. After her divorce from Mr Winchester she remarried, becoming Mrs King.